The Honest Always Stand Alone

The Honest Always Stand Alone

CG SOMIAH

NIYOGI BOOKS

Published by
NIYOGI BOOKS
Block D, Building No. 77,
Okhla Industrial Area, Phase-I
New Delhi-110 020, INDIA
Tel: 91-11-26816301, 26818960
email: niyogibooks@gmail.com
www.niyogibooksindia.com

Design: Write Media

ISBN: 978-81-89738-71-6

Year of Publication: July 2010
First Reprint: September 2010
Second Reprint: 2014
Third Reprint: 2015
Fourth Reprint: 2016
Fifth Reprint: 2018
Sixth Reprint: 2019
Seventh Reprint: 2021
Eighth Reprint: 2024

Printed at: Niyogi Offset Pvt. Ltd., New Delhi, India

Publisher's Note

The mandate of Niyogi Books is to provide a platform for a variety of opinions and we respect the sentiments of our authors. CG Somiah has desired that the content of this book is not edited drastically or toned down as these words are an honest expression of his views. He stands by what he has written and takes full responsibility for it.

Contents

Being sworn in as the Comptroller and Auditor General of India by President R Venkataraman, 1990.

Preface

It is not easy to write the story of an eventful life, especially after reaching the age of seventy-five, as memory is usually a casualty. For one who had never kept any notes, the task of writing a book was all the more difficult. My memory, however, has served me well and I could weave into the narration several interesting and humorous incidents that took place in my life and career. These incidents are factual without any embellishment. Any errors are due only to a less clear recollection of events.

I have to acknowledge the help received from my daughter Pria in deciphering my handwritten manuscript and getting a dozen copies printed for private reading. I thank my friend, K Srinivasan, retired IAS Officer of the Orissa cadre, for his help and support. Finally, a special word of deep gratitude to my beloved wife Indira whose affectionate companionship and lively encouragement made this book possible.

This book is dedicated to the dwindling band of honest officers who are battling heavy odds to maintain their integrity and dignity to extend corruption-free good governance to the people of India. They need all our support.

CG Somiah

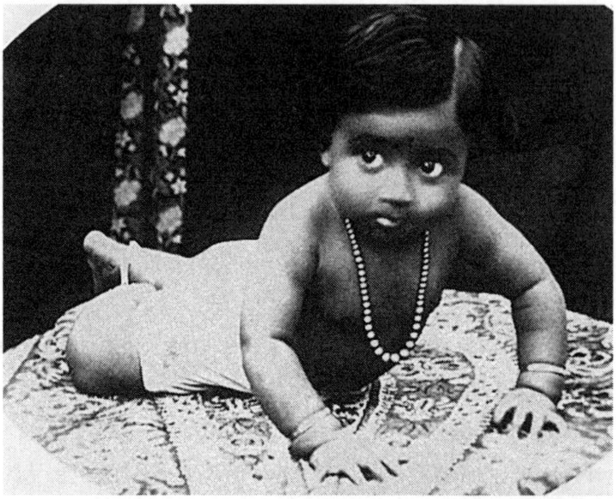

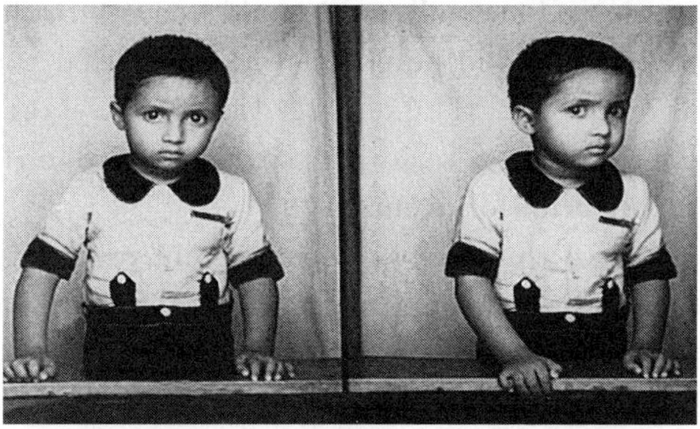

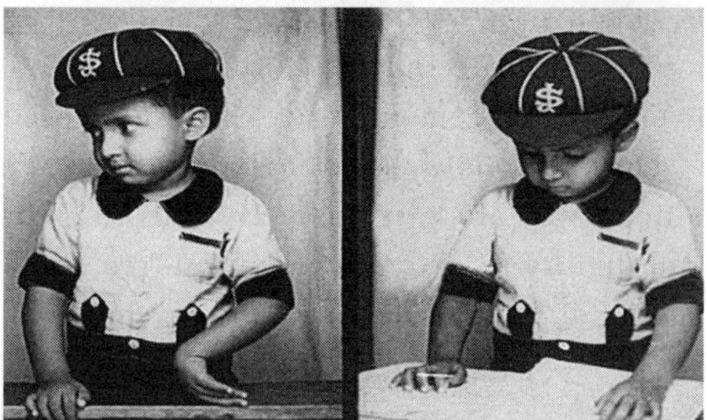

I was born a little dark unlike most of the Kodava community: as a one-year old, 1932 (above) and as a four-year-old, 1935.

1

Early Memories

On 1 April 1936, there was much rejoicing in Berhampur. The State of Orissa was constituted on that day by the British Government who took out areas from West Bengal, Central Province (now Madhya Pradesh) and the Madras Presidency. Koraput and Ganjam Districts, which were part of the Madras Presidency, became the two southern districts of Orissa. I was five years old then and, as I saw the flags and buntings go up with people in a celebratory mood, I never thought that later in life I would serve the new State as an administrator. The birth of a State is not an ordinary affair and I was witness to a great historical event.

Another childhood memory is of riding on horseback. When my father was posted as Range Forest Officer in an interior place called Baliguda in Koraput District, he was provided with a horse for his touring (jeeps and good roads in the jungle area were unknown then) and I used to be taken on horseback by my father. Baliguda was a back-of-beyond place where there was no primary school and my schooling was at home, learning the alphabets from my mother. The area was full of tribals and there were fearsome stories of human sacrifice done by them. In the small hamlet we lived in the name Baliguda was indicative of human sacrifice. In the night, while we slept in the forest quarters, we could hear jungle noises including the roar of tigers and the trumpet of elephants. The fact that the tribals were active till late in the night was evident from their drumbeats. After nightfall no one stirred out of the house and my father always kept his loaded double-barrel gun, which I now possess, near him when he went to bed.

My memories now take me back to 1935, when a cyclone hit Berhampur. Heavy rain and raging winds made a peculiar eerie sound on that terrifying night when we all sat huddled together waiting for the nightmare to end. When we got out in the morning after the cyclone had abated, we found that part of our roof had blown off, but the damage we suffered was nothing compared to the all-round destruction the cyclone had caused. Several houses had collapsed and many people had been killed. For the first time I saw dead bodies carried out of the houses with weeping relatives in attendance. This is a memory I would love to forget.

When we moved to Dachur, we found the Ranger's bungalow to be like a palace in comparison to the cramped conditions we lived in at Berhampur. I have two childhood memories of Dachur. I was still not going to school but I remember taking part in a children's race where I stood first. The second experience was more interesting. At the back of our house from the twenty feet-wide verandah there were stone steps equally wide leading to the backyard. As I was playing in the backyard I noticed a snake's head dart out of a small crevice in the steps. I immediately brought this to the notice of my parents and they sent for a snake charmer to catch the snake. The snake charmer, who was a tribal, came with minimal dress and a turban on his head. With his music he enticed the snake to come out of the crevice. It was a small cobra. I think the smallness of the snake made the snake charmer complacent and when he tried to catch the snake by its tail without pinning its head first with his iron tongs, the snake in a quick reflex action bit him on his forearm. The snake charmer was cursing himself for his carelessness and he quickly put the snake into the small basket that he carried. He brought out some herbs from his bag and started grinding them on the steps with a round stone. He ate the herbal paste and cautioned us not to wake him up. Gradually he lost consciousness and fell flat on his back on the steps and his breathing became laboured. My father told us to keep quiet and allowed the snake charmer to have his rest as desired by him. After an hour the snake charmer opened his eyes and started stretching his limbs before getting up. He was gone in ten minutes, suitably rewarded by my father for his timely help. I shall never forget the calmness with which the tribal snake charmer reacted when he was facing death.

I was born on 11 March 1931 a little after mid-noon in Karkal, a small *taluk* (administrative division) headquarter of the South Canara District. At the time of my birth my father was posted in Karkal as the Range Officer of the Forest Department of the old Madras Presidency. It is a small village township but it was famous in the neighbourhood as it had the second highest Jain statue of Mahavir, the highest statue is in Sravanabelagola in Karnataka. My mother told me that before my birth she used to visit the statue and pray that I may grow up tall like him. Her wish was fulfilled for I am six feet tall with an athletic build. My mother, however, overlooked one fact when she wished that I take after Mahavir. The statue was made of black granite and I was born a little dark unlike most of the Kodava community who are of a fairer complexion. I used to joke about this with my mother whenever she scrubbed me hard in the bath to make me look fairer!

I am a Kodava by birth and I belong to the Codanda family. Every Kodava, male or female, carries a family name and that acts as a *gothra* (lineage or clan assigned to a Hindu at birth) to prevent marriage between a man and woman with the same family name. The Kodavas are a small community and it is estimated that the total population of Kodavas living in Coorg and also outside it is not more than two lakhs; this small number is distributed under about six to seven hundred family names.

It is a traditional practice among Kodavas to fire a gun to announce the birth of a son in the family. I was told that when my father fired a gun to announce my birth, the neighbourhood was alarmed and information was lodged in the local police station that guns were being fired in my father's house to settle a dispute. The local Station House Officer (SHO) came to our residence with a couple of constables to see what was happening. He was charmed to learn that his colleague was celebrating the birth of his son in the traditional manner. I was told that the SHO wished that I should join the Police and be a good policeman. This incident came to my mind when many years later I was appointed as the Union Home Secretary, a post mainly dealing with law and order and the Police. I was indeed lucky to have surpassed the policeman's expectation.

My father's name was Ganapati; he was the thirteenth child of his parents. My father's father was Somiah, an agriculturist owning a vast tract of land in Kottoli Village near Virajpet, one of the prominent towns of Coorg. I have inherited about thirty-seven acres of this property and also have a share in the ancestral house in Kottoli Village. My grandparents have been buried in a very prominent place a little away from the house and our stay there is not considered complete without a visit to the cemetery. When my father died in 1961, we buried his ashes next to his parent's cemetery in accordance with his wishes.

My mother's name was Ponnamma and her pet name was Polly. She was the eldest in the family of four children. She belonged to the Kelapanda family and her father Muddappa held the important post of Public Prosecutor. She was born in 1908, educated at the Mercara Convent and later at the Good Shepherd Convent in Mysore. She told me that as a child she would travel to Mysore in a bullock cart and it used to take six days from Mercara to Mysore. The same journey today takes two hours by car! After her schooling she went to the Women's Christian College in Chennai. I do not think she completed her college as her father died suddenly under mysterious circumstances. According to my grandmother, he attended a wedding at Pollibetta where she suspects he was poisoned by criminals whose prosecution he was handling. He returned late at night after attending the wedding and by the morning he was dead. He was just thirty-five. He was highly respected for his professional integrity and his untimely death came as a great shock to the Coorg community. From a relatively comfortable life my mother's family turned poor overnight. My grandmother, who became a widow at a very young age, was of indomitable courage and she started managing the affairs of the family. My grandfather had acquired an old house with about two acres of land (one acre under coffee) in a beautiful location near Raja Seat in Madikeri. He also owned a few acres of paddy land in his village. My grandmother managed these resources well and continued to look after the education of her children.

My mother got married in 1927 when she was nineteen; my father was much older to her. With this marriage, the burden of looking after the entire family fell on my father who was a very generous-hearted person. He used to tell me stories when

I was young and he was my mentor as I grew up. He took a lot of interest in my studies and, knowing that I was a good student, he would encourage me to perform better and give my best. Mathematics was my favourite subject and invariably after attending the Maths examination we used to get together to analyse and discuss the paper. More often than not I used to score hundred per cent in Maths and on the few occasions I did not succeed in doing so, his disappointment was as great as mine.

2

Blessings from Kollegal

The first time I went to school was at the age of eight. That was when my father was transferred to Kollegal in the Sathyamanagala Forest Area, which was in Madras Presidency, now located in Karnataka. The medium of instruction in high school was Kannada and, while I was proficient in Telugu, I did not know a single word of Kannada. I think I was permitted to join the school only because my father was an influential Government officer of the locality.

My father engaged a private tutor to teach me Kannada. I could not understand a word of what was being taught. I scored good marks only in Maths and in the other subjects I got zero! With the tuition my knowledge of Kannada gradually improved but not enough to pass the final examination of the Ist Form (Class Six). However, my father sent generous supplies of coffee and oranges to the headmaster and that proved to be a major factor in ensuring that I was promoted to the next class. Thereafter, I was on my own and was invariably at the top of the class in the subsequent examinations. When I topped the IIIrd Form final examination, I heard the headmaster tell my father that I would go a long way in attaining success. He blessed me by reciting a Sanskrit *sloka* (verse). These blessings, I believe, have guided and guarded me throughout my life. I remember my headmaster every time success graces my life. Although I liked company, I did not have many friends in school. I was a dreamer and a voracious reader. One of the few friends I did have was S Subbaraman who, later in life, joined the archaeological department and was part of the Indian team that went to Cambodia in the early seventies to help with the restoration of the world heritage monument, Angkor Vat. I followed my classmate's footsteps in visiting Angkor Vat thirty years later as a tourist.

At Kollegal I had my first lessons in tennis. My parents were members of the local officers' club and my mother, more than my father, was fond of playing tennis. Konganda Achaya, the sericulturist, was the presiding deity of the club and my father used to play poker with him. The club did not have any independent existence but was centred round the tennis court behind the imposing red building housing the *tehsildar*'s (revenue collector's) office and the treasury. The wide verandah of the building had a table and a few chairs for the poker players.

My mother was the only lady tennis player and she made a graceful figure in her Coorg sari as she played the game. Surprisingly, she never wore any shoes while playing. I used to accompany her to the tennis court and help in fetching the ball most of the time. When the game finished I used to pick up my mother's racquet and practice on the adjacent wall. At times, when the tennis quorum was not full, I was invited to play with the members. That is how I started tennis and later excelled in the game, winning many tournaments.

Overlooking Kollegal was a huge stone hill called Murudi Gudde. It was a great adventure for me to climb the hill and visit the small temple perched on its top. My mother and I used to often pray at this temple. I particularly enjoyed the view from the top as everything below looked so small. Other memories of my childhood at Kollegal include a visit to the nearby Sivasamadram waterfalls. The Cauvery River was at its majestic best as it cascaded down the mountain in three different streams, enveloped in swirling mist and the sound of roaring waters. An open-seated iron carriage, mounted on sloping rails and controlled by an iron rope and a winch, took us down the mountain side to the powerhouse located below and I witnessed for the first time how electricity was generated.

Visiting Mysore, the nearest urban centre, was indeed a great event for me as a young boy nurtured in the village atmosphere of Kollegal. As the bus entered Mysore, the splendour of the city looked magical to my youthful eyes—the wide roads, neatly-built houses in big compounds, the gleaming palace, which passed by as a blur, the large number of motor vehicles mingling with horse-driven carriages called *tongas*, the stately-looking big clock tower and the drive down the wide Sayyaji Rao Road that ended at the bus stand.

While in Mysore, I visited the Kolar gold fields. I remember going deep down to the lowest level of the mine in a lift to see the mining and making of gold. An Englishman was in charge of the mine and most of the workers were Anglo-Indians. I was ten years old when I visited the mines and I still remember the liquid gold draining out of the smelter into the lead-lined ingots. It was a rare sight. Thanks to the kindness of one of the workers I was allowed to handle a cooled ingot of gold. My education of the mining of precious metals was complete when years later, as the Central Vigilance Commissioner (CVC), I visited the copper and silver mines of Malanchkhand in Madhya Pradesh while on my way to the Kanha wildlife game sanctuary.

I spent three years in Kollegal from 1939 to 1942. In 1941 my father was transferred to Puttur near Mangalore. My mother, my sister Rani (who was three years younger to me) and I moved from the official residence of the Range Officer to a private rented accommodation in the new extension in Kollegal as my father decided that I should continue my education in Kollegal until he was ready to take me to Mangalore for further studies. We had a Coorg servant boy, Subbiah, to help with the work at home. My mother continued her tennis and I, in turn, became more proficient in the game. I remember the long walks I used to take with my mother to reach the tennis court. It was a peaceful but isolated life that we led in the absence of my father. When I finished the IIIrd Form in April 1942, I passed with distinction. While we were in Kollegal we were vaguely aware of World War II that was raging in Europe and I used to visit the school library to read the newspaper about the progress of the war.

In May 1942 my father decided that it was time for us to move to Mangalore. We took up residence in a three-bedroom independent house at a place called Collector's Gate. The residence of the Collector and District Magistrate was located nearby but all that we saw was the imposing gate leading to the residence of the Collector who was held in awe. In my daily walk to school, a mile away, I would pass this gate and dream that one day I would grow up and be a Collector.

I was admitted to the St Aloysius School in Mangalore in 1942 and enrolled in the IVth Form. The school had an imposing façade and was located in a grand building on a hillock near the lighthouse, from where one could see the Arabian Sea. It was run by the Jesuit order and the college of the same name was located in an adjacent hollow connected by a corridor and steeply descending steps from the school. The playground of the school and the college was located on the adjacent hollow. There was an athletic track, a football-cum-cricket ground and a basketball court. Coming from a village school I was spellbound by the size and scale of the school building. Adjacent to the school was the school chapel where Catholic students offered prayers. It was an imposing building with religious paintings on the walls and the entire ceiling, giving the place a grandeur that no other chapel I visited in India possessed.

When I revisited the school fifty years later, in 1995, I was personally conducted round the premises by the principal who led me to the chapel where all the paintings were under restoration by the Indian Trust for Art and Cultural Heritage (INTACH). It was indeed a memorable visit. One of the founder members of St Aloysius School was Joachim Alva, the great grandfather of Nikhil Alva who married my daughter Pria in 1997. Nikhil's grandfather was also called Joachim Alva, who was a well-known associate of Pandit Jawaharlal Nehru during the freedom movement. Without my realising it, the strands of the past were being carried to the future in a very happy outcome of marriage between our two families. I again visited the heritage church in January 2007 when I went to the school along with Indira, Pria and her children and Nikhil's father Niranjan Alva.

While in school in Kollegal my name was registered as Krishnaraj, a pet name given to me by my mother after visiting the famous Sri Krishna temple in Udipi. On the day I was taken by my father to join the St Aloysius School my father asked me whether I would like to use my Coorg name 'Somiah'. I agreed and my name was registered as Codanda Ganpati Somiah. When we returned home and my mother learnt that I had changed my name, she was furious. I pacified her by saying that I will retain my pet name in a shortened form as Raja. I fared very well scholastically and was one of the top three in the class of forty students. I actively took part in games mainly badminton, basketball and cricket. I did not get much of a chance to play tennis as the school tennis court was not in use.

During the summer vacations and Christmas holidays we would visit Puttur, a couple of hours' bus journey from Mangalore. The Range Officer's quarters were spacious and located in an acre of land nearby, outside the bustling township. I remember chasing monkeys from the mango trees and distracting the bats hanging upside down on the tall trees in the garden by making a noise with a long bamboo pole. I loved my days in Puttur.

It was in Puttur that my father introduced me to a lawyer friend who had a fairly large library of general books apart from a very big collection of law books. My father recognised my interest in general reading and wanted me to spend time with books during the holidays. This helped to considerably enrich my knowledge. I recollect there was a huge globe in the library and I would twirl it to see the names of the various countries of the world and their capitals. Standing in front of the globe, I used to dream about visiting these countries. Little did I know that I would visit sixty-eight countries, in all the five continents, in the years to come.

I spent four years in Mangalore from 1942 to 1946 studying in St Aloysius School and College. I remember the Quit India movement of Mahatma Gandhi in 1942 when our school closed for a day. There was agitation in the town and I saw a vast procession on the streets with people carrying Congress flags. My father explained to me the Independence movement started by Mahatma Gandhi and led by Pandit Jawaharlal Nehru and he suggested that I read about it. The school library, however, did not have any books on the subject. Instead, I read about Alexander and Napoleon the two romantic figures of history. I used to read a lot of stories by GA Henty who wrote about the Vikings and the Romans. My interest in general knowledge was kindled by my History teacher Father Monteiro who used to ask us questions by referring to a small notebook that he always carried. I thought I might get a shortcut to general knowledge by borrowing this notebook. My request, however, was turned down with the advice that I read and develop my own general knowledge. That started my reading adventure, which has not diminished with age.

The year 1944 was a joyous one for us. We had a new arrival in the family and I had a baby sister who was named Rathi. She was a happy child and every day, back from school, I would gather her in my arms and play with her. It was great having her in the house and there was never a dull moment. My other sister Rani, three years younger to me, was born in Madikeri when I was too young to recollect her birth.

Next year, I completed my school education by passing the Secondary School Leaving Certificate (SSLC) examination with high distinction, averaging eighty-one per cent. I was now looking forward to entering college. My application to St Aloysius College was rejected as I was under-age. When my father consulted Father William Sequera, the headmaster, for guidance he advised him to file an affidavit to increase my age from fourteen to fifteen years. My father came back home dejected as he was a firm believer in the truth and it was against his nature to file a false affidavit. He went back to the headmaster and a compromise was struck. I was given admission to college as a private student, not officially recognised. This meant that I did the two-year intermediate course in three years. The first year was devoted mainly to learning French. My father presented me with a new bicycle and I would proudly ride to college on it. Since I knew I could not appear in the annual examination I spent the year improving my sports abilities. I played badminton, cricket and basketball regularly. Unfortunately, there was no opportunity to play tennis.

At college, I struck up a close friendship with a Catholic boy called Hugh Aranha. He also had a new cycle and as he was not fond of studies he induced me to bunk classes. I was not averse to his suggestion as I knew that the year in college was not meant for serious studies. We used to take off immediately after attendance and go on long bicycle rides in the streets of Mangalore, going as far as the Bunder area where the Mangalore Port was located. Aranha was a religious-minded person and he and I used to spend quite some time in the school chapel. While he prayed I would admire the fabulous paintings depicting the life and times of Jesus Christ. I will not be wrong when I say that in India there is no church that can rival the paintings in the St Aloysius school chapel.

After completing my one-year course in college in 1946, I migrated to Madras Christian College in Tambaram. The college was huge and immaculately maintained. The principal was Dr Boyd, a Scot with an amiable nature and a merry glint in his eyes. He taught English and his teaching of Shakespeare was superb. He was a strict disciplinarian but students loved him for his friendly attitude. I was allotted a room in Selaiyur Hall as hostel accommodation.

Here I was able to play tennis again and as I played a good game, I was immediately taken to the first court. I also played cricket. I still remember a closely-fought cricket match at the St Thomas Cricket Ground facing the St Thomas Mount. St Thomas was an apostle of Christ who came to India, and lies buried in the hillock in St Thomas Mount, which is between Tambaram and Chennai. In college I was doing well both in studies and in sports.

Juniors in college used to be ragged and my cousin and classmate Ratna and I had a taste of it when, on returning to our hall after a late dinner walk, we were 'pillowed' by seniors.

The pillow cover had within it old slippers and shoes and we were really battered. The same night some other gang of seniors wanted me to come out of the room for further ragging and I resisted, brandishing a hockey stick. One of the seniors of that group was a Sinhalese by the name of Kanakalingam and we later became very good friends. He was the cricket captain of Selaiyur Hall. I lost touch with him after leaving college and I was surprised to receive a letter from him when I became the Home Secretary, Government of India. I was in the news as we had started a dialogue with the Liberation Tigers of Tamil Eelam (LTTE) and we had secretly brought Velupillai Prabhakaran, the LTTE chief, for discussion to Delhi before the induction of the Indian Peace Keeping Force (of the Indian Army) into Sri Lanka. Kanakalingam in his letter, written from Jaffna, wondered whether I was the same Somiah who had confronted him with the hockey stick in Selaiyur Hall. I replied to him but never heard from him again.

While I was in Christian College, the country attained Independence on 15 August 1947. Ratna and I went to Chennai to take part in the celebrations. The city had turned delirious with joy and the streets of Chennai were packed with people who were going round the town to see the illumination on Government buildings and fireworks at the parade grounds. Ratna and I walked the length of Mount Road, came to the Central Station, which was beautifully illuminated and walked up to Parry's Corner before catching the last train back to Tambaram. The previous night Pandit Jawaharlal Nehru, the first Prime Minister of Independent India, had addressed the nation and we heard his famous 'Tryst with Destiny' speech while we were in the quadrangle of Selaiyur Hall. A few months later, when Gandhiji was assassinated we heard the anguished voice of the Prime Minister sharing his sorrow with the nation.

Cricket fever was as high then as it is now and I remember attending a test match between India and the West Indies at Chepauk Cricket Grounds, Chennai. We woke up at four in the morning and reached Egmore station at five. From there we trudged three miles to get to the Chepauk Grounds and stood in a queue for nearly four hours for tickets. It was a real high to see the great Mustaq Ali field in his silk shirt as also Vijay Hazare, Vijay Merchant and Vinoo Mankad—the famous three Vs of the Indian team. This is the only test match that I have seen on the cricket field. All subsequent cricket watching has been done on television except when at Lords in England I saw the thrilling finals of the First Prudential Cup heralding the one-day limited over cricket—that was in 1974-75 during my year's sabbatical in Oxford.

My life in Christian College and in Selaiyur Hall was happy and eventful. My father had been transferred to the Beypore timber depot near Calicut, located next to the Beypore River. My summer vacation in 1947 was happy and it was a good time for bonding between me and my two sisters. We as a family used to visit the riverside and play in the sand along the bank.

While in Calicut my father and I got into a discussion about my future. My father mentioned to me that he had seen a news item that the Union Public Service Commission (UPSC) was reviving the civil services entrance examination, which had been suspended during the War years. The last of the Indian Civil Service (ICS) got into service in 1942. The new service of Independent India would be called the Indian Administrative Service (IAS). My father mentioned that I had a very good scholastic record and I should try and get into the Indian Administrative Service after I completed my degree course. He also suggested that since I was good in Maths, I should join Maths Honours for my degree course. He apparently had in mind the fact that Maths was a high scoring subject in a competitive examination and would provide me a natural advantage. I was hazy about my own future until then and was thinking on the lines of taking up engineering or medicine. I told my father I would give his suggestion further thought and tell him about my choice by the time I complete my Intermediate course the following year.

Back in Selaiyur Hall and in college I used to often think of my father's advice and in the process started making enquiries about the Maths Honours course. The head of the Maths faculty was Professor Kibble, a brilliant mathematician of Scottish origin who used to teach us Catechism (moral values and good thoughts and ideas). He was a good teacher but he had the mannerism of an absent-minded professor. He was also a butterfly collector and maintained a private museum with butterflies of different sizes and colours neatly pinned to the board enclosed in glass. He would catch butterflies early in the morning with a net and keep them captive under his sola hat. Occasionally he would stroll into class in the morning with his catch and when he absent-mindedly removed his hat the butterflies would fly out.

When I finally decided to opt for Maths Honours I told my father about Professor Kibble and his absent-minded ways. He then advised me that I should change my college and join Loyola College for Maths Honours. I was extremely sorry to leave Christian College but for the sake of my career I had to abandon the college that I loved very much. While in Loyola College I won the South India Junior Tennis Championship for players under eighteen years of age, which was a high point in my athletic career.

Nearly forty years later Christian College was celebrating its centenary celebrations. The college extended an invitation to

Playing tennis at Loyola College (above) and at the South India Junior Tennis Championship, Chennai, 1948.

Prime Minister Rajiv Gandhi to be the Chief Guest but received no response. On learning that I was an ex-student of the college, the principal met me in Delhi to seek my help to get the Prime Minister to accept his invitation. At that time I was the Home Secretary and I used to meet the Prime Minister almost every day. I conveyed the principal's request to Rajiv Gandhi and mentioned to him that by accepting the invitation he would be honouring a great educational institution of South India and in turn would feel honoured by his association with the celebrations. The Prime Minister readily agreed to attend the function and asked me to accompany him. The principal was happy and so was I at the prospect of visiting my alma mater after four decades. But unfortunately this visit did not materialise. A couple of days before the event Delhi witnessed serial blasts organised by Khalistani terrorists and I stayed back in Delhi while Rajiv Gandhi attended the function.

The summer vacation of 1948 was spent in Coorg in my grandmother's place at Fairdale, Raja Seat. She was a wonderful grandmother, very hospitable and fond of cooking Coorg delicacies for her children and grandchildren. She knew a little English but used to write to me in Kannada. As a widow she was always immaculately dressed in a white *sari* and when guests arrived she had a habit of rushing to the mirror to powder her face. I remember her with much affection and love. Her house used to be full when her grandchildren got together and we all used to sleep on mattresses on the floor in the hall while the elders occupied the two bedrooms. After a lovely vacation at Granny's place, I joined Loyola College.

Loyola was very different from Christian College. There were no manicured lawns and well-maintained hedges. The entire campus was spread across fifty acres, housing a cricket ground, ten tennis courts, a hockey-cum-football field, a chapel, Bertram Hall, the Father's Lodge, the hostel buildings and the more recently-constructed science blocks. The college was located in the heart of the town in Kodambakham and the main gate faced Sterling Road, which had the Railway Officers' Colony on either side. I had an upstairs room in the second block of the hostel. There were five mess halls housing the English, Cosmopolitan, Tamil I, Tamil II and Andhra messes—the last three were vegetarian.

I took up Maths Honours where Father Racine, a French priest, was the head of the department. We had a Mathematics teacher called Adivarahan whom we nicknamed 'ancient pig'. I was fascinated by Adivarahan's geometry classes. I was hardly fifteen days in the college, when I got a call from the principal to meet him. The principal, Father Jerome D'Souza, was an imposing personality with an extraordinary command of English and a booming voice. Father D'Souza informed me that from the marks list of the Intermediate examination, it appeared I had done well in Chemistry in addition to Maths and Physics. He also said that owing to a student not having joined the Chemistry Honours course after being selected for it, there was a vacancy there that I could fill in.

I was completely taken aback by this offer. Noticing my hesitation, Father D'Souza told me that there were only fifteen seats in Chemistry Honours in the entire Madras University and that it was a much coveted seat that was now being offered to me. I was relieved that I had not been summoned for disciplinary action and, regaining my courage, I told the principal that Maths was my favourite subject and, as I wanted to join the IAS, I felt that it would help me to score high marks. He looked at me with an indulgent smile and asked me how I could be so sure of joining the IAS when only about thirty candidates out of more than a lakh were selected for the service every year. In case of failure, qualification in Maths would not provide me a good opportunity for an alternate job whereas with Chemistry, job opportunities were boundless, he continued. Seeing my hesitation to accept his offer, he gave me two days time to decide.

I wrestled with the problem as I had no means of consulting my father who was in Mysore. Consultation over the telephone was not an available option as my father did not have a telephone. I talked to my friend Venu (grandson of VT Krishnamachari) who said he had a friend in Mysore who had a telephone. I contacted his friend and explained to him the offer made to me by the principal and requested him to consult my father and let me have his opinion. I got an answer from my father asking me to decide for myself. Finally, I thought that there was considerable force in Father D'Souza's advice and joined Chemistry Honours—a complete change in my scholastic career.

Chemistry Honours was fun. The laboratory work, which was half the course, was very interesting. My scholastic record in the first two years was excellent. I seemed to have mastered Chemistry and I stood first in my class two years running. At the annual college day functions I was proud to receive two silver medals in recognition of my achievement. By this time I had come to be known in college as the South Indian Junior Tennis Champion, College Tennis Captain, Hostel Champion in table tennis and a meritorious student of Chemistry Honours, all rolled into one. My parents were very pleased with my performance.

I had my first encounter with the Police on Sterling Road. My friend Vaz and I, both hostellers, decided to see a late night movie and borrowed bicycles for our outing. We were on our way back, cycling hard on Sterling Road, when I saw a police constable who signalled us to halt as we had no lights on our bikes. I decided to make a run for it and pedalling fast I ducked under the outstretched baton of the constable. Vaz did not see the baton and ran straight into it. He fell off his bike and injured his nose. The constable said he would book a case against us for riding without lights, expecting a tip from us to be let off. We did not have any money. Seeing us penniless he marched us to the nearest police station and booked a case against us. He asked us to appear before the court in Mylapore the next day and we trudged back to the hostel very late that night.

The next day both of us bunked class and appeared in court and there were eager lawyers to take up our case for as little as four *annas*. A friend of ours had advised that in order to cut short the court proceedings and repeated appearances in court the best course of action would be to plead guilty. Our case came up before the magistrate late in the afternoon and we both were in the accused dock when he asked us whether we plead guilty or not. We pleaded guilty and each of us was fined a rupee.

This story has a sequel. When I was applying to the UPSC years later, to appear in the civil services competitive examination, there was a query in the application form whether the applicant had at any time been convicted by a court. This was an embarrassing question to answer and I thought it would prejudice my application if I answered in the affirmative. When I consulted my father, he was clear in his mind that honesty was the best policy and advised me to fill up the form truthfully, owning up to a minor traffic offence when I was a student. My honesty in replying to this question was appreciated when I later appeared for the interview but that is yet another story.

A year after I joined Loyola College my father retired from service and took up a small house on rent in Krishnamurthy Puram in Mysore. Rani finished her education in Maharani's College and Rathi did her schooling in the nearby convent. During my Christmas and summer vacations I used to spend time with my parents and sisters. We lived a very simple life. My father had a bicycle and he used to do the day's shopping on it. We went to Devraj Market in Sayyaji Rao Road by bus and visited Bollu Uncle's small condiments shop. Occasionally we visited the Gaity Theatre to see a Tamil or Hindi film. My parents were members of the cosmopolitan club where I used to join them for tennis. I enjoyed playing singles with the local tennis champion ML Rama Rao. Ours was a happy middle class existence and I remember we had a special celebration when we bought our first radio in 1949.

While I was in Loyola College hostel, my monthly budget was Rs 100, which used to come regularly by money order. It was a tight fit to manage with this amount as my tennis used to cost me extra for maintenance of the racquet and purchase of the tennis shoes. As captain I had to pay the bus fares of my team when we visited other colleges for inter-collegiate tennis and on some occasions we used to celebrate our victory by visiting the local hotel for a *dosa* (South Indian snack) and coffee treat. One day, I was sitting in the canteen and enjoying a morning cup of coffee. D Srinivas, who was doing Chemistry research, was with me. He said he was an astrologer and palmist and asked me to show him my palm. After a few minutes of studying my palm he looked at me with wonder and said that I have a very bright future in India and internationally and I would travel widely by the time I was seventy, at which age I would receive State honours. It was an amazing prediction, which has been proved true in every way.

I appeared for the final year examination in 1951 with the confidence that I would lead the class again as I had done in the first two years of the course. I did well but, in the crucial practicals, the crucible in which I was conducting the experiment fragmented while cooling and I could not complete the experiment. I was in tears and brought it to the notice of the external examiners hoping for some relief. All that they said was that I could repeat the experiment by taking a new crucible. I told them that I was in the final stages of the experiment and there was no time to repeat it. I requested them to note in my answer sheet that the crucible had broken on its own while cooling and not due to any mistake of mine. Later I was to learn that I lost my rank due to this mishap.

I went home dejected but I was greatly relieved when the results were announced—I had obtained a first class and sixth rank in the university. It was time for celebration and celebrate we did by going to the Chamundi Temple located on the Chamundi Hills nearby. We also spent some time with my grandmother at Fairdale.

Inevitably, after my results were out, my father wanted to discuss my future plans. I had just turned twenty and was under age to appear for the civil services examination. Our financial situation was precarious and I knew I had to take up a job immediately. I told my father that I would work as a lecturer in Loyola College after the summer vacation and while on the job would prepare for the civil services examination. He suggested that I appear for the Indian Police Service (IPS) examination in October 1951 as the age limit for that was twenty. I told him that I had been successful in all my examinations the first time around and what would I do if I got selected for the IPS. Would I be able to give it up for the IAS the next year? My father agreed that I make my first and best shot at the IAS examination in October 1952.

3

The Turning Point

I joined as a lecturer in Loyola College on 3 June 1952 for a princely salary of Rs 100 per month. When I received my first month's salary, one *anna* was deducted as the cost of the revenue stamp on which I had to sign the receipt. I chose Organic Chemistry for my lectures as I could easily memorise the chemical formula for teaching my students.

I was enjoying my work as it also involved supervision of the students in laboratory work. I continued to play tennis in the first court, won a hundred metre-race for teachers at the college annual day function (I still have the the long three-cell torch won by me as a prize) and simultaneously prepared for the General Knowledge and General English papers of the civil service examination. It was a do-or-die mission for me to succeed in this examination. I had to appear in five papers apart from General Knowledge and General English. It was a busy year for me and I longed for the summer vacation to take a break and visit home in Mysore. News had spread in Kodagu that I was appearing for the IAS and much was made of me as people were eyeing me as a potential son-in-law!

When I left Loyola College I had handed in my resignation as lecturer as I had no intention of continuing in the next academic year. I returned to Chennai after my vacation and sought accommodation in the newly-opened Catholic Centre near Parry's Corner. Soon I was down to the grind of studying very seriously. As luck would have it, I received unexpected help from Sivarama Reddy, a fellow resident of the Catholic Centre who was appearing for his Geography Honours examination. He gave me all his books and extensive notes and I am ever grateful to him as I scored high in Geography.

While I was preparing for the examination, I gave myself an hour of free time every evening for a walk on Marina Beach. The sea breeze was like a tonic and I would return refreshed. My companions during the seaside walk used to be Chennira Ponnu and Chonira Cariappa. We used to walk together sometimes up to the St Mary's College in the hope of seeing some pretty girls there.

When the examination was a week away, I started relaxing the rigour of my studies and from fourteen hours a day, it came down to nil on the day preceding the examination. On that day I just went to see a film in the nearby Midland Talkies, which was the only air-conditioned movie hall in Chennai at that time. I saw *Razor's Edge*, had an early dinner at the canteen and was off to bed by 9 pm. I had a wonderful and restful sleep. The next day I got up at 6 am, said my morning prayers and after an early breakfast I set out for the examination centre by bus, reaching there at least half-an-hour early. I sat under a tree, quietly contemplating the scene around me with many aspirants reading and making last-minute preparations. Many of them looked at me with surprise for I was sitting under the tree motionless, as if I had no care in the world. When the first bell rang I got up and went inside the examination hall. I greeted the boys seated next to me and wished them luck. They acknowledged my greetings with a grin but there was no return wish! I then realised that in a competitive examination each man is for himself and there was no place for sentiments here.

In preparation for the interview I became an avid reader of newspapers. I would jot down points for possible questions and that helped me to think and react in an orderly manner. I got the call for the interview towards the end of January 1953. I arrived in Delhi by train two days in advance and stayed at Madras Hotel in Connaught Place. It was my first visit to Delhi and it took me a day to adjust to the intense cold. The next day I took a bus to Shahjahan Road to familiarise myself with the approach to Dholpur House, which was the venue of my interview. I did not know a soul in Delhi then. The room rent was Rs 10 a day and the food was South Indian vegetarian, which was not alien to my taste.

The interview was to start at 10 am and six candidates were seated in a large waiting room that was kept warm with *angeethis* (charcoal burners). When I was called in I leaned back on my seat and placed my hands on my lap under the table. I was advised to keep my hands hidden as hands have a knack of revealing the tension and nervousness of a candidate. The first few questions from the Chairman were matter-of-fact and affable, on my journey, how I found Delhi on my first visit and so on. He was glancing at a factsheet about me and he enquired whether I came from Coorg, the fabled land of generals. I answered in the affirmative. His next question was whether there was any rail connection to Coorg and, in the absence of railways, how does one reach Coorg. Then he asked me how many main roads are out of Coorg and when I answered there were three main roads out of Coorg in addition to subsidiary roads he disputed the fact and said he had visited Coorg when he was Home Secretary and there were only two main roads out of Coorg, one to Mysore and one to Mangalore. When I tried to explain, he cut me short by banging his fist on the table. That triggered a reaction from me that he did not expect. I brought my hand from my lap and, with a closed fist, I banged the table, asserting that since I am from Coorg, I should know better. I saw the other members gape at me in disbelief and I thought my interview was headed towards disaster. A smile appeared on the Chairman's face and he asked me to show him the roads on a map hung on the side wall. I got up confidently, pointed out the third exit out of Coorg from Virajpet to Cannanore. From there onwards the interview went off well and, as I got up to leave, the members of the interviewing board smiled at me. I knew then that I had fulfilled my father's wish. Later, when I got the marks, I found that I had obtained the third highest interview marks in our batch. Natwar Singh, who joined the Indian Foreign Service (IFS), got the highest marks in the interview; Venkatramanan was second.

After the interview, I travelled back home by train and en route did some sightseeing in Agra and Gwalior. I saw the Taj Mahal, of course, visited Nur Jehan's tomb, the Agra fort and Fatehpur Sikri. I sat on the marble platform where the great Tansen used to sing for Akbar. I prayed at the beautiful mausoleum of Chisti, tying a thread on the marble frieze surrounding the tomb, praying for my success in the examination. I visited the historic fort of the Scindias of Gwalior and headed home to Mysore. My parents were eager to know the details of my interview and my father was pleased when I told him that in my reckoning I had done well. As I waited for the results to be announced, we had a stream of visitors, including friends and relatives, some with match-making intentions.

On 13 February 1953, the results were announced. My father had gone out in the morning to pick up the milk and the newspaper from the shop diagonally opposite our house. He came back and shouted for me, announcing that my name had figured in the combined list of successful candidates for the IAS and the IFS. I was shaving at that time and as the general jubilation increased in the house I continued to shave while simultaneously offering a quick thanksgiving prayer for my success. My mother and sisters dragged me out, congratulating me and I went and hugged my father and thanked him for the motivation that he had provided. As I sat in their midst I realised it was a big turning point not only for me but for my entire family. We lit a lamp and prayed together and thanked God. That evening we went to a temple before everyone started coming to our house to congratulate me.

In the first week of March 1953, I received a telegram from the UPSC asking me to report to a Joint Secretary in South Block in New Delhi and that a letter explaining the position would follow. I waited three days and as my journey to New Delhi via Chennai would take at least three days, I set out by train on the fourth day without receiving the letter. I was under the impression that I had been called for training in the IAS and I went with my entire luggage. I was travelling third class in the Grand Trunk Express. At Bezwada (now called Vijaywada) Railway Station, a nattily dressed young man got into the same compartment and took his seat a few feet away from me and in his hearty Malayalee accent announced that he was going to Delhi for the IFS interview. He had, apparently, received the letter following the telegram and there it was clearly written that he had been invited for the IFS interview. During the initial years of the constitution of the IFS, Pandit Nehru took a personal interest in interviewing the candidates after the UPSC interview. I then realised that I was heading for a similar interview. Taking advantage of the fact that the train was halting for half-an-hour at the station for stocking the pantry car I got down and went in search of a telegraph station. Not finding one I approached the station master and sought his help to send a telegram to my father to inform him of the real purpose of my visit to Delhi. Two days later, when after reaching Delhi I checked in at the Madras Hotel, a telegram was awaiting me asking me not to join the IFS and to return home. Armed with this telegram I went to South Block and reported to Rajeshwar Dayal, Joint Secretary in the Ministry of External Affairs. I showed him the telegram and sought his permission to withdraw from the interview. He was emphatic in not giving me permission as he said it was not in his powers to grant my request. As I sat in his antechamber, seven other candidates trooped in, including Natwar Singh. There was another person who caught my eye, it was Shyam Sunder Nath, who was from Peshawar. I also met A Damodaran who had stood second in our batch, a person very much older to us. He had been given age concession as he had the credentials of a freedom fighter who took an active part in the freedom movement led by Mahatma Gandhi.

We were called in one by one for the initial interview with RK Nehru, the Foreign Secretary who was assisted by MJ Desai, ICS, Secretary, External Affairs Ministry. I was called in fifth and, as I entered the room, I saw both of them seated on a sofa in a corner of the room. I was asked to sit opposite them on another sofa. The first question I was asked was why I was interested in joining the Foreign Service. To their bewilderment, I answered that I did not want to join the Foreign Service. I saw RK Nehru cup his ears and say, 'Come again.' He thought he had heard me wrong. I repeated my answer and also told them of my earlier conversation with their Joint Secretary, seeking permission to withdraw from the interview. I produced before them the telegram from my father.

They had apparently never faced a candidate who was declining the invitation to join their service. They asked me the reason for my disinclination to join the Foreign Service and I mentioned that since I was the only son I had commitments in India. They tried to persuade me to change my mind and when I held firm, they bade goodbye to me. I came back to Rajeshwar Dayal's room and told him what had transpired. He said the final interview was with Pandit Nehru. I told him that I did not have the courage to meet Pandit Nehru with a 'no' and after shaking hands with him and the other candidates, I returned to Madras Hotel. The next day I caught the train back to Chennai and then on to Mysore. I have preserved my father's telegram to this day.

4

God's Hand

Finally, official orders reached me to join the IAS and I was directed to go for my probationary training to Metcalfe House in Delhi on 14 April 1953. My appointment made news in the local newspapers as well as in Coorg. Within a week we received a letter from a Coimbatore businessman seeking alliance with his daughter. My parents of course ignored the letter but it provided some ammunition for my sisters to make fun of me. In Mysore, I was invited by the local Kodava students to address them and to provide them an opportunity to felicitate me. This was my first function as a Chief Guest and I still have the group photograph that was taken with the students.

With the blessings of my parents and the good wishes of friends and relatives, I set out a third time to Delhi to join the IAS. I was eager to meet my batchmates, all of whom had come through a gruelling test. We could easily call ourselves 'the crème of the crème' of the Indian universities. We had representation from almost all States. I was not the only one from Karnataka, there was another from Dharwad and his name was PR Dubashi. I mention his name in particular as he was the most inquisitive among us. We had a number of guest lectures by eminent people of Delhi and used to wait with relish for Dubashi's encounter with them. At the end of the lecture, even before the announcement was made inviting questions, Dubashi would have raised his hand and asked his question in a pompous manner. Some of the questions were erudite and some were silly and we used to sit back relieved that there was somebody to ask the questions. He has recently been honoured with the Padma Bhushan award.

We were housed in what used to be the Army barracks in the vast compound of Metcalfe House. Each probationer had a spacious room with a verandah in front and with an attached dressing room and bathroom. There was a primitive flush system with an overhead tank. The furniture was essentially utilitarian and minimal. There was one bearer attached to two probationers and he used to bring our morning tea, make the beds, polish our shoes and generally be at our disposal for running errands. I felt this was the height of luxury as I had never before enjoyed such comforts.

We were a total of thirty-eight trainees including seven IFS probationers who trained with us for the first four months and one officer promoted from the State civil service to the IAS from Gujarat. The Vice-Principal was JD Shukla, a senior ICS Officer from the Uttar Pradesh (UP) cadre, whose residence was within the campus. He was short and dapper with a thick face and intelligent eyes. He used to smoke a cigar after dinner. He was well-versed in Urdu poetry and he recited it in the elegant Lucknavi style. He used to teach us the basic nuances of administration in general and district administration in particular. We had a lecturer to teach us Economics and a retired Sessions Judge by the name of Munir to teach us Criminal Law. We had language teachers to teach us the basics of the spoken language of the State we were assigned to. There were visits from Bapat, ICS, who was doubling up as the principal of the school while functioning as an Additional Secretary in one of the Ministries. He gave us insights into the ICS and how they functioned as administrators. He had a relaxed way of talking and a peculiar mannerism of doodling on the blackboard behind his back while addressing us.

The day for a probationer started at 6 am. We were woken up by the bearer with a hot pot of tea. The reporting time for morning Physical Training (PT) was 6.30, followed by a brisk workout for half-an-hour on the spacious lawns next to the barracks. After PT, I would run round the barracks six times, covering a mile in about ten minutes. I was the only runner as the others felt tired after PT. We used to brush up our studies for an hour in the morning and present ourselves for breakfast by 9 am. The table setting was immaculate and we learnt the art of using forks, spoons and knives.

After breakfast we all used to troop into the classroom next door where, apart from the regular subjects taught, we used to get the senior officers from various Central Ministries as guest lecturers. Afternoon classes ended at 4 pm when we were required to play games. There was tabletennis, tennis and volleyball. I used to play all the three games.

It was decided to hold a tournament in tennis before the departure of the IFS probationers to Oxford and Cambridge for further training. I was given the task of arranging the tournament. I paired the probationers by lots and arranged a handicap doubles tournament. I had a lot of fun umpiring these matches as the line calls were mostly disputed and I had to adjudicate. Shyam Sundernath, an IFS probationer because of his American study background, considered himself to be a great player but there was great mirth when his team was defeated by the girls' team. We had three girls in our batch—who provided the romantic interest for us.

The Vice-Principal, who witnessed the doubles tournament, decided that Natwar Singh and I would play an exhibition match and a date was fixed for the match. Natwar and I used to practise playing singles and I found him to be an accomplished player with neat strokes. He was a consistent and good baseline player. As the day for the exhibition match approached there was much excitement. The other probationers had seen us play and they were expecting a good match. I won and there was general jubilation in the IAS camp that we had inflicted a defeat on the IFS. Our outdoor activities included horse riding, rifle and revolver shooting practice at the police lines and attending motor mechanics classes at the Basrurkar's Garage in Connaught Place. I also learnt driving.

By the third month of the IAS training we were unofficially advised about the States to which we had been allotted. I was allotted to West Bengal along with Penn Anthony and Mihir Chowdhary. It was the rule to allot candidates in such a way that at least fifty per cent were from outside the State. I started learning Bengali. A couple of months later we were deputed for attachment with the Army for training. Half of us went to Kashmir and the other half to Assam for attachment with Army units for two weeks. LI Parija, VT Chari and I were attached to an infantry division on the Baramulla, Poonch and Uri sectors. We were in the frontline, sharing Army bunkers dug into the mountain slopes.

Our last programme in Kashmir was to have tea with the Prime Minister of Jammu and Kashmir (J&K), Sheikh Abdullah. He was designated as Prime Minister at that time as J&K had its own constitution even after its merger with India in 1948. A week before our appointment with him we learnt he had been taken into custody by the Indian authorities and his deputy Bukshi Ghulam Mohammad was made the Prime Minister. The tea appointment was cancelled and we missed the chance of a lifetime of meeting the charismatic leader of Kashmir. Years later he made his peace with Pandit Nehru and regained his political standing in J&K as its Chief Minister.

On reaching Delhi I learnt that my cadre allotment had been changed from West Bengal to Orissa. There were three vacancies in West Bengal and they had earlier ordered that one Bengali and two non-Bengalis would be posted from our batch. In the revised orders, BC Mukherjee, who was slotted to go to Orissa, was ordered to go to West Bengal and I was asked to go to Orissa instead. I took the orders in my stride without any resentment and started learning Oriya instead of Bengali. Parija was also happy that I was going to Orissa as we had struck up a close friendship by that time. Later we came to know that BC Roy, the Chief Minister of West Bengal, had suggested the cadre change. Mukherjee obviously felt bad that I had been displaced from West Bengal and he visited me a number of times in my room but I never raised the issue with him. In retrospect it was God's hand again working in my favour. None of the three persons who went to West Bengal distinguished themselves either in the State or in the Centre.

Our batch had a fifteen-day outing or Bharat Darshan to see India. We were divided into three groups with a team leader and a faculty member for each team. I was nominated as a team leader. On the tour we had to call on dignitaries and it was the responsibility of the team leader to ensure that the team assembled in time and was introduced to the dignitary. As I was not very good at remembering names I told the members of my team that if I made any mistakes in the introduction they should keep quiet. We went in a special coach by train and had a magical tour of Rajasthan, visiting Ajmer, Jaipur, Chittorgarh, Udaipur and Pushkar. Our next outing was to the Police Academy at Mount Abu in Rajasthan where our IPS batchmates were being trained. We were attached to the academy for fifteen days and put through our paces in horse riding, rifle and pistol shooting and vigorous bayonet practice. We were taught the basics of Police administration and learnt how to inspect a police station.

During those days the District Magistrate was the supreme leader in the district with the Police under his general supervision and control, a fact resented by the IPS Officers to this day. We got along with our IPS colleagues and they treated us with respect when we beat them in all the games we played—cricket, tennis, tabletennis, shuttle and volleyball. Parija and I led our batch to victory.

On completion of our training we had to appear in a written examination, which we had to pass and we also had to undergo a second interview conducted by the UPSC. The marks scored in the interview together with the impression marks given by the Vice-Principal were added to the total marks originally scored by us in the selection examination to determine one's revised ranking in the batch. I gained about four or five places in the overall ranking and the highest impression marks as a probationer, given to me by the Vice-Principal, helped me to improve my position. I was happy to learn that the Vice-Principal considered me to have the best overall personality in the batch.

The last day at Metcalfe House was celebrated on the lawns till well past midnight. I took the evening train to Chennai the next day. It was the same Grand Trunk Express in which I had travelled to Delhi to take up my new job. I came home to a hero's welcome in Mysore. My sister Rani had completed her studies and was a graduate in Psychology from Maharani's College, Mysore and Rathi was in school. All of us went on a brief holiday to Coorg to spend time with my grandmother. Before I knew it, I was back on the train to join duty in Orissa, my State cadre.

5

Posting in Orissa

I reached Cuttack, the old capital of Orissa and its largest town, a little past midnight. I had written to the Collector and informed him of my travel plans. When I got down from the train in the deserted and sleepy railway station, I found to my surprise that there was no one to receive me. The porter informed me that there was not a single taxi in Cuttack and even the horse-drawn *tonga* was not available at this late hour. It was a very depressing landing in Cuttack as I had visions of being officially received and driven to the circuit house. I asked the porter to guide me to the first class waiting room where I took refuge for the night and slept on a wooden chair with rattan backing and foldable leg rests, an item of furniture that was standard in all the Government rest houses in Orissa. Mosquitoes were a nuisance and the next day, when I was served tea by the waiting room attendant, I found that his right leg was swollen with filaria. It was a horrible welcome that Cuttack gave me but, surprisingly, despite this initial setback, my official life in Orissa proved to be most enjoyable.

The day after my arrival I set out on foot to call on the Collector. I was invited to have breakfast with him at eight in the morning and my two-mile walk took me past the Cuttack Club. V Ananthakrishnan and his wife received me with warmth and I found them to be a delightful couple. Ananthakrishnan gave me the necessary guidance about how I should conduct myself in my official and civil life. He advised a series of courtesy calls to all the senior officers in town. When I called on the seniormost civilian in town, Sri Senapati, ICS, he noticed my formal attire and told me that it neither suited the climate nor the ethos of Orissa, and advised me to dress informally. He was the Member, Board of Revenue and I was astonished when he returned my courtesy call the following Sunday, clad in half-pants! I also called on Justice R Narasimhan, ICS. He was a judge of the Orissa High Court.

The Cuttack Club was the centre of all social activities for officers posted there. I joined the tennis club and soon found there was no one to match my game. I ventured to learn other club games such as billiards and bridge. It was at the bridge table that I met Biju Patnaik who at that time was the most prominent industrialist of the State. He owned Kalinga Industries and Kalinga Airways. He was a flamboyant character with a magnetic personality. He was also an aviator who conducted a daring mission on the request of the Central Government to rescue Sukarno, the future President of Indonesia. Biju Patnaik undertook a solo flight to Djakarta in a Dakota and rescued Sukarno from the thick of the battle of independence being waged by his followers against the Dutch. Jawaharlal Nehru became his personal friend after this event. Later, on entering politics, Biju Patnaik became the Chief Minister of Orissa.

I was new to bridge at that time and I learnt the game under the tutelage of Mrs Narayanswami, wife of the Director of the State Postal Services. I used to play at the club with her and also at the bridge parties held at her house. I soon developed a passion for the game and started taking part in tournaments.

Bridge has sustained me all these years. A few of the interesting hands that I played have been reported in the bridge columns of *The Hindu*. I won the All Orissa Singles Championship in badminton and tennis and also won in billiards in the club tournaments. I am now past my seventy-fifth year, I continue to play bridge six days a week and I derive great pleasure matching my wits against very good players in Bengaluru. I am also happy that my wife Indira has taken to the game. Mathematically there are 635,013,559,599 possible hands in a game of bridge. In my second year of playing bridge in Cuttack, I was associated in a game where my partner K Srinivasan held all thirteen cards of a suit, a rarest of rare happenings.

When I joined duty in Cuttack for field training I was designated as Assistant Collector and was conferred with Class III magisterial powers to try criminal cases. My initial days of training were spent in being attached to the various sections of the collectorate to give me firsthand knowledge of how the district administration functions. Ananthakrishnan used to take me on tours to the sub-divisional and *tehsil* (administrative division) offices in the district. I very vividly remember our tour to a sub-divisional town of Athgarh where I was a witness to an enquiry being conducted by the Collector into an allegation of molestation by a tribal Adivasi girl against the local *tehsildar* (administrative officer) named Guru.

I held court in a low-ceiling, thatched barrack next to the main collectorate building. I used to cycle down every day to attend court, equipped with a sola hat to guard against the sun and, on rainy days, I used to wear a raincoat. I would cycle with as much dignity as I could muster, being a magistrate and was delighted when after a few days the traffic constable near my court started saluting me as I passed by. I was surprised when, one day, he appeared before me as an accused in a simple trespass case in a property dispute filed by his neighbour. Being pleased with his deference to me on my cycle, I was happy to acquit him and that was my first judgment as a magistrate!

My room had a *punkah* (fan) and the *punkah* puller sat on the verandah with the rope in his hand. When the lawyers were on their feet arguing before me the *punkah* could not be pulled due to the low ceiling. The lawyers who appeared before me were third-rate and they were in the habit of prolonging their presentation to impress their clients who did not understand a single word of English. In the beginning, as I was new to my job, I used to patiently hear them out though there was much bombast and no substance in their presentation. In the third month as a magistrate, I thought of an idea to cut them short, by having an arrangement with the *punkah* puller who would start pulling the *punkah* when I gave him a signal by pulling out my handkerchief from my pocket. When the *punkah* was pulled, it forced the lawyers to sit down. The lawyers got wise to this arrangement and when they saw my hand approach my pocket, they used to plead with me to give them a minute's time to conclude their argument, which I gladly granted. I was nicknamed the '*punkah*-magistrate' and years later one of the lawyers met me in Delhi and asked me whether I was the same person who induced the lawyers in my court to shorten their argument with the judicious use of the *punkah*.

Next door to me, in the main building of the collectorate, was located the revenue court of the Additional Collector, the officer next in rank to the Collector. The incumbent of the post was a very colourful character named DD Suri who got into the IAS as an emergency recruit. Legend has it that after hearing a revenue case for three days he passed the most famous and eccentric order: 'Heard both parties. Both speak nonsense. Case dismissed.' For obvious reasons he did not do too well in service.

My field training period as Assistant Collector was for a year but, in December 1954, I was posted as Special Magistrate with second class powers.

Three decades later I met him in Delhi when I was Additional Secretary, Finance. After his retirement, he had settled down in Delhi and was functioning as an informer to the Customs and Excise Department, earning a commission for the tax collection made through the information furnished by him. He told me that his earning this way was much more than his salary as an IAS Officer.

My field training period as Assistant Collector was for a year but, in December 1954, I was posted as Special Magistrate with second class powers. I was to head a section of the armed Police in charge of a *havildar* (a non-commissioned officer corresponding to a sergeant), at a place called Chandbali in Bhadrak Sub-Division, Balasore District. My instructions were to tour the area with the armed force to control the lawlessness in the Kanika area, fomented by the tenant's agitation against the *zamindar* (landlord) of Kanika. The agrarian unrest was led by Chakradhar Behera and the lawlessness that followed had claimed six lives. I reached Chandbali by bus after getting briefed by the Sub-Divisional Officer at Bhadrak and took up my residence there in the local *dak* bungalow (rest house).

The armed Police reported to me the next day. Chandbali was a port on the Baitarani River and the only other officer present at Chandbali was the Port Officer. I called on him and obtained a map to familiarise myself with the topography of the area. The Kanika area was approachable by boat and I, along with the Police, set out in two boats. For the next fifteen days we route-marched in the area, covering about fifteen to twenty miles daily. The policemen carried their own rations and I used to eat with them, paying for the food consumed by me. At nightfall we used to rest in the primary schools. I met a large number of villagers, the village head and local *patwaris* (land record officers). The march brought peace to the area and we learnt that the ringleader Chakradhar Behera had gone into hiding when we visited his village. I returned to Chandbali earning the respect of the local population and also of the Police contingent that I led for the physical stamina that I had exhibited. The Raja of Kanika later became a Minister and, when I met him as Collector, Balasore District, during his visit to Balasore, he praised my efforts for bringing peace to his area. When he expressed his displeasure that I had not called on him while I was on duty earlier at Kanika, I silenced him by saying that an officer has to maintain an aura of impartiality while on sensitive duty. He had a bad reputation as a *zamindar*.

I received a promotion and was posted as Sub-Divisional Officer, Bhadrak, after a month's stay in Chandbali. As Sub-Divisional Magistrate, I had first class powers to impose punishment of up to two years of imprisonment. The local doctor of the Government hospital, Prakash Rao, became a close friend of mine. I used to discourage him from drinking in my presence as prohibition was in force in the sub-division. After inspection of the sub-jail in Bhadrak, I asked him to visit the prisoners once a week to treat them. There was a prisoner convicted of murder who was awaiting the confirmation of his death sentence by the Orissa High Court. I allowed his family to visit him once a week. When the High Court confirmed his death sentence I was present at his hanging inside the prison along with Dr Rao. The hanging was fixed at 6 am and I vividly remember the sombre scene, which I had to supervise and send a report to the Session's Court in Balasore. The man walked steadily up to the gallows, he greeted me with folded hands before the black hood and the rope were slipped on his head. I gave him a minute to pray before signalling for the opening of the trapdoor underneath his feet. I, too, prayed before giving the signal. We waited for fifteen minutes as per jail regulations and inspected his dangling body for the doctor to pronounce him dead. It was a magisterial duty that I would prefer not to perform again.

I had the misfortune to face drought and floods in the sub-division in the same year. Relief camps were started in the drought areas and starvation deaths were avoided. The unprecedented floods that followed the rainy season covered all the four coastal districts of Orissa—Balasore, Cuttack, Puri and Ganjam. Half my sub-division was underwater, flooded by the swelling water of the Baitarni and Subarnarekha Rivers. I mobilised boats to undertake relief operations and the distribution of food. I was about to set off in a boat to personally supervise the operations when I got a wireless message to await the arrival of Nilamoni Routroy who was a Deputy Minister elected from the Bhadrak constituency. He expressed a desire to tour with me and we set off together in a big rowing and punting boat. We were on water for the next ten days. To our surprise we learnt that there were more deaths due to snake bites than drowning. The poisonous snakes found refuge along with the people in the available small bits of dry land in the villages. We used to sleep on the boat and sustained ourselves on the food packets that we were also distributing to the flood-affected people. Nilamoni had a tin of State Express 555 cigarettes. Finding me tired one day he offered me one and that was the first cigarette I smoked in my life. This led to my becoming a confirmed smoker for the next thirty-two years until I kicked the habit in 1987. Nilamoni became the Chief Minister of Orissa. He used to remind me about the first smoke I had with him.

After the drought and floods were over, administration in the sub-division returned to normal until the publication of the States Reorganisation Commission report. It appeared that the verdict of the Commission that two predominantly Oriya speaking areas, Kharsuan and Seraikella, would form part of the adjoining Bihar State, was perverse. The statewide agitation that followed resulted in police firing in Puri and Cuttack. I imposed a ban against the assembly of people and processions under Section 144 of the Criminal Procedure Code. On learning that the student leaders of Bhadrak College had started gathering at the playing field of the college to start a procession defying the ban, I drove up unescorted to the college premises and, seeing the student leaders playing volleyball, joined them in the game, much to their surprise. By that one friendly action I gained their confidence and I was able to convince them in the discussion that followed that it was best not to defy the ban and a serious law and order situation was thus averted.

The people of Bhadrak were greatly excited that Acharya Vinoba Bhave would pass through the sub-division while he was on his *padayatra* (pilgrimage by foot), collecting land for the poor. He and his entourage of thirty people would be passing through my sub-division for two days, covering about fifteen miles each day. Their itinerary was drawn up in such a way that they reached a big village at mealtime so that they could rest in the local schools. Vinoba Bhave entered my sub-division at Bonth Village and I received him personally and garlanded him. I walked about a mile with him and then got into my jeep and returned to Bhadrak.

The next visitor of importance to my sub-division was VS Hejmadi, ICS, Chairman, UPSC, who was a botanist and a naturalist. The Collector, Balasore, instructed me to show him the crocodile sanctuary. It was a natural sanctuary at the confluence of the Baitarani and Brahmani Rivers at a place called Dhamra, a mile from the sea where the rivers ended their flow. I requisitioned a motorised boat with a cabin that belonged to the Port Officer at Chandbali. Hejmadi and I witnessed a rare sight—nearly a hundred crocodiles lazing in the mudbanks of the river on either side, enjoying the winter sun. A few crocodiles were in a frolicsome mood and they surrounded our boat, catching the passing fish. It was literally a sight for the Gods and Hejmadi thanked me profusely for arranging this visit. I was equally delighted.

While I thought I was doing a good job in Bhadrak, I received my orders of transfer in the first week of April 1956. I was being sent for settlement training for two months in Bolangir District. Through the official grapevine I learnt that I was being groomed to be the next Settlement Officer, a senior post. I got a rousing send-off from Bhadrak, especially from the student leadership of Bhadrak College, who had become my friends. Before my posting in Bhadrak I had acquired a second-hand car, a mini Hindustan 10. Bundling my meagre belongings into the car I set off to Sambalpur via Cuttack, a drive of about two hundred-and-fifty miles with a ferry crossing across Mahanadi as there was no road bridge across the river. At Sambalpur I called on the District Magistrate, KS Ramachandran and his pretty wife Neela, had dinner with them before proceeding further on to Bolangir, the district headquarters and then on to Sonepore, a *tehsil* headquarter where I had to report for duty. I joined the settlement camp located in an adjoining village. My tent was pitched next to the tent of the Assistant Settlement Officer. I got a lean-to constructed out of bamboo and bamboo matting to house my car.

Within a week I had learnt the basics of the settlement and mapping operations and the Assistant Settlement Officer permitted me to hold court under his supervision. The field work was hot and backbreaking, while the court work, entailing interacting with the villagers, was exciting. After returning to camp, to beat the heat, I used to drink half-a-bottle of locally brewed double-distilled Mohua liquor (looked like misty gin but more potent) and fall into deep sleep. I used to get up at 3 pm and eat a roast chicken (chicken in the village was available for four *annas*) prepared by my peon and get ready for the evening court proceedings. Once while camping in the open under a mohua tree, I had a close encounter with a bear, who was attracted by the honey-sweet mohua flower. I could only ward off its attack by frantically waving a fully-lit lantern in its face. I had no time to reach for my gun, which was tucked away under my camp cot.

After an interesting and adventurous training period I was happy to get away from the intense heat of Sonepur from where I was posted as Charge Officer, Settlement, Cuttack. My jurisdiction extended till Angul on the Sambalpur Road on one side, to Chilka on the road to Berhampur on the other side. During my years tenure as Charge Officer I completed the settlement of the Angul sub-division.

Chilka is the largest salt water lake in India and in winter it attracts migratory birds such as the Siberian duck. I have done bird-shooting at Chilka, which is quite an art as you have to be amid the birds stealthily, well before sunrise.

Chilka was also the pleasure ground of Snodgrass, the British Collector of Ganjam District, during the rule of the East India Company. He embezzled the revenues of the district, spending it on wine and women. He was finally arrested, tried and convicted. After imprisonment he was cashiered from service, denied a pension and deported to England. His fight to regain his pension was historic. He took to sweeping the streets before Parliament House, drawing attention to the breach of covenant by the Company in denying him pension. Parliament passed a special resolution ordering the Company to pay him.

I appeared for my departmental examination in Oriya Language and Treasury Account, which I could not take earlier as I had been suddenly posted out as Special Magistrate, Chandbali. The Oriya examination proved easy as I had gained proficiency in reading, writing and speaking the language. Accounts was a bore but I got through. The passing of these examinations was essential for my promotion to the senior scale, which was imminent.

In Cuttack I played bridge regularly and gained expertise in the game in the company of Justice Narasimhan and Mrs Narayanswami. I took part in the All Orissa Tennis and Badminton Championships and was the single's champion in both. That year (1956) I visited Puri to attend the Rath Yatra of Lord Jagannath and mingled with the crowd to pull the ropes of the chariots down the road called 'Bada Danda'. I witnessed the ceremony of the Raja of Puri sweeping the floor of the three *raths* (chariots) of Jagannath, Balabhadra and Subhadra, before the idols were installed on them. I also heard the priests of the temple singing obscene songs in Oriya as encouragement to the crowd to pull the huge wooden *raths* better with added vigour! The crowds were thick and heavy and there were excellent Police arrangements to control them.

I made friends with George Patnaik, the elder brother of Biju Patnaik. They were a contrast in style; the younger brother was flamboyant while George had a very low profile, riding a bicycle to work. That year I met Dr Pranakrishna Parija, father of my batchmate Lulu Parija. Dr Parija was a distinguished educationist who retired as Vice-Chancellor of Utkal University. I also made the acquaintance of Bhairab Mohanty who, through the help of the Orissa State lottery, raised funds to build a grand cricket stadium in Cuttack called 'Barabati Stadium'. On his invitation I became the Chairman of the Orissa State Badminton Association for a year after winning the State badminton championship. I was simultaneously the Vice-President of the Orissa State Bridge Association.

In October 1956, AD Pisharody (Sub-Divisional Officer, Post Offices; I had stayed at his official residence in Cuttack) and I decided to have a holiday in Darjeeling. We arrived there when the weather was turning cold but the sunshine was bright and beautiful. I had the unforgettable sight of the Kanchanjunga range of mountains looming over Darjeeling, the snow-clad hills literally glittering in sunlight. We made a trek to Tiger Hill, to view the mountain ranges at sunrise. As the sun rose in a cloudless sky we saw Kanchanjunga turning pink and then orange in the morning light for a fleeting five to ten minutes, a fabulous sight. Our guide pointed out to us the various peaks including Mount Everest, which was seen as a speck in the far horizon.

Before taking charge as Collector and District Magistrate, I went to Mysore to spend time with my parents and sisters, Rani and Rathi.

Towards the end of March 1957 I got my transfer orders, posting me as Collector and District Magistrate. Before taking charge I went on leave to spend some time with my parents in Mysore. From there it was a short trip to Mercara to visit my grandmother. The Chief Commissioner of Coorg was holding a tennis tournament in his residential premises and had invited some players from Mysore to take part. My mother and I took part in the mixed doubles tournament, which we won.

I also called on General KM Cariappa who had retired and settled in Mercara. Attired in my long-sleeved silk shirt, I walked the distance to the General's house and knocked at his door at 12 noon sharp. The General himself opened the door and, on seeing me attired informally, he asked me to wait outside. A minute later he opened the door with a tie in his hand and ordered me to wear it. I donned the tie and went inside and found him fully attired in a three-piece suit to receive me! He was a very gracious host and I was served a three-course lunch with a butler in attendance.

When I joined duty in Balasore I did not know that my tenure there would be so short. BC Mathur was to proceed to Delhi after his leave; he was posted there as Deputy Secretary, Government of India. Just on the eve of his departure the deputation rules were changed, prescribing eight years minimum service for an IAS Officer to be posted as Deputy Secretary at the Centre. Mathur, who had spent his holiday with his family touring the South, expressed a desire that he would not like to go to Delhi as Under-Secretary. The Chief Secretary rang me up and told me that Mathur would be reposted to Balasore as Collector and asked me whether I would like to go to Delhi in his place. I said I had no objection and in June that year, after a three-month stint as Collector and District Magistrate in Balasore, I was on my way to Delhi on my first deputation posting.

While in Balasore I disposed of a large number of revenue cases pending in the collectorate and reorganised the civil supplies wing of the collectorate to better serve in relief work during floods and drought. I toured the district extensively and inaugurated Balasore's first cinema hall. I also visited the defence establishment in Chandipur where an offshore firing centre had been established to test-fire long-range shells from the heavy guns of the Army. Chandipur has now developed into a major rocket launching centre.

6

Life in Delhi

This was my first posting to Delhi on deputation and two more were to follow. My expectations of a posting to Delhi were romantic but the romance was squashed on the day of arrival at the Old Delhi Railway Station. I had brought with me my car and luggage in an attached motorcar van. I had also brought along a cook from Balasore. No one met me on arrival and later in the day, when I reported for duty at the Ministry of Finance, I was shocked to learn that it would take months to get official residential accommodation. I had left my luggage in the first class retiring room and had asked my cook to keep an eye on it.

In the afternoon, when I returned to the station to unload my car and luggage, I did not know where I could store them. It was a daunting task. I called Madras Hotel from a telephone kiosk at the railway station but no one was willing to give me a room and storage space for my luggage. I was coming out of the booth dejected when the person next in line asked me whether I was in search of a house. He said he could help me and asked me to wait until he finished his telephone call. I heard him make two or three calls enquiring about houses and on coming out of the kiosk introduced himself to me as Chopra. He said that there were some vacant houses in Patel Nagar, which we could see immediately.

I had heard of conmen duping newcomers to Delhi and had kept a big spanner under my car's front seat in case my new friend was up to any mischief. We reached Patel Nagar at dusk and scoured the area for three hours in search of a house. At three vacant houses we drew a blank. The fourth vacant house, which we visited at about 10 pm that day, was a two-bedroom flat on the first floor with the landlady, a widow, occupying the flat above. My friend, speaking in Punjabi, convinced her about my credentials and we were happy when she agreed to have me as a tenant. With the help of my cook and the driver of the tempo my luggage was moved into the flat. It was midnight by the time we finished the work.

The restaurants in the area were closed and my friend suggested that we have dinner at the famous Moti Mahal restaurant in Daryaganj, which would be open till 2 am. Moti Mahal was a very well-known restaurant serving chicken delicacies and Peshawari food. We had a midnight repast of excellent *tandoori* (barbecued) food at the end of a tension-filled day. God had sent an angel in the shape of Chopra to help me out of an impossible situation on my first day in Delhi. He has continued his friendship with me even to this day and I can never forget the timely help he rendered to a total stranger.

Since my deputation to the Centre was so sudden, my workplace had not yet been determined. Lalvani, an officer of the Rajasthan IAS cadre, to whom I reported, sent me to the Ministry of Irrigation and Power to work as the Assistant Financial Advisor (AFA). They, however, sent me back as their Minister had already chosen his favourite for the post. I was then sent to the External Affairs Ministry where I joined as an AFA, sharing the same office room of another AFA named Soni from the Central Secretariat Service. I was allotted the work relating to the fixation and revision of foreign allowance, capital acquisitions and lease of premises abroad and budgets for our foreign embassies. My immediate boss was Raj Kumar who was Deputy Financial Advisor and above him was AS Bhatnager, the Financial Advisor (FA). After a week at work when I called on the FA, I mentioned to him that since I play tennis, I would not like to sit late in office unless there was work to do. He smiled at me and said, 'Young man, I do not come to office in the afternoon, because I play golf!'

I played tennis at the YMCA and that year our team beat the team representing Delhi Gymkhana Club in the annual inter-club tournament. They had been unbeaten champions for a number of years.

In December I was allotted a D-II type flat in Moti Bagh, a residential area about three kilometres from the Secretariat. The drive to Moti Bagh was by Shantipath and on either side of the wide road and expanse of greens were the newly-built embassy buildings of the prominent countries in the world.

Shortly before I shifted to Moti Bagh, I got news that my father, who had settled down in Mysore after retirement, had suffered a mild heart attack. I wrote to my parents and requested them to wind up their establishment in Mysore and live with me. My sister, Rani, had finished her college and Rathi was on the verge of completing her school. After considerable persuasion, they all agreed to live with me. It was also a financially sound proposition as it was difficult to maintain a double establishment with my meagre salary. From the day I drew my first salary in the IAS even as a probationer I had started sending money home.

The cook who had accompanied me from Balasore could not stand the Delhi cold and decided to go back. A couple of days before the arrival of my parents and sisters, I engaged a Nepalese cook. He was also able to cope with the extra work of the large family. Everything seemed perfect. On Sunday I took my parents and sisters out for a drive to India Gate. We were out for about three hours and when we came back home dinner was served. My mother, for some reason, did not eat. She had a glass of milk and noticed that within a few minutes of having eaten dinner, we were all showing signs of drowsiness and, to her horror, fell asleep at the dining table. In the neighbouring flat lived an IPS Officer, Warty. My mother sought his help. It took Warty no time to realise that we had been poisoned and as a trained Police Officer he acted swiftly in arranging our shift by ambulance to the nearby Safdarjung Hospital. We were immediately given a stomach wash, which saved our lives. The next day, when we got up in the hospital, we could not see a thing clearly and regained our eyesight twenty-four hours later. Our condition was diagnosed as 'Dattura poisoning'. Our servant pretended he had similar symptoms and he was also admitted to the hospital. The Moti Bagh Police let him off after questioning but we sacked him as we were certain that he had tried to put us to sleep as a prelude to burgling the house.

I took my parents and sisters to Agra to see the Taj Mahal. I also took them around Delhi and on one such trip, while we were passing the impressive circular Parliament building, my father expressed a desire to see it. It was late in the evening but not yet dusk. I parked my car at the main entrance and, after introducing myself and showing him my official pass, I requested the liveried guard on duty to let us to see the Parliament building. He not only allowed us in but escorted us inside the deserted building (Parliament was not in session). He also took us inside the chamber of the Lok Sabha. The general décor was green and we all took turns to sit on the first seat of the front row where the Prime Minister sits. Those were the days when one could meet the Prime Minister, rushing up the stairs of South Block to attend office, as I did many times.

I had my first trip abroad in 1958 when I visited Lahore in Pakistan. I was deputed there along with Lakshminarain Vadhera, Under-Secretary, External Affairs, to sort out the snag that had arisen in the lease agreement of the building that housed our consulate office in Lahore. We went by train, crossed the Wagah border checkpost and got into the Pakistan train waiting across the border. We reached Lahore in the evening and were put up in the consulate guest quarters where we stayed for three days. Along with attending to official work, we did some extensive sightseeing.

Lahore is a very pretty city with many Mughal gardens. The best kept, among the many visited, were around the tomb of Jehangir. We walked the length of Anarkali, the old shopping centre resembling Chandni Chowk of Delhi. I was particularly impressed with the deportment of the traffic police in Lahore. Smartly turned out in grey uniform, their hand signals were given with commanding authority. At Anarkali I bought a shawl and some dry fruits. The local consul took us to the Lahore Gymkhana Club where I played bridge. The atmosphere was friendly and belied the tension existing between the two countries. At the Gymkhana Club I met some of the prettiest women of Pakistan, some of whom were sophisticated enough to smoke cigarettes through dainty ivory cigarette holders. The ladies had Persian features and beautiful translucent skin.

On return from Pakistan, I was invited to one of the biggest diplomatic functions in Delhi—the inauguration of the beautiful marble and white stone building on Shanthipath to house the US Embassy. More than five thousand people were there. That year we also had the historic visit of Nikita Khrushchev and

Nikolai Bulganin from the USSR. Delhi gave them a rousing welcome, cheering as they drove by in an open car. Nehru was in his heydays of the non-aligned movement and India was a popular destination for visiting dignitaries.

During the Puja holidays in 1958, I set out on a five-day motor trip to Punjab with my parents and sisters. Accompanying us was Victor Perianayagam, a Postal Service Officer, whom we had met in Agra. He was one of the nuttiest characters I have ever seen—a friendly and honest soul who was a delightful companion. My parents and sisters liked him very much and there was never a dull moment during our trip. We went to Chandigarh and drove up to the Bhakra Nangal Dam that was under construction. From Bhakra we proceeded to the Anandpur Sahib gurudwara. Our last visit in Punjab was to the Golden Temple in Amritsar. Little did I realise then that this peaceful abode of God would provide sanctuary to criminals and terrorists who would turn it into a battlefield for the Government to regain control twice in the future in the security operations that were code-named Bluestar and Black Thunder. The latter operation was conducted under my supervision when I was the Home Secretary.

The people of Punjab charmed us with their active lifestyle, robust outlook and innate hospitality. Both the Sikhs and Hindus lived in harmony and we were delighted to learn that in the earlier days the firstborn in a Hindu family would adopt the Sikh religion. We also tasted the food at the roadside *dhabas* (local restaurants) including 'Makki ke roti' and 'Sarso ka Saag'. We witnessed the *bhangra* dance as also the more delicate dance of the Punjab women. We were completely charmed with Punjab and its people.

On our way back to Delhi, just a mile outside Karnal, our car broke down. We had the car towed back to Karnal as major repair was involved and we sought shelter in the circuit house, the official guest house for senior officers. As we were sitting down for lunch, a cavalcade of cars drove up to the circuit house. It was Partap Singh Kairon, Chief Minister of Punjab, making an unscheduled halt. As he walked into the sitting room, he was surprised to see us and I saw him making enquiries about who we were. I went up to him and, after introducing myself, mentioned to him that my parents and I were taking temporary shelter here as our car had broken down just outside Karnal. When he learnt that my parents had come from the South to visit Punjab he was pleased and exchanged a few pleasantries with my father.

My parents, sisters and I witnessed the grandeur of the Republic Day parade and the Beating Retreat against the backdrop of the Secretariat for two years consecutively. The latter is probably the grandest defence services show on earth and the change of guard at Buckingham Palace, London, pales into insignificance in comparison. I attended the function celebrating the Independence Day at the Red Fort and I saw Pandit Nehru unfurl the national flag from the ramparts of the fort. Hearing him extol the benefits of Independence, my hopes soared that the country was poised to achieve great things.

At the External Affairs Ministry my batchmates in the IFS, Natwar Singh and Shyam Sundernath, had joined as Under-Secretaries; RK Narayanan, the future President of India, was a Deputy Secretary. PN Haksar was the Joint Secretary, Administration and Subimal Dutt, the Foreign Secretary. BN Chakraborty and YN Gundevia were the other two Secretaries in the Ministry. While Subimal Dutt and Chakraborty were always formally dressed, Gundevia was in shirt-sleeves and, with his boyish looks, did not look like a Secretary. We heard stories of his being flippant even with Pandit Nehru.

The deputation post as Under-Secretary in the Government of India is a tenure posting for a period of three years. Half-way through my tenure I was assigned the task of framing the rules of service conditions of Foreign Service Officers, rules governing their entitlement and allowances, their travel on duty and transfer, leave entitlement, accommodation and furniture entitlements when posted abroad. All these issues were covered by Government orders issued periodically but there were no set rules. It entailed the voluminous scanning of the existing orders and reframing them in different sets of rules and in the process covering new areas where no orders existed to make the rules comprehensive. I was authorised to discuss the rules framed by me with the Joint Secretary, Administration and in case of disagreement, the matter would be taken up for discussion by my boss Rajkumar, the Deputy Financial Advisor, with the Joint Secretary, Administration. Any disagreements at that level would be resolved by discussion between the FA and the Secretary, Administration. I was present in all these meetings since my proposals were being discussed. My term of office was coming to an end and the External Affairs Ministry took the initiative to move the department of personnel for a three-month extension, citing my indispensability for the finalisation of the IFS rules. The rules were finalised and published at the end of my extended tenure.

The Ministry honoured me by organising a send-off party with the Foreign Secretary personally in attendance, along with many senior officers of the Ministry. I have a photograph taken at the party prominently displayed in my house. This was followed by an official letter from the External Affairs Ministry placing on record its appreciation of the part played by me in the finalisation of the IFS rules. The letter has also been preserved by me.

I applied for a month's leave, which was sanctioned, as we were all planning a visit to Coorg in May. Early in April I woke up one morning with an unexplained burning desire to visit Badrinath in the Himalayas. I had heard of Badrinath, but did not know where exactly it was located and the means of transport to reach it. I went to office and during the lunch hour rang up the Uttar Pradesh tourist centre to find out all the details. While I was making this call, it so happened that a colleague of mine, who was an Under-Secretary in the Ministry, was in my room and he heard me. At the end of my conversation, he said that he would like to accompany me. Within a week the number of pilgrims had gone up to five. The Under-Secretary's name was AS Mani and accompanying him was his brother and another acquaintance, a senior engineer from Bhilai, all South Indians. The fifth pilgrim was Dr Rao who was the personal physician of the President of India.

We reached Rishikesh in the morning and, after taking a morning dip in the clear waters of the Ganga, we caught a bus that took us to Joshimath. From Joshimath to Badrinath it was another two-day trek. This part of the trek was most exhilarating as we moved along the ridge with the Alaknanda River flowing in the gorge below, keeping us company along with the murmur of the casuarinas trees, lining the route with the mountain breeze blowing through them. I was twenty-eight years old, in prime health and I was a strong trekker, always on the lead, even ahead of the experienced porters. I used to halt on the way, waiting for my party to catch up with me, as I sat on the wayside rocks. There was a constant flow of pilgrims from different parts of India and I heard almost all the major Indian languages being spoken. After a hard and strenuous climb, we reached near Badrinath, the abode of Lord Vishnu. It was a bustling place of many tents and *chatrams* (free abode for the pilgrims) with thousands of pilgrims in transit to and out of Badrinath. We pitched camp and visited the temple area late at night to absorb the sanctified air of the place. There were *kirtans* and *bhajans* (devotional songs) conducted by the *sadhus* (holy men). We went round the bathing tanks opposite the temple, which were continuously fed by a sulphur spring. It was indeed a wonder of nature that boiling water was coming out of a spring barely two hundred feet away from the ice-cold Alaknanda River flowing down the mountain gorge.

The next morning, after taking a bath in the hot spring, smelling of sulphur, we stood in a queue. After an hour's wait we gained entry into the temple to shouts of 'Govinda' from the assembled pilgrims. I saw the small stone statue of Vishnu being worshipped, gleaming in the glow of the *arati* (candles lit for prayers). It is a memory I treasure for life. We had a sense of fulfilment in seeing the Lord after an arduous journey. Following this trip we visited Talecauvery in Coorg. On return to Delhi I immersed myself in framing the draft IFS rules.

In January 1960, we had visitors from Coorg who stayed with us. Baby Accia (Chatrangada Appanna, my father's sister's daughter) was full of news of Coorg and Bengaluru. In the course of a conversation with my father she mentioned Dr Konganda Chittianna who had a pretty daughter who was also Lata's (Baby Accia's daughter's) classmate. My father asked Lata to send us her photograph. It was a cut-out from a group photograph and only a one centimetre square framing a pretty girl with curly hair. First impressions were good and my father suggested that when we next visited Bengaluru or Coorg we could look up the family who was well known to him. This was the start of a fairytale whose glamour has not worn off even today. The girl's name was Indira.

7

Back in Orissa

A fortnight before our departure from Delhi to Orissa I received the State Government's orders posting me to Sambalpur as Collector and District Magistrate. Orissa then had thirteen districts and Sambalpur was considered a coveted posting to head the district. Rajkumar, Deputy Financial Advisor and my boss, along with my entire office staff, were present at the railway station to see me and my family off. It was a very touching farewell. We changed trains in Nagpur and arrived at Jharsaguda station in Sambalpur District after two nights of train travel. The local *tehsildar* received me at the station with pomp and a welcoming garland.

We drove to Sambalpur and moved into the residential bungalow of the District Magistrate. The bungalow was very large, the ground floor occupied by the residential office of the Collector with the top floor housing the residence. As my father was a heart patient and I did not want him to climb stairs often, I interchanged the office and residence and we lived on the ground floor.

The mystery of my posting to Sambalpur was revealed to me when I landed in Orissa. Biju Patnaik had entered politics as a member of the Congress. He was the young bull pitted against the ageing bull Harekrishna Mahtab, the leader of the State

Congress Party and the Chief Minister of Orissa. The two fell out in a *kendu* leaf deal (*kendu* is a minor forest produce used for wrapping in the manufacture of *bidis*—cheap cigarettes) of Sambalpur District. When the corrupt District Magistrate of Sambalpur, Misra, who favoured the man backed by Biju Patnaik in the *kendu* leaf deal, was transferred from Sambalpur, Biju Patnaik raised the banner of revolt against Mahtab. I, who was returning from Delhi, was readily available and I was posted to Sambalpur by the Chief Minister. Within a few days of my taking over as District Magistrate, Biju Patnaik staged a walk-out from the Congress Party with his followers. This made the Congress a minority party in the assembly, forcing Mahtab to resign. Governor's Rule was enforced under Governor Khosla. I had unwittingly been caught in a fight between the political stalwarts, Biju Patnaik and Mahtab.

On taking over as District Magistrate, I settled the *kendu* leaf deal in favour of the rightful party, displacing the man backed by Biju Patnaik. This was done purely on merit but I had to pay a price for it later. I was busy touring the district and getting to know its people and places. My neighbouring district was Bolangir, which I visited to discuss some border issues with the Collector. While driving back I saw a string of carts going single file with the cartmen asleep. As I approached the carts my headlights revealed a tiger silently walking underneath the carts. When I honked to wake up the cartmen the tiger slunk away into the darkness. Saving these men from a maneater was my good deed for the day.

The daily report that I received from the District Police showed that a large number of the rich and irrigated farmlands of Bargarh subdivision were being acquired by Andhra farmers, displacing the local farmers and making them landless. It struck me as strange that people in large numbers were selling their irrigated farmlands to persons coming all the way from Andhra. During my tours of that area, I visited the villagers to find out from them why they were selling their lands. The villagers had not seen a Collector in their lifetime and there was a huge turnout. In those days a Collector was held in high esteem. It was an exhilarating experience to be taken in a procession in the village with the women ululating in unison, welcoming me, while modestly hiding their faces with the *pallu* (loose end of a *sari*). I had a meeting with the villagers, sitting in the courtyard of their school. I sanctioned them a much-needed drinking water well and also money to desilt the village pond. Even after becoming a Secretary to the Government, I never felt as powerful and capable of doing good work as when I was Collector and District Magistrate. It is a very heady experience.

At the meeting I enquired from the villagers why they were selling their land when they have received the blessing of irrigation from the nearby Hirakud Dam. The local *tehsildar* was also present and I saw the villagers looking at him and not answering my question. I sensed that the *tehsildar* had warned them not to and this intrigued me. I called the oldest person in the crowd to come and sit next to me. His reply astounded me. The Hirakud Dam is also a hydro-electric project and the irrigation water flows into the canal after turning the turbines to generate electricity. A strong rumour had been spread among the villagers that, with electricity having been extracted out of the water, the water had become dead and was not useful for cultivation. It was also rumoured that the water would damage the seeds planted in the fields. This was the reason why the farmers were selling their land. I realised that the *tehsildar* was a party to the conspiracy to deprive the farmers of their rich irrigated land. I explained to the villagers that there was no truth in the rumour and promised them a new school building if they stopped selling their land. On coming out of the village I took the *tehsildar* to task and told him that he would be suspended if any more land was sold in his area.

With the fall of the Mahtab Government, the Election Commission fixed the dates for fresh elections to the State Assembly in Orissa and, as the District Returning Officer in charge of the elections, I was busy touring and supervising the setting up of polling booths. Orissa was the first State to enact the Zilla Parishad Act to usher in Panchayati Raj with devolution of administrative and financial powers to the Zilla Parishad at the district level, to the Block Parishad at the block level and to the Panchayats at the village level. It was a new experiment for wider people's participation in the development activities of the nation. I was kept very busy conducting these elections prior to the State-level elections. I was on tour and out of headquarters for more than a fortnight in a month.

We had torrential rains, especially upstream of Hirakud Dam in the higher reaches of the catchment area of the Mahanadi River falling in the State of Madhya Pradesh and the river started to swell. There was panic in Sambalpur with the rapid spread of a rumour that the dam was breaking up. Within an hour I got into my Land Rover and was driven to the Hirakud Dam site to make a spot inspection and to discuss the situation with the dam engineers. It was an awesome sight with the dam disgorging water from its twelve sluice gates. Even the approach road to the dam was slowly getting flooded. I left the dam only when the water level had stabilised by about 9 pm and, on returning home, I found that the rising waters of the Mahanadi had swamped the front area of my bungalow. By morning the water started receding and we had narrowly escaped a natural disaster of a dam burst.

Sambalpur was not only the district headquarters but was also the headquarters of the Divisional Commissioner and the

Range Deputy Inspector General (DIG) Police. DIG Dharma Raj and I became good friends. The District Superintendent of Police (SP) was Bannerjee, who was senior to me in age and length of service and this resulted in a rather ticklish problem. A District Magistrate was Number One in the district and, according to protocol, the SP had to call on him for the first meeting. The SP's house was next to mine and though a week had passed since I took charge of the district, there was no sign of him, though I heard he was in town. He was obviously hesitating to call on me first. I knew I had to break the ice and one day, in the course of my evening walk, I saw him sitting on the lawn and having tea. I stopped by his gate and greeted him and he immediately came to me and shook my hand. I accepted his greeting but not his invitation to have tea. I invited him to drop in and have a drink with me the next evening, which he readily accepted. Thus the ice was broken with the protocol intact for the district administration to function smoothly.

Dharma Raj used to share a drink with me occasionally and he was good company. He was a devout Christian and his efforts to convert me to Christianity by saying that only Jesus can save us was countered by me with the rhetorical question whether all humanity, born before Jesus, had gone to hell.

The State elections held in the searing heat of May gave a landslide victory to Biju Patnaik and he and his Ministers were sworn in to form the new Government. One of the decisions they made in their first Cabinet meeting was to bring back Misra as the Collector and District Magistrate of Sambalpur and I was transferred to Mayurbhanj. Misra was eager to take over the very next day but I held my ground despite telephonic directions from the CM's office in Bhubaneshwar. I had seven days joining time in addition to journey time to take over at the new place and I made Misra, who had arrived in Sambalpur, wait in the circuit house. On the seventh day we drove from Sambalpur to Mayurbhanj District via Lohardega, Simdega and Ranchi in Bihar. We halted a night in the Ranchi circuit house and reached Baripada, the district headquarter, by evening the next day. Misra was arrested by the CBI a year later after a house raid and was convicted on charges of corruption.

Mayurbhanj is the prettiest district in Orissa, largely covered by forests. Its major roads were well maintained and the Government rest houses dotting the district were also well kept. It had a majority tribal population; the largest tribe was known as the Santhals. Within a few days of my arrival my Divisional Commissioner decided to pay a visit to my district. He was an ex-Army officer and an Anglo-Indian named Barren, whom I had met earlier when I was posted in Cuttack. He was fun loving and while on tour with me, insisted on witnessing and betting during a cock fight organised by the local villagers, even though it was banned.

One Sunday morning, while I was relaxing in my house, the Additional District Magistrate, who was my deputy, came to my residence in an agitated manner. He told me that, on opening the treasury strongroom for his monthly inspection, he saw that rats had got into the room and had damaged the revenue stamps stored there. I asked him about the safety of the currency and he replied that it was safe as it was locked in the currency chest. I told him to consult the treasury code and inform all concerned about the damage to the stamps, as prescribed in the code. The next day he told me that he had made an inventory of the damage in the prescribed form in triplicate, sending one copy each to the Commissioner of the Division, the Finance Department and the Accountant General (AG), Orissa. I forgot about this incident in the rush of work until I got a letter from the AG's office two months later asking for a clarification as to why the rats had attacked only the higher denomination stamps and not the lower, although they were stacked alongside. I initialed the letter and sent it down to the officer for putting up a suitable draft reply. Two reminders followed from the AG's office and both of them were sent to the officer for action. Finally, I got a demi-official letter from the AG, chiding us for the delay in furnishing a reply and threatening to include the item as an audit para if an immediate reply was not forthcoming.

In the old days, officers were generally afraid of an audit para against them and I sought the explanation of the Additional Collector for the delay in replying. He appeared before me scratching his head and he said that he had no adequate answer to the query raised by the audit. I smiled, appreciating his difficulty and calling for my stenographer. I proceeded to dictate a reply to the AG. I expressed regret for the delay in replying to the audit query and then, tongue-in-cheek, I wrote that on receiving his irate reminder, I had gone to the treasury strongroom, called a meeting of the rats who had damaged the stamps, and the king rat had replied that they nibbled only the higher denomination stamps since they found the gum behind these stamps to be sweeter! I later learnt that, on receiving the reply, the AG's office exploded in laughter and that was the end of the audit objection. The Accountant General of Orissa at that time was Sandilya, the son-in-law of President Radhakrishnan. I met him later and one could not find a better gentleman than him to laugh over the incident. Little did I realise at that time that in the distant future I would be on the other side of the fence, heading the Audit organisation in India and also that of the United Nations (UN).

A bye-election was also to be conducted in my district for the State Assembly. A month before the elections I received a resignation letter from a clerk in my office on the plea that he was contesting the elections to become a Member of the Legislative Assembly (MLA). He was a tribal named Majhi and on enquiry I found him to be an efficient clerk who had joined service twenty years ago. I invited him through the office superintendent to meet me to discuss his resignation. I spent quite some time with him to try and persuade him to withdraw his resignation letter but I was unsuccessful in my effort. He lost the elections and appeared before me again a few days later requesting that he be reinstated in his job. I was genuinely sorry for him but I did not have the necessary powers to reappoint him. I told him I would forward his case to the Government for sympathetic consideration. I did send it up with a strong recommendation that he be reinstated. I lost sight of the case when I was transferred from the district.

I met Majhi again sixteen years later in the strangest of circumstances. I had returned to Orissa after my second deputation to the Centre and had done a year as Chairman, Orissa Forest Corporation, when I decided to call on the new Minister, Forests. On being ushered into his room, I was dumbfounded to see Majhi. I learnt about his success in the subsequent elections contested by him and his rise as a politician. Much to my surprise he continued to address me as Sir whenever we met.

In Mayurbhanj I had a very fine officer as my SP. Prafulla Rath was active and young like me, both bachelors. The Civil Surgeon of the district was Dr Ghoshal, a fun-loving middle-aged doctor. We used to meet often at my place to share a drink. Mayurbhanj had a small officer's club, which I used to visit occasionally to play bridge and billiards. The tennis court was not functional as the cement court had developed big cracks due to long disuse and poor maintenance. When I inspected the District Jail I found a disused tennis court next to the Jailer's house. I told the Jailer, Rama Rao, to get the tennis court back into shape, using the jail inmate's manpower. Within a fortnight the court was made ready for play. Just before the discovery of this tennis court I received a letter from a friend of mine from Kolkata that Sumant Misra, former India's Number One tennis player, was planning to visit the tiger reserve in the Simlipal hill range located within the district and requested me to make the necessary arrangements for his visit. I invited Sumant to bring his tennis partner with him and inaugurate the court. As luck would have it, Chief Minister Biju Patnaik was planning to visit my district around the same time and I requested him to be present at the inauguration. I teamed up with the third tennis player in Sumant's team and we had an interesting exhibition match in the Jail tennis court witnessed by Biju Patnaik and the elite of Mayurbhanj.

Makar Sankranti is a big festival for the tribals and once, while on tour in the district, a band of dancing Santhal men and women stopped my car and invited me to visit their village. They offered me their local brew, *handia*, and soon after that I joined them in dancing to the beat of drums. Much to their surprise I could easily match their steps. Tribal grapevine was quick to spread the news that the new Collector was informal in his ways and was friendly with the tribals, earning their lasting love and trust.

On 29 July 1962, my father suddenly passed away in Jamshedpur. The next day we brought his body to Baripada. As I gazed at the funeral fire, I broke down and started crying. My father was my philosopher and friend; he was an exceedingly good man.

Hardly two months had elapsed after my father's death. I received orders from the Government deputing me for a month's training along with other Collectors at the National Institute of Community Development (NICD) in Mussoorie. It was a welcome break for me to get over my sorrow. We were trained on how to handle the newly-formed Zilla Parishads and the block development activities under their charge. The Institute was headed by IDN Sahni. Indeed, his initials stood for 'I do nothing' and we hardly saw him during the training period. The training provided me the opportunity to catch up with my general reading as the library was well stocked.

While in Mussoorie I came across an advertisement in a newspaper put out by the British Council, Delhi, inviting applications from administrators for a scholarship at Oxford. The application had to be endorsed by the applicant's Government. I applied for the scholarship, which was duly sponsored by the Orissa Government. I received an invitation from the British Council to appear for an interview in New Delhi. I was informed of the results of the interview two months later and was happy to learn that I had been selected. I also received the good news that the Census Commissioner of India had commended my work in the 1961 Census operation and had awarded me a medal.

In the meantime my term in Mayurbhanj had come to an end and I was transferred to Bhubaneshwar as Additional Secretary, Home; I joined in April 1963. Five months into the job I took leave to visit Coorg before I left for Oxford. I had hardly spent a week there when I received a telegram from the Chief Secretary, Orissa, cancelling my leave and summoning me to come to Bhubaneshwar immediately to report to the Chief Secretary, B Sivaraman, ICS. I was told by him that following the brief war with China and, as part of the exercise to beef up the security of the country, an MiG factory to manufacture fighter planes had been sanctioned to be set up in Orissa at Sunabeda, in

Koraput District. The Chief Secretary explained to me that this was a prestigious project and he had chosen me for heading it. I stood before him with mixed feelings (pride at being selected and sorrow at the prospect of losing the opportunity to study at Oxford). I was appointed Special Project Officer.

My camp life for the next two months reminded me of my settlement training days. Often, when sitting alone in the tent, I used to think of Oxford and the comforts I had left behind to do my duty. Before leaving Bhubaneshwar I had written a letter to the British Council with a copy to the State Government that due to exigencies of service I was not in a position to accept the scholarship. In the concluding part of my letter I requested them to let me avail of the scholarship after a couple of years. This elicited a response that I never anticipated. The British Council addressed a letter to the Chief Secretary, urging him to relieve me immediately as the grant of scholarship could not be postponed.

After two months of very hard work of survey and forest clearance in Sunabeda, I drove back to Bhubaneshwar to personally report to the Chief Secretary. This provided me an opportunity to meet my family and also visit my bank as I drew no pay during this period. On the basis of sanction of my post issued by the Ministry of Defence, the Controller of Defence Accounts, Patna, had to issue me a pay slip—the authority to draw my pay. In fact, for the entire four-and-a-half months I stayed on the job I drew no salary! I drew it much after I left.

Sivaraman appeared distant when I met him to report the progress of work. He heard my narration and then coldly told me that after having accepted the job he did not expect me to petition to the British Council to have me relieved from it. He threw the British Council letter at me and asked me to read it. I lost my cool. I literally shouted at him saying that he was being mean to me. I yelled that I had not pleaded with the British Council as he had imagined, but had only informed the British Council of my inability to accept the offer and had requested them to defer this offer to a later date. I asked him whether he had ever lived in a tent in the middle of a jungle in Koraput, being eaten up by mosquitoes. I glared at him defiantly. He then understood that he had wrongly accused me and had deeply offended me. He got up from his chair and offered his apologies and asked me to calm down. The great Sivaraman, whom we revered so much, was asking my forgiveness! I clasped his proffered hand and forgave him. Peace was established by the time I left his office room to return to Sunabeda.

The task assigned to me was completed within four months and I was back in Bhubaneshwar for receiving further instructions from the Ministry of Defence. The instructions were totally unexpected. The Chief Secretary, Orissa, was informed by the Secretary, Defence, that a high-level decision had been taken to entrust the project work to an Air Force Officer and I could be spared from deputation. Sivaraman was shocked to hear this, especially since he had persuaded me to accept the job. He felt very contrite when he conveyed the news to me.

I was posted as Additional Secretary, Finance Department, on my return from Sunabeda. I also shifted residence to a better bungalow. It was while I was here that I had a surprise visitor—RN Bannerjee, former Chairman, UPSC.

Chief Minister Biju Patnaik had embarked on a bold initiative to modernise and industrialise Orissa. He brought about a refreshing change in administration, which though efficient was not dynamic. He thought big and also had the ability to follow through with bold action. He dreamed of building a world class export-oriented port at Paradip. He, however, failed to convince the Centre and the Central Planning Commission of the need for such a port. I remember the day he returned from Delhi with their negative response; he was angry and he convened a meeting of all top officers of the Secretariat. In the meeting he announced his decision to go ahead with the project without any Central assistance and I was given the task of finding adequate resources for the project within the State Budget.

Biju Patnaik was an exciting person to work with. He was bold and honest. I have also played bridge with him, both before he joined politics and much later when he had retired. He was a flamboyant player.

8

Marriage and Beyond

Years after we got married, Indira told me that she had seen me earlier taking part in a tennis match in Mercara. That must have been in the year 1956 when I won the Coorg Tennis Championship—both singles and mixed doubles, the latter in partnership with my mother. Even before that, our paths had crossed in a very strange manner. In 1946 I was going home to Mysore to spend the Christmas vacations with my parents, when I struck up a conversation with a Coorg couple. They had two little girls who were playing hide-and-seek and I remember luring the elder of the two from underneath the seat with the promise of a chocolate. She was none other than Indira, eleven years younger to me. The happy coincidence was that it was my father who chose her to be my life partner.

Our engagement ceremony was simple. After a small prayer before a lit lamp, I sought Indira's hand. She was so confused that she extended the wrong hand for the engagement ring and I still tease her about this. There was general bonhomie and high tea followed.

By the time I was engaged to Indira I had been transferred out of Bhubaneshwar and was posted as the Commissioner, Commercial Taxes, Cuttack. I was to succeed SMH Burney, an officer five years my senior, who was going on transfer to Delhi.

This meant not only being given a senior, coveted post but also a very big house next to the Mahanadi River. This was the house that was once occupied by Naba Krishna Chowdhary, former Chief Minister of Orissa, when Cuttack was the capital of the State and before the shifting of the capital to Bhubaneshwar. The first year in my new job was spent mostly on tours—inspecting my offices that were located in all thirteen districts of Orissa. These tours were conducted by road (the only railway line was along the coastal belt) and we generally organised joint tours to the outlying districts. There were five bridge-playing officers, including Lulu Parija, my batchmate. During the day we used to attend to our respective work and after nightfall, settled in the comfortable circuit houses, we would play bridge late into the night. As all of us had our own Ambassador cars (no staff cars, only drivers were provided at that time) during our return journey five of us would get into one car with one of us acting as a driver while the rest played bridge, using a light attaché case as a table on the lap of the person occupying the middle back seat. The other car would follow with our drivers in it. They must have wondered at the madness of their bosses. Some of my colleagues who came to know about our bridge escapades used to say that Parija and I spent more time playing bridge than working during our tours. Little did they know that we slogged hard during the day and did not ever neglect our work. My intense supervision of my officer's work paid rich dividends. The sales tax collection increased by twenty per cent within a year of my taking charge and I received a commendation letter from the Government.

During one of these tours Parija and I decided to visit Koraput via Phulbani where Captain Mohanti, a good bridge player, was the Collector and District Magistrate. The next day we were off to Koraput for the inauguration of the chromium factory put up by industrialist Dr Panda. The Chief Guest on that occasion was Morarji Desai, who was then the Industry and Commerce Minister. On the way back we passed by Sunabeda where once a virgin forest stood! I parked by the roadside and recollected the hard life I had spent there in a tent, years ago, in preparation for the MiG factory. Instead of the twinkling lights of the new township, my eyes could only see the ancient forest that once occupied the land with its majestic trees. This is the forest that I had once helped to uproot in order to make way for the township.

A year or so later I was transferred as Director, Industries, in Cuttack. With no major industries in Orissa, it was a lacklustre post and my main job was to promote and look after the smallscale industries of the State. The distribution and allocation of scarce raw materials such as steel, copper, aluminium and zinc was one of the functions of this job. The Secretary, Industries, was three years my senior and he used to ring me up often to convey the Minister's suggestions for the allotment of raw material to the smallscale industries. Some requests, if they were in tune with my plan of distribution on merit, were complied with, but most requests were ignored by me. The Secretary apparently was not amused and he got even by giving me an average rating with minor adverse remarks, which I got to know about years later. When I became the Comptroller and Auditor General of India he rang me up to congratulate me and, while accepting his congratulations, I told him that his adverse remarks on my work were a minor irritant in my career. I did, however, forgive him his lack of honesty.

On the home front, after our engagement, Indira and I started corresponding with each other and my first gift to her was a learner's book on bridge with the advice that she must learn the game that I passionately loved. In December 1965, I visited Coorg to attend my cousin's wedding and on the way I broke journey in Bengaluru to meet Indira and her parents. During my private chat with Indira I told her that I would be coming again in May to marry her.

Back in Orissa, Indira and I continued our conversation through letters. Indira informed me that the wedding date was 22 May and it would be held in the guesthouse of the Raja of Nepal, which was nearby. I had six hundred invitation cards printed in the name of my mother and she and I again set out by car to Bengaluru and Coorg in the third week of April. All of us met two days before the wedding in Bengaluru. After the beautiful ceremony, Indira and I drove off to Ooty for our honeymoon.

Soon after that I got transferred to Bhubaneshwar as Secretary, Department of Forest and Cooperatives. This was in the summer of 1967 when the Congress had suffered a defeat at the hustings and the main Opposition party, the Ganatantra Parishad headed by RN Singh Deo, the former Maharaja of Bolangir, was in power. The new Government was trying to do some springcleaning in the area of corruption. The Chief Minister summoned me and asked me to prepare a transparent scheme for the sale of *kendu* leaf collection rights from the forest of Orissa. *Kendu* leaf had been the bane of successive Governments who fell prey to the inbuilt corrupt practices in the scheme. In a month's time I had a Cabinet note prepared. This was placed before the Cabinet for approval. Under the new scheme, the geographical areas of the *kendu* leaf were clearly demarcated, the annual lease rent would be determined by open auction and the lease would be for a period of three years. When the auctions were held the annual revenue increased twofold and the Chief Minister was extremely happy.

The new Government with its rightist philosophy had appointed a high-level Committee to go into the working of the public sector undertakings of the State. A number of loss-making units were recommended to be closed and, surprisingly, the Committee also recommended the closure of the Orissa Forest Corporation, which was making a profit. I fought successfully against this recommendation, pointing out that the forests were better protected under State management, depriving the forest contractors the opportunity of largescale timber theft. The Chief Conservator of Forests and the officers of the forest department were all for bringing back the contractors for obvious reasons. I stalled the proposal and finally got it rejected by the Cabinet, to the dismay of the forest officers.

As Secretary, Forest and Cooperatives, I became aware that all was not well in the cooperative banking system and vested interests were milking it. Abani Roy, four years junior to me, was the Registrar, Cooperative Societies. I asked him to inspect the cooperative banks and verify the rumours. His inspections revealed serious irregularities in at least three banks. Using his inherent powers he superceded their management, which made headline news. Under my instructions a First Information Report (FIR) was lodged against a Chairman of the Cuttack District Cooperative Bank who had misappropriated a crore of rupees. The clean-up in the *kendu* leaf regime and in the cooperative sector was hailed by the media and the public as a helpful step to clean governance.

Fortunately, for the two years of the three that I functioned as Secretary I had a very good Minister. He was MP Misra, an advocate from Sambalpur who had earlier practiced in my court when I was the District Magistrate, Sambalpur. He was an unusually honest politician, but honesty in politics does not pay and he was abruptly removed. Years later he rang me up and told me he was ill and that he could not afford to buy his medicines. I sent him a cheque of Rs 1,000.

The Orissa Forest Act was enacted when we were under the British rule and it had many regressive provisions with regard to the tribals who lived in the forests. I undertook a complete revamp of the Act, also bringing in modern ideas of forest management and protection. It was a two-year exercise that was completed at the end of my tenure. The enactment was passed in the legislative assembly a year later, giving me the satisfaction of a job well done.

9

Simply Unforgettable

Indira went home for her confinement. One evening in August, while I was playing bridge at my residence, a telegram arrived informing me that I was the proud father of a baby girl. I received the telegram while I was in the midst of playing a grand slam contract. I pocketed it without saying anything and resumed the game. I completed the grand slam to the satisfaction of my partner and then announced the good news. We stopped the game, cigars were distributed and there were rounds of drinks in celebration. I was overjoyed and after the bridge players had left I walked up to the main telegraph office and sent Indira a telegram of congratulations. I was keen to know whether she had inherited the beautiful brown eyes of the mother so I asked about the colour of the eyes of my little princess. Promptly I got an impish telegram saying she had blue eyes and she looked Chinese! I have preserved that telegram.

A couple of days later I was on the train to Bengaluru, via Chennai. While I was travelling third class, Chief Minister Singh Deo was travelling in the first class. We met at the Bhubaneshwar station. He told me that he was going to Bengaluru to meet the famous Bala Yogi who was breaking his six-month fast. He also said that he had something to discuss with me. He was surprised to learn I was travelling third class (I had exhausted all my resources performing the twin marriages of my sisters). I reached Bengaluru in forty-eight hours and I was in the joyous company of Indira and the baby, both of whom I gathered in my arms with a prayer of thanks to the Gods. In joy and sorrow I always think of God. We decided to name her 'Pria', denoting abiding love. Indira was radiantly happy as a mother.

I returned to Bhubaneshwar after a three-day stay. I found that I had a new Minister named Mohapatro whose house was next to mine. When I called on him, I briefed him about the work in the department. He made detailed enquiries from me about the *kendu* leaf leases and casually mentioned that there may be a case for giving some remission and relief in the lease rent in the final year of the three years' lease as the *kendu* leaf contractors who had met him complained of a poor crop this year. I made no comments as I took leave of him, except to say that the *kendu* leaf contractors had made good money in the last two years of the lease with good crops and had enjoyed good prices.

A month later I got a call from the Chief Minister's office to put up the file examining the plea of the *kendu* leaf contractors for remission of lease rent in the last year of their three-year lease, citing bad crop as the reason for this remission. In the beginning of the *kendu* leaf collection season, I had introduced a system of obtaining a report from the District Forest Officers about the crop and the likely out-turn from each unit. These reports did not indicate any significant fall in output except in about three or four units where the fall in output was marginal. When almost all the *kendu* leaf dealers filed petitions for remission of lease rent it became clear to me that it was a political move initiated by the Chief Minister to make money, sacrificing the revenue of the State in the shape of remission to contractors. I sat over the file as long as I could and when pressure mounted on me from the Minister and Chief Minister's office I recorded a long and well-reasoned note why there was no case for remission. When the file reached the Minister he sent for me and in an oblique way suggested that it could be in my interest if I took back the file and changed my advice recommending remission. I told him that it was the Minister's prerogative to overrule the advice tendered by the Departmental Secretary and since he was a lawyer by profession he could easily make out a case for remission, overruling my advice. He had an incredulous look on his face when I told him that and I withdrew, never to meet him again. Within fifteen days, I received orders transferring me to Cuttack as Excise Commissioner. I had no trouble in complying with the order but little did I realise then that it was just the beginning of my troubles.

We moved to Cuttack. The annual excise auctions were held within a month of my taking charge and when I sensed that a cartel was working to get some lucrative units at a low price I put them to retender (not auction). The retendering of the units inviting the bids in sealed covers broke the cartel and we got record prices. I had taken care to note on the file the reason for retendering as I suspected cartel formation and that saved the Government when some of the disgruntled contractors challenged my decisions in the High Court. The overall excise revenue increased by twenty per cent. One of the unsuccessful contractors told me that he was the fundraiser for the Chief Minister and he wanted me to cancel the retendering of units and revert to the auction mode. I am mentioning this case because of his fascinating eyes—cold and venomous, like a serpent's. He lost the case in the High Court but he had the last laugh. Soon after the High Court decision I was abruptly transferred to Delhi. He had the audacity to call on me at my residence while I was busy packing and, fixing his venomous gaze on me, informed that he had got me transferred. He was evil and I still remember his serpent eyes with a shiver. He was the most unforgettable character I have met in my life.

I got the orders transferring me to Delhi at the end of May 1971. Earlier I had received an order promoting me to the super-time scale in a leave vacancy arising on 1 June. The transfer order also cancelled my promotion order and, on the day I was to take over the promotion post, I was relieved from my duties and asked to proceed to Delhi on transfer.

I was given the post of Director, Budget, in the Finance Division of the Ministry of Defence. It was June and blazing hot when I reached Delhi and on arrival I stayed at Orissa Bhawan. After a month I shifted to the transit accommodation at the Constitution House, pending the allotment of regular residential accommodation. In August I received the happy news of the birth of Prince Anand. I saw Anand for the first time when he was about seven to eight months old when Indira rejoined me in New Delhi, after I was allotted a residential flat at Moti Bagh.

Within a couple of months of my transfer to Delhi, Abani Roy, who had succeeded me as Secretary, Department of Forest and Cooperatives, was sent to Delhi when he did not oblige his political masters when asked to reexamine the case of grant of relief to the *kendu* leaf contractors. This is what I had earlier recommended for rejection. Abani Roy was a lawyer by profession and he, too, recommended the rejection of relief to the *kendu* leaf contractors, buttressing my earlier reasons with legal arguments. He was banished out of the State with a posting to Delhi. The Secretary who succeeded him did not have the spine to oppose the case and it was finally decided in favour of the contractors. The local press, who were following the case closely, mounted an attack on the Government and the Opposition parties took to the streets to criticise the corrupt practices of the Government. After a month of violent protests inside and outside the assembly the Government, headed by Bhanj Deo, was forced to resign. His royal ire having been aroused, he recorded scathing adverse remarks in my character roll, which were soon communicated to me.

It was a crucial year in my career, as my batch of IAS Officers were due for empanelment in the Joint Secretary's panel, when the adverse remarks landed on me as a bombshell. I appealed against the remarks to the State Government and simultaneously filed a petition addressed to the Secretary, Personnel, giving the entire background of the case, leading to the remarks from a vengeful Chief Minister, seeking his protection in the empanelment procedure. The empanelment is done by a Committee headed by the Cabinet Secretary with the Secretaries of Home and Department of Personnel to assist him as members of the Committee.

Soon I learnt that I was not included in the panel for Joint Secretaries though the Committee had unanimously recommended my name. Seeing my excellent previous record of service, the Committee had not given any credence to the adverse remarks of the Chief Minister of Orissa. At the Prime Minister's Office, however, I was unlucky and the panel put up for the Prime Minister's approval did not contain my name.

Undeterred by this adversity, I busied myself in my new job in the Finance Wing of the Defence Ministry. It was not a glamorous post but while on the job for two years I learnt how the Central Budget was prepared and what constituted the Defence Budget. I had an important role to play when war broke out between Pakistan and India in December 1971.

My mother and I were shifting house; we had hired a van to move our household baggage to Moti Bagh and by the time we had unloaded and shifted our baggage to the first-floor flat, dusk had set in. Pakistan had conducted sneak air raids on our Air Force bases as a prelude to declaring war on India. The Indian Government's immediate response was to declare a blackout in cities in Punjab and Delhi. The citizens were advised by the Civil Defence authorities to observe a strict blackout and soon after we entered our new residence, we were in pitch darkness. As we had no curtains on our windows and doorways, we could not even light a candle and both my mother and I spent a miserable night. As it was the month of December it was dreadfully cold.

In office, with the war on, there was hectic activity and as Director of the Defence Budget, I was summoned to attend the high-level meetings of the Defence Secretary with the Service Chiefs. KB Lall was the Defence Secretary and the Service Chiefs of the Army, Air Force and Navy were General Sam Manekshaw (with the twinkling eyes), Air Chief Marshall PC Lall and Admiral SM Nanda, respectively. More money was required for conducting the war and I was the key figure in the Ministry to find the money, which I did in consultation with the Finance Ministry. The war was over in three weeks and following it a new nation, Bangladesh, was born with East Pakistan severing its ties with mainland West Pakistan. It was indeed a historic moment.

In Delhi, I resumed playing bridge and took part in many tournaments. My regular partner in these tournaments was Hedda, an ex-Member of Parliament and I won the pairs tournaments with him in the Delhi State Championship.

In Orissa my appeal against the adverse remarks in my character roll lay dormant. The Congress Government, which succeeded the Government headed by Bhanj Deo, bowing to public pressure, set up a Commission of enquiry under Justice Mitter to probe into the scam relating to the *kendu* leaf contracts. After a year-and-a-half the Commission submitted its judicial finding, indicting the action of the previous Government in granting relief to the *kendu* leaf contractors, which in the Commission's opinion was unwarranted and mala fide. In their report they quoted at length the note that I had recorded as Secretary, Forest, rejecting the demand of the contractors for relief. They praised the effort made by Abani Roy and me to prevent loss to the exchequer and for our probity in rendering the correct advice to the Government. The action of our successor in succumbing to political pressure was condemned by the Commission. After this report was made public, the State Government took up my petition for review and the State Cabinet unanimously resolved that the adverse remarks appearing in my character roll should be completely expunged.

All this took two years and during that period not only my batchmates but also IAS Officers a year junior to me were promoted as Joint Secretaries while I stagnated at the level of a Director. I had full faith that truth will prevail in the end and I had no regrets about my action to fight corrupt practices, which resulted in a loss of promotion for two years. My colleagues in service were upset about my plight and some of them were of the view that it was not prudent to defy corrupt politicians who can harm one's career. I heartily disagreed with them.

I was first promoted as Additional Financial Advisor in Defence, Finance and after a couple of months I joined the Home Ministry as Joint Secretary in June 1973. I was designated as Joint Secretary, Police and was in charge of all the paramilitary forces in the country. Prominent among them were the Border Security Force, the Central Reserve Police, the Assam Rifles officered by Army Officers, the Indo-Tibetan Border Police and the Central Industrial Security Force. I was responsible for their proper equipment and provisioning and for their deployment in the country. The Bureau of Police research and development was also under my charge as was the management of the entire IPS cadre. I was the interacting point in the Home Ministry for all law and order matters in all the States of the Union and I was in charge of distributing grants to the States for the modernisation of Police forces and for Police housing. I was Secretary to the Indian Police Service Board whose Chairman was the Home Secretary. The crime branch of the Central Bureau of Investigation used to report to the Home Ministry through me. The promotion of State Police officers to the IPS was under my charge and I had to visit the States every year. Being in charge of all the paramilitary forces under the Home Minister, ninety per cent of the Home Ministry's budget was under my charge. All this not only involved very heavy work and responsibilities, but the job also enjoyed a lot of prestige and power.

At the time I joined the Home Ministry, Govind Narain was the Home Secretary. Within three or four months of my joining the Ministry, he was transferred to the Defence Ministry as Secretary and the youngest and the last person to join the ICS in 1942, Nirmal Mukherji, took over as Home Secretary. Within a few days, we faced a serious law and order crisis in Uttar Pradesh with spreading unrest among the Police forces of the State. It culminated in open rebellion by many battalions of the Police Armed Constabulary (PAC). They held their commanders hostage in their barracks and the State Government in desperation called for Army help. While a Major in the Army was parlaying and negotiating with the rebellious troops, a shot was fired at him, injuring him. All this happened suddenly and when the Intelligence Bureau (IB) reported the matter, the Home Secretary convened a late night meeting with the Central Police Chiefs in attendance. I was the convener of this meeting. After detailed deliberations it was decided that a firsthand assessment of the situation in Uttar Pradesh was necessary before making any decision. This task was assigned to KF Rustomji, Director General, Border Security Force, who would be assisted by me.

We took an early morning flight to Lucknow and called first on the Chief Secretary of the State, Sarwan. He seemed to be unaware of the gravity of the events happening round him. We then called on the Home Secretary, RK Trivedi. He had a full grip of the situation and we spent more than an hour with him. Overwork, not granting of timely leave, insensitive handling of the constabulary by its officers and the lack of proper housing were the main grievances but what set off the revolt was the largescale employment of constables to do menial work in the residences of Police Officers. We were horrified to learn that constables were widely used in the private agriculture farms of Police Officers and there were also instances of illicit relationships of officers with the wives of the subordinate staff when they stayed with them. Before we left the Home Secretary's room we suggested to him that the Inspector General (IG) of Police should be changed but not before the revolt was brought under control. We also held discussions with the local Army commander and suggested that while the Army may be in charge of the overall operations, the actual negotiations may be done by Police Officers who had earlier commanded the battalions of the PAC and who had earned the respect of their men. We flew back to Delhi with a new plan of operation in place in the State.

Within three days the situation was brought under control and, with the transfer of the IG and with strict instructions issued to prevent misuse of the constabulary in domestic work, harmony was brought back in the ranks of the State Police. I gave higher grants from the Centre to the UP Police under the heads of Police Housing and Police Modernisation.

One of the positive spinoffs of my job was that I came across and made friends with some of the outstanding Police Officers of the country. The best and the most charismatic of them was Rustomji who was considered the father of the Border Security Force, which was raised by him following the war with Pakistan in 1961. He was a Parsi and an Indian Police (IP) Officer of the old British Raj. He belonged to the Madhya Pradesh cadre. He had a commanding personality and great leadership qualities.

The Railways had many trade-wise unions and for the first time all the unions except one decided to strike together; it was an all-India strike. In the Home Ministry we were keeping track of the gathering storm and when the final strike notice was received by the Railways, the Prime Minister directed the Home Ministry to take charge and deal with the strike firmly. George Fernandes was one of the prominent Railway union leaders spearheading the strike. Home Secretary, Nirmal Mukherji, convened a meeting of all the top Police Officers of the Centre, including the Director, IB, and, in consultation with them, worked out a strategy to break the strike. Prime Minister Indira Gandhi gave us clear instructions to end the strike at all costs and this mandate was conveyed to Rustomji who was placed in overall charge of the operation after the strike was notified under the Essential Services Maintenance Act (ESMA).

He moved fast. He got a list of all the union leaders from the Railway Ministry and asked me to flash their names and addresses to all the State IGs, using the wireless network of the IB. I was told to direct them to arrest the union leaders under the provisions of the ESMA. This was done twenty-four hours before the commencement of the strike and about seventy-five per cent of the top union leaders were taken into custody. The kingpin among them, George Fernandes, escaped our best efforts to arrest him in the initial drive but he was arrested within the next two days from his hideout in Hubli. He was found dressed as a Sikh to escape detection. With his arrest and after a few strong-arm tactics such as physically evicting non-Railway men from the unauthorised occupation of Railway quarters allotted to the Railway union members, who had illegally rented out the quarters to outsiders, the Railway strike fizzled out in a week's time. If the strike had been allowed to continue any longer some parts of the country would have suffered food shortages and, with the suspension of the coal traffic, it would have led to the shutdown of power stations, resulting in an industrial shutdown and widespread unemployment.

One of my duties was to function as Secretary to the Board chaired by the Home Secretary to manage the affairs of the IPS. The Board used to assess each year's batch of the IPS to prepare panels for promotion to the level of Deputy Inspector General and Inspector General in the paramilitary forces, the Central Bureau of Investigation (CBI), the IB and the Bureau of Police Research and Development (BPR&D). Though the Research Analysis Wing (RAW) was under the Cabinet Secretary, as its officers were mainly from the IPS, the Home Ministry was responsible for preparing panels of eligible officers for promotion in their organisation. In the year of the Indo-Pakistan War of 1971, a panel of eligible officers of RAW was prepared by us for promotion to the rank of IG. In the case of one officer named Mullick, the Board decided that he was not yet suitable for promotion and there may be a special review of his case a year later. The normal review of rejected cases was held after a lapse of two years. The IPS Officers used to keep in touch with me to ascertain whether they stand included in the panel or not and Mullick dropped by to make a similar enquiry about himself. I told him that his overall record was good and the Board had decided to review his case after a year. He was, no doubt, disappointed on hearing this, but his reaction astounded me. He told me that his astrologer had predicted the exact date of his promotion four month's hence and he had the fullest faith in him. With a smile and a shake of his head, he took my leave.

Four months later Mujibur Rahman, the newly-elected Prime Minister of Bangladesh who was popularly called 'Bangabandhu', was assassinated. RAW, which had a big presence in Dacca, had completely failed in its intelligence and the Prime Minister ordered an overhaul of the RAW set-up in Dacca. RN Kao, Head of RAW, rang me up to ascertain the status of Mullick for promotion as IG as we had not yet sent the list officially to him and on learning that Mullick was not in the approved panel, mentioned to me that he was the only officer available for posting in Dacca as he had worked there earlier for several years and had the requisite experience and contacts. On his request, the review of Mullick's case was hastened and he was included in the panel to enable RAW to place him in Dacca as the head of the organisation. I never had occasion to meet Mullick after that, but I still remember his absolute confidence in the prediction of his astrologer.

In 1974 I learnt that the Department of Personnel, at the request of the British Council, was in the process of preparing a panel of four officers for the British Council Scholarship for a year's study in Oxford. This was the same scholarship that had been awarded to me more than a decade ago. I met the

Home Secretary and he included my name in the list of three officers he recommended for selection. The Department of Personnel, after scrutinising all the recommendations received from various Ministries, numbering about two hundred, finally selected four officers for the scholarship, two from the IAS, one from the IPS and one from the Education Service. I was happy to learn I was among them.

I decided to take Indira with me as there was a provision for spouses to accompany the scholar to Oxford and the spouse received a small maintenance allowance in addition to the scholarship. Our children, who were too young to be taken, were left behind with Indira's elder sister Vina who very graciously agreed to look after them during our absence. Indira decided that if she gets an opportunity she will seek employment in Oxford. She told me that she had learnt typing and shorthand after graduation and during the long wait before her marriage and she wished to brush up her knowledge and expertise by attending a coaching class nearby.

We were booked to fly by the BOAC flight leaving at 7 am. We partied the whole night at a friend's place where all our close friends had gathered to bid us farewell. All my bridge friends were there and we had a very long session. For Indira it was her first trip abroad and we sat hand-in-hand, savouring the beautiful moment. As the plane gained height and Delhi was disappearing from our gaze I recollected how, more than a decade ago, I had missed the chance of a scholarship in Oxford. In hindsight it proved to be for the best since Indira was there to keep me company this time. Indeed, all my seeming reverses in life turn out to be blessings in disguise.

10

Oxford Days

It was in the airport bus that was ferrying us across London that we met up with three other Indian scholars who had travelled in the same plane. They were Chauhan, an IAS Officer slightly junior to me, Natarajan, an IPS Officer from the Madhya Pradesh cadre and LR Mull, an officer working with the University Grants Commission. On arrival at Oxford we were told to report to the Queen Elizabeth House where we were warmly received. Natarajan, Chauhan and Mull were provided single rooms while we were led to our apartment located on St John Street, hardly a stone's throw away. And the very next day, Indira got a job as a shop assistant in the soft furnishing section of the local Cooperative Departmental Store in High Street Oxford.

Our classes in the forenoon, on 'Development Economics', were held in the lecture hall of Queen Elizabeth House. In the afternoon we were free to attend any class in any of the two dozen colleges in Oxford, a privilege given to the scholars of the Queen Elizabeth House Fellowship. I chose to attend lectures of general interest such as international trade, the politics of oil, environmental issues raised by the Club of Rome, political thoughts and insights into the strife in the Middle East, the world food programme and so on. I found the lectures fascinating and used to spend hours in the Bodleian Library reading the reference literature mentioned during the lectures. I thoroughly enjoyed my scholar days in Oxford; they really helped broaden my knowledge.

Midway into our studies, Dr Paul Streeten, Head of the Queen Elizabeth House, asked us to write a short thesis on our area of interest and I chose 'Socialisation of Land and the Commune System in China' as the subject of study. My thesis was highly appreciated by Dr Streeten and he decided to keep it as part of the library of Queen Elizabeth House. I played bridge, watched a number of plays, attended a musical evening with Cliff Richards at the Old Victoria Theatre in London and listened to guest lectures. We visited Wales and Scotland, the latter during Christmas holidays and also went on a trip to the neighbouring countries in Europe in April 1975.

We found that the residents of Oxford had no knowledge of India and thought of it in the colours of the old British Raj. I decided to organise an 'India Day' in Oxford in the premises of the hostel where we stayed. I went to London and discussed this idea with Natwar Singh, a batchmate of mine who was functioning as India's Deputy High Commissioner in the UK. He was equally enthusiastic and gave me full support in my venture. He offered to send an Embassy team to Oxford with a projector to show films about the industrial growth in India, including the advances made in atomic energy and space research. There was an excellent film showcasing the Taj Mahal, Ajanta and Ellora and Kashmir. I roped in my cousin in London to perform a Bharatnatyam dance to taped music and it proved to be a huge hit. We served Indian snacks. We had invited all the prominent Coorgs in the UK. They came from far and near and we had a gathering of about twenty of them for drinks and dinner that night in our small flat.

My course in Oxford was coming to an end and we were invited to a farewell party at the Queen Elizabeth House. Dr Streeten delivered the farewell speech; he praised the work of the Indian scholars and he highlighted the excellent work done by me on my China study. He paid me an extraordinary compliment in comparing me to a Mercedes Benz car, silent but efficient.

My studies in Oxford ended on a high note. Indira and I decided to have a fortnight's holiday in the USA, before returning to India, using the reserves of our savings from Indira's earnings.

11

The Emergency

At the custom's counter in Delhi airport, the officer asked me whether we had anything to declare. I mentioned that we had nothing to declare. When the officer recognised from my diplomatic passport that I was a high ranked officer of the Home Ministry, he drew me aside and cautioned me to declare goods attracting custom duty as he was under instructions to search everybody's baggage. He reminded me that an Emergency had been declared in the country by the Government headed by Indira Gandhi and the customs check did not spare anyone. When I stuck to my guns, he shrugged his shoulders and ordered that our baggage and hand luggage be searched. At the end of it he looked at me in wonder, stating that I had not even stitched a new suit abroad.

Immediately after my arrival I reported for duty at the Home Ministry and soon became aware of the full contours of the Emergency. Nirmal Mukarji was suddenly transferred from the Home Ministry and posted in a relatively unimportant post as Secretary, Civil Aviation. His successor was ML Khurana who was earlier the Chief Secretary of Rajasthan. Mukarji was not even aware that he had been transferred when Khurana called on him at his office and announced that he had been appointed and suggested an immediate changeover. The gentleman that he was, Mukarji, after checking with the Cabinet Secretary, vacated his chair in half-an-hour—barely enough time to collect his personal papers lying in the office.

When the country was brought under the Emergency in May 1975, thousands of arrests were made across the country, including Opposition leaders such as Jayaprakash Narayan. Indira Gandhi had been unseated from the Parliament by the historic judgment delivered by Justice Sinha of the Allahabad High Court dealing with the charges in the petition made by Raj Narain about the alleged malpractices committed by her in the elections. After obtaining a stay order from the Supreme Court, she ordered the Emergency under the legal guidance provided by Siddharth Shanker Ray and support from her son Sanjay Gandhi who soon turned out to be an extra-constitutional authority in running the Government.

When I reported to Khurana, the new Home Secretary, he asked me to take back my previous post as Joint Secretary, Police. The Home Minister at that time was Brahmananda Reddy, a senior Congressman and the former Chief Minister of Andhra Pradesh. Indira Gandhi, under Sanjay Gandhi's advice, had brought in Om Mehta as Minister of State in the Home Ministry and I learnt that he was wielding all the power in the Ministry with Brahmananda Reddy acting as a figurehead. I missed my senior colleague Srinivasa Varadan who was sent packing to his parent cadre of Madhya Pradesh. We learnt later that he and Bishan Tandon, Joint Secretary in the Prime Minister's Office, were the unofficial advisors in the case against her in the High Court and, when the verdict went against her, she had them summarily transferred.

Countrywide arrests were still on under the draconian Maintenance of Indian Security Act (MISA). These were being made on the recommendation of the IB to be finally approved by Om Mehta after the file had passed through the Joint Secretary, Internal Security and the Home Secretary. During the temporary absence of the Joint Secretary, Internal Security, I was handling his work and on seeing some of the old files I found that the IB's recommendations for arrests were being approved 'in toto' without any examination at the level of the Joint Secretary and the Home Secretary.

After I took over as Joint Secretary, Police, I started to examine the proposals of the IB and suggested some changes while sending up the file to the Home Secretary. When a second such proposal was received by him he summoned me to his office in the evening and, after allowing me to share a cup of tea with him, raised the issue regarding the files submitted to him, differing with the IB's recommendation. He suggested that it would be better if I take back the files and resubmit them without any detailed examination, as was being done earlier. I argued with him that as administrators we should critically examine all proposals received by us and he was well within his rights to overrule my suggestions while submitting the file to the Minister. On the other hand, if he found that there was substance in my suggestions, he should endorse them for the Minister's decision. I also reminded him that the scale of arrests throughout the country had been enormous and that was all the more reason for us to ensure that there is no illegal detention. I told him that, after the lifting of the Emergency, if the Opposition came to power they are sure to appoint a Commission of enquiry to look into the misdeeds of the Emergency and our files would be under judicial scrutiny. Finally, I declined to reexamine the files already submitted to him and offered to step down from the job. I said that he could relocate me in the Home Ministry or, if that was not possible, I was prepared to return to my State cadre.

My reference to a future Commission of enquiry seemed to have struck home and the files continued to be examined by us for the Minister to make appropriate decisions. When the Justice Khanna Commission was appointed in 1977, after Indira Gandhi lost the elections, Home Secretary ML Khurana was summoned before it and he was grilled. He and the Home Ministry were absolved of all wrongdoings, blaming it on the illegal action of the Minister. Khurana, who had returned to Rajasthan, rang me up and thanked me for the good advice I had given him.

There are many stories of atrocities committed during the Emergency. Though the Lieutenant Governor of Delhi, Kishan Chand, toed the official line, he was not considered to be dynamic and was replaced by Jagmohan, a Haryana State Civil Service Officer. Jagmohan was completely under the thumb of Sanjay Gandhi.

Sanjay Gandhi wanted to check the growing population of the country by rigorous family control measures including forcible vasectomy and tubectomy on men and women of childbearing age. Under his guidance, instructions were issued to all States by the Centre to fix district-wise targets for the operation, which led to forcible enforcement in many cases. I had a small part to play in saving some of the intended victims from vasectomy. The veterinary department of the Rajasthan Government had sent a team of their officers with about three or four trucks to Punjab to get pedigreed bulls to improve their livestock. When the team did not return to Rajasthan even after a fortnight, they found out that the trucks and the officers had been detained at a border checkpost. The Home Secretary, Rajasthan, rang me up to request my help to get the staff released from Police custody as ascertained by them. When I rang up the Home Secretary, Punjab, he, after checking the position, informed me that the Rajasthan trucks had been detained at the border and the veterinary staff had been taken to a nearby vasectomy camp. On my specific instructions to the Home Secretary, Punjab, he got them released but not before one of the six veterinary staff had been put under the knife!

We were getting reports of similar highhandedness from other parts of the country and the very people who had originally welcomed the Emergency were turning against it. The Emergency had initially led to more efficient governance. A large number of corrupt officers were sent packing home after review and, surprisingly, even the higher ranks from the IAS and IPS were not spared. In Orissa, my home State, VS Mathews, Chief Secretary, was sacked after the end of the three-month notice period. Such actions were generally appreciated but gradually, with mounting disillusionment with the negative aspects of the Emergency, there was growing disenchantment among the people. As the media was being subjected to censorship, some of the leading dailies such as *The Statesman* of Kolkata countered it by publishing blank front pages.

In the Home Ministry we realised that we could not hold the country together any longer and our informal advice to the Prime Minister was to revoke the Emergency and call for general elections. This was communicated to her through Om Mehta and we were happy to learn that she was likely to accept our advice. This was during the end of 1976, but we soon found out that Sanjay Gandhi had vetoed the proposal. The Prime Minister ordered that the IB conduct a secret survey to gauge her chances of success in the elections. Within two months the IB had produced a report, painting a very rosy picture of her victory in the elections. I suspect the report was doctored to please her but the end result was for the good of the country.

Two years after the declaration of the Emergency, Indira Gandhi took a plunge to seek a fresh mandate of the people and the rest is history. The Congress party got the worst drubbing at the elections and her Government was thrown out of power. For the first time an Opposition Government had been sworn in with Morarji Desai as the Prime Minister. Raj Narain defeated Indira Gandhi and became a Cabinet Minister. Charan Singh, the prominent leader from Uttar Pradesh, became the Home Minister.

Substantial changes were made in the Home Ministry and Khurana was sent back to Rajasthan where he occupied a relatively insignificant post. Srinivasa Varadan was recalled from Madhya Pradesh and made the Home Secretary. Within five years of my stay in the Home Ministry I worked under four Home Secretaries! Some of the Additional Secretaries in the Home Ministry, who had identified themselves closely with the previous regime, were sent packing. Varadan, who was earlier a senior colleague of mine in the Ministry, was now my boss. He proved good in his job and I especially admired his unflappable nature in times of crisis.

The Parliament took the extraordinary step of summoning Indira Gandhi. She was given a reprimand for declaring Emergency in the country when there was no need to do so. The income tax agency raided her farmhouse. It was rumoured that metal detectors were used to unearth hidden gold, but they found nothing incriminating. They arrested RK Dhawan, her Personal Secretary and tried to pump information from him to incriminate Indira Gandhi but he held firm and remained silent. MO Mathai, the former Personal Secretary of Pandit Nehru, published his autobiography, which had a secret chapter titled 'She'. This chapter was not published but was privately circulated.

One morning, the Commissioner of Police rang me up and asked for the deployment of an additional Central Reserve Police

(CRP) battalion in Delhi. Delhi had no law and order problem then and I asked the Commissioner to explain to me the reason for his request. Though he was speaking on the secure Rax telephone, he said the purpose was top secret and he could not reveal it to me on telephone. I was surprised at his reply and told him that I cannot accede to his request without his clarifying to me the need for an additional force in Delhi. A few minutes later I received summons from the Home Secretary, asking me to come to his office immediately. The Home Secretary told me that the Home Minister had decided to pass orders for the arrest of Indira Gandhi that afternoon and he directed me to provide the additional force to Delhi immediately. This order was complied with promptly.

At about 4 pm that day I got a call from Venkatramani (an IAS Officer of the Orissa cadre who was a year junior to me), Joint Secretary, Ministry of Petroleum, that the CBI officers had come to arrest his Secretary BB Vohra, an IAS Officer belonging to the 1948 batch, the seniormost batch of the IAS. Vohra who knew me well had asked Venkatramani to seek my help as he was unable to comprehend why he was being arrested. I was greatly shocked to learn that the CBI was seeking the arrest of Vohra who was known to be impeccably honest. I told Venkatramani to advise Vohra to buy time and I raced to the chamber of the Director, CBI, who was also personally known to me. He told me that the Home Minister had suggested to him that along with the arrest of Indira Gandhi, the CBI should arrest two senior officers of the Government of India against whom there were allegations of corrupt practices, so that Indira Gandhi's arrest could be viewed by the public as part of the cleaning-up exercise conducted by the new Government. CV Narasimhan, Director, CBI, informed me that he had decided to pick up two senior-level officers of the rank of Secretary to the Government of India against whom certain enquiries were pending with the CBI. He had selected Vohra and Agarwal, who headed the Postal Department. In official circles Agarwal was known to be corrupt but the image of Vohra was clean. When I mentioned this to the Director he said that there were some allegations against Vohra in a petroleum deal, which were under investigation by the CBI. When I pressed him further whether the CBI enquiry had revealed any wrongdoing by Vohra, he replied that the enquiry had not been completed. I tried my best to plead with the Director on behalf of Vohra but when he appeared adamant, I lost my cool and told him that he was not fit to hold a high office in the Police and stormed out of his office.

I rang up Venkatramani to brief him about my failed efforts and Vohra and Agarwal were arrested. They were both released on bail the next day. In the cases that followed Agarwal was convicted on corruption charges but Vohra was honourably discharged as the court found that there was inadequate material to chargesheet him.

Nemesis caught up with the Director of CBI in a very strange way. The CBI had made arrangements to spirit away Indira Gandhi outside Delhi after her arrest to prevent any local agitation. While being escorted out by the Police, they got stalled at a railway crossing, which had been closed to traffic. When the people assembled there, waiting for the barrier at the crossing to open, saw Indira Gandhi under arrest, they surrounded the Police and prevented them from proceeding further. At this unplanned setback, the Police retreated with Indira Gandhi and she was finally lodged for the night at the Public Works Department (PWD) rest house near Qutub Minar on the outskirts of Delhi. The next day she was produced before the court in Delhi where there was a dramatic end to the case.

The court held that the chargesheet filed before it was inadequate and Indira Gandhi was discharged.

It was the most absurd and clumsy handling of the case by the CBI and Charan Singh, the Home Minister, lost face and his political image was gravely dented. The Director, CBI, paid for his ineptitude and he was immediately transferred and sent back to his State cadre. Nearly thirty years later I met him in Chennai at a wedding ceremony and he spoke to me as if nothing untoward had taken place in the past. Even now I have no sympathy for his fall from grace, which he richly deserved.

Morarji Desai as Prime Minister was soon open to criticism as his son Kanti Desai emerged as an unholy power centre. Charan Singh, the Home Minister, was also ambitious to become the Prime Minister. There were powerful forces at work in New Delhi, when my tenure in the Home Ministry came to an end in April 1977. A month earlier I met the Home Minister and bade him goodbye. A few days later I got a call from the Home Secretary, summoning me to his office. He said he wished to retain me for one more year and he had discussed the matter with the Home Minister who had approved the proposal. He also mentioned to me that the Home Minister was aware of the correct advice rendered by me during the period of the Emergency and that he liked my straightforward ways. As my children were still studying in school, I readily agreed to the proffered extension.

Sometime in the early 1970s the petrol prices were suddenly hiked by fifty per cent and, though I was a high-level officer in the Government, I could not afford to commute to work in my own car. I took to travelling by bus to office before some of us living in Moti Bagh started a car pool. One day, I got into the bus at Moti Bagh and I had standing room only. At an intermediate bus stop the person sitting next to me vacated his seat and as I was about to sit on that seat, I suddenly received a powerful push from behind and I went sprawling forward. When I got up I found that a constable in uniform had taken the seat, pushing me aside. I was enraged at his assault and I got hold of his collar. I then raised him up and pushed him aside to claim the seat. Fortunately, the other passengers in the bus who had witnessed the incident supported my action and the constable meekly got off at the next halt. Realisation came to me then that I had committed the grave offence of assaulting a Police constable in uniform and if he had arrested me it would have made headlines that a senior Home Ministry official was arrested for assaulting a constable in uniform!

During our car pool days three of us—all Joint Secretaries in the Home Ministry—decided to break off from office a little early to listen to a lecture being delivered by the noted anthropologist Margaret Mead at the Nehru Auditorium at Teen Murti House. I was driving my car and, when I did not find a parking place nearby, I drove up to a nearby Police sub-inspector. Introducing my friend sitting alongside me as Joint Secretary, Police, I requested him to get the car parked and deliver the keys inside the auditorium. He gave my friend a smart salute and took the keys from me, had the car parked and delivered the keys to me, again with a smart salute to my friend. Later I told my friend that if I had introduced myself as Joint Secretary, Police, the sub-inspector may not have believed me.

When I was Joint Secretary, Police, there occurred an unusual incident of law and order on the lawns adjoining Rajpath near India Gate. A prominent leader of Uttar Pradesh, Mahendra Singh Tikait, had made known his intention to march to Delhi when the Parliament was in session to protest against low farm prices. He took the Delhi Police by surprise when one night about four hundred bullock carts loaded with about two thousand farmers entered Delhi unnoticed and parked themselves on either side of Rajpath with the intention of marching towards Parliament to press their demands. In the morning the Delhi Police swung into action and cordoned off the area by a heavy deployment of force. The strike of the farmers lasted for four days. In desperation, the Police offered to allow a small delegation to visit the nearby Krishi Bhawan to meet the Minister, Agriculture, but Tikait was adamant in taking his procession to the Parliament. On the fifth night the Police thought of a unique plan to make the farmers retreat without using force. They set up a dozen loudspeakers and played very loud hard rock music. The farmers were taken by surprise but they stood their ground. Near midnight, the cows and bullocks showed signs of unrest and began breaking their tethers to run away from the music. It was then that the farmers decided to retreat and by dawn they had disappeared from India Gate, heading back home. It was the most unique method of crowd control practised by the Police; this could have happened only in incredible India!

Prime Minister Morarji Desai decided to visit the North East. He flew to Mizoram in a Border Security Force (BSF) plane accompanied by his personal staff and ML Kampani, Joint Secretary, North East, escorted the party. Nearing Jorhat, the plane developed a snag and started losing height and crashed in a wooded area. By skilful piloting a major disaster was averted and the plane landed with a thud, with both its wings damaged by the surrounding trees. Kampani narrated to us the great composure exhibited by Morarji Desai who, though badly shaken up, walked out of the wreckage of the plane unaided. He was past his eightieth year. I was the first to be informed of the plane crash by Kampani by telephone and when I called on Charan Singh to inform him of the crash, he did not appear to be very concerned about the Prime Minister's safety. Such was his political ambition to become the Prime Minister. He eventually unseated the Prime Minister and became the Prime Minister himself but did not last long. He was the first Prime Minister to have avoided a test of his strength in the Parliament. He resigned without even attempting to pass the test.

The extended period of my tenure was getting over and the last important assignment I handled in the Home Ministry was the setting up of the National Police Commission. The Home Minister ordered that such a Commission be set up to bring about an improvement in the working of the Police in the country. I delineated the terms of reference and the setting up of the National Police Commission was notified with Dharama Vira as its Chairman and Rustomji as one of its prominent members.

Indira and I started discussing our future course of action on my transfer back to Orissa. It was agreed that she and the children continue to stay in Delhi in the interest of the children's education.

12

Facing Challenges

During my flight to Kolkata and then on to Bhubaneshwar I had the company of a colleague of mine, UC Agarwal, who was also returning to Orissa after his deputation stint as Establishment Officer of the Government of India. This was a powerful post in the Department of Personnel in the rank of an Additional Secretary, dealing with the placement of all civil servants in the various Ministries. We were received at the airport by the Joint Secretary, Protocol. After welcoming us he drew me aside and revealed that the Chief Minister did not wish me to join as Secretary, Forests, for the Minister, Forests, had raised an objection. I myself had been surprised when I received the State Government's orders, sending me once again to the same post where I had a confrontation with the Chief Minister and from which post I was transferred away suddenly when I refused to toe his political line. The present Minister, on learning of my reputation, had demanded a change in my posting.

I waited at the circuit house in Bhubaneshwar where I was staying, when I received revised orders posting me as Chairman of the Orissa Forest Corporation in Bhubneshwar. I did not call on the Chief Minister or the Minister, Forests, deliberately not following the official protocol. They had dumped me in a job that did not have much work as there was a full-time Managing Director running the Corporation.

After taking charge of the new job I decided to tour the State extensively, visiting the various field divisions and the timber stock depots of the Corporation to get a good working knowledge of it. This allowed me to interact with the officers and staff in the field, leading to many improvements in the management practices of the Corporation.

We had very large orders from the Railways for the supply of wooden sleepers but the problem that faced the divisions was about not getting enough wagons to get the sleepers lifted from our stockyards. The odd fact was that though the Railways were badly in need of the timely supply of sleepers for their ongoing projects, the commercial wing of the Railways—that was in charge of the allotment of wagons—did not seem to realise the urgency of the matter. The commercial wing, located at Khurdah Junction near Puri, was highly corrupt and wagons were supplied only when palms were greased. This fact was brought to my notice by the Divisional Managers of the Corporation. On my return to Bhubaneshwar I conferred with the Managing Director and a senior officer of the Corporation to find a solution to this problem but they were bereft of any ideas. I mentioned to them that, since the Corporation was a commercial organisation, we have to follow commercial practices. It was finally agreed that a special hospitality fund would be created in the Corporation and withdrawals from this fund, with the joint signatures of the Chairman and the Managing Director, would be utilised for bribing to ensure a timely and adequate supply of wagons. I staked my reputation in creating this special fund and we faced no problem after that! This was, no doubt, rather an unorthodox solution, but it was necessary.

Six months in my new job I was invited to attend a meeting especially convened by the Chief Minister for all senior officers of the Forest Department to discuss measures to protect our forests. The Chief Minister, JB Patnaik, had just returned from Delhi after attending a meeting with Sanjay Gandhi who had informally raised this issue. The meeting lasted three hours and there were several suggestions such as increased staff for patrolling in the forests, setting up extra checkposts, more intensive checks, supervision over private timber sawmills, providing extra jeeps and wireless sets to the field forest staff for improving mobility and reach and so on. I listened quietly, not offering any suggestions, until the Chief Minister turned to me and asked for my views. I told him that the suggestions made so far appeared impressive but in actual fact were ineffective. To the shock of the top brass of the Forest Department, I bluntly told him that the nexus between the contractor and the Forest Department in overlooking illegal activities was the main cause for the depletion of forests. I also said that the area of operation of the Orissa Forest Corporation was limited to cover only one-third the area of the forests in the State and the only effective way to protect the forests was to extend the area of operation to the entire State. The forest officers present at the meeting were miffed at my suggestion and the Chief Minister, sensing their hostile mood, quickly closed the meeting but not before extending an invitation to me to meet him separately to discuss the matter further.

I met him a week later and he said he was appreciative of my suggestion. He asked me to extend the area of operation to the entire State, starting from the next financial year. I thanked him for his offer but informed him that I have to plan in advance to make the takeover a success and would hence need two years to implement the suggestion fully, extending my operations gradually from year to year. A Cabinet decision followed this and in two years the area of operation of the Corporation was extended to the entire State except the Angul Forest Division, which was reserved for departmental management as a sop to the forest officers. This was a major achievement in forest protection in Orissa, of which I am proud.

Kendu leaves grow wild in the forest and are collected annually, processed and sold at a considerable profit by the Orissa Forest Corporation. We used to export *kendu* leaves to Pakistan and during the period I was Chairman, we received enquiries from Sri Lanka. Cyril Mathews, Sri Lankan Minister of Industries, came to Orissa to hold preliminary discussions with us about the export of *kendu* leaves and he invited us for the final round of discussion in Sri Lanka. We learnt that he was an important political figure and the right-hand man of President JR Jayawardene.

During my inspection of the divisional offices I found that there was a large number of sundry debtors and huge sums had remained uncollected from them for years. A staggering Rs 80 crore was shown as total outstanding—Rs 60 crore was owed to us by the Railways and this backlog was substantially cleared after a year's sustained efforts; Rs 15 crore was owed by the public sector coalfields and it was obtained after mounting a special drive. The remaining Rs 5 crore was the amount that Government officers of the IAS, IPS and IFS (Indian Forest Service) owed the Corporation for the supply of timber for the building of their houses. I personally rang up the officers after issuing individual notices to them and, except for one senior officer, we managed to get the money owed from all of them.

The Corporation extended its operations to the entire State during my tenure and this yielded rich dividends. The forest revenue increased twofold. I had got into an informal understanding with the Finance Department that, instead of collecting annual charges from me for working the forest coupes, I would give ninety-five per cent of my increasing profits, thus maximising Government revenue. In this process we got the advantage of paying less income tax, a mutually beneficial arrangement.

When I took over as the Chairman of the Corporation, I was astonished to see that we were in arrears of audit for four years. I employed a local firm of chartered accountants to update the accounts quickly and I approached the office of the Comptroller and Auditor General of India to appoint an auditor to audit the accounts of the Corporation for two years at a time. I made two visits to the Comptroller and Auditor General's office to obtain this special sanction. I had no inkling then that I would, many years later, grace the august office myself!

As the Corporation was making good profits and had surplus cash, I decided I would start some plantation activity. I obtained the lease of about three thousand hectares of degraded forests on the border of Puri and Ganjam Districts and took up cashew cultivation there. The Managing Director of the Corporation and I paid a visit to the cashew research station in Karwar and went to Mangalore where I had studied years earlier. When I visited Orissa years later as the Central Vigilance Commissioner I travelled by helicopter from Bhubaneshwar to Damanjodi in Koraput District, where the National Aluminium Company (Nalco) had its manufacturing unit. I was delighted to see that I was flying over the cashew plantation, which was then in full bloom.

Once, during my tours, I camped in the Simlipal Tiger Reserve along with three bridge players, including the Divisional Commissioner Sunderrajan and his wife Sudha. The log hut where we stayed was built on stilts and we could clearly hear the jungle noises at night. In the morning we were witness to the beautiful mating dance of the peacock and, on our return journey, we ran into a herd of elephants. Once they passed, a lone tusker chased us head on and I had to frantically reverse my jeep for more than a hundred yards to escape its charge. This was an unforgettable experience.

I had read an advertisement that the Cashew Corporation of India, a Government of India undertaking, was giving out loans to encourage cashew cultivation in the private sector. I decided to call on Vinod Pande, Joint Secretary in the Commerce Ministry, to ascertain the terms and conditions of the loan being extended by the Cashew Corporation of India. On entering his room I introduced myself, mentioning my name and official designation and asked for information on the loan. He looked at me condescendingly and said that he would discuss such matters only with the Secretary of Orissa's Forest Department and not with me! I smiled and quietly told him that I had functioned as Secretary, Forest, in Orissa for three years. He immediately recognised that I was a senior IAS Officer and his demeanour changed and he was forthcoming with all the information I needed. Vinod Pandey later became Cabinet Secretary and he was the one who rang me up years later to tell me that the Prime Minister had decided to appoint me as the Comptroller and Auditor General of India and sought my consent before obtaining presidential approval for the proposal.

Within a month of my return to Orissa from Delhi in 1978, I heard that in response to my application for the allotment of a plot in Bengaluru made five years ago, the Bengaluru Development Authority (BDA) had given me a plot, measuring sixty feet by forty feet, in Indira Nagar. I visited Bengaluru to take possession of the plot, but on inspection I was dismayed to find a high-tension electric wire above the plot, making construction hazardous. I went storming to the BDA office and entered the room of the Chairman, Somanna, unannounced and sought his explanation. He was about to get me thrown out when I introduced myself, mentioning my official designation. He was quite impressed when I told him that one of my batchmates was the State Finance Secretary and the other occupied the high post of Divisional Commissioner. After this introduction, further discussions were carried on quite smoothly. Somanna assured me that I would be allotted another plot nearby and I soon took possession of the new plot, paying the royalty and rent. Construction proceeded briskly and the house was ready within a year. We are comfortably settled in this small but beautiful house.

Early in 1979 I came across a newspaper advertisement that the Indian Institute of Management, Delhi, was organising a ten-day management course in Srinagar towards the end of April for executives of public sector undertakings. My Managing Director and I enrolled for this course and I alerted Indira to accompany me to Srinagar. We went on a trekking trip to Amarnath, by the newly-opened Baltal route. After an invigorating stay in Kashmir, we returned to Delhi and went for a holiday to Bengaluru and Coorg with the children.

Three years is the prescribed 'cooling off' period to be spent in a State before an officer can go back to Delhi on Central deputation. In November 1980, I got a call from VB Easwaran, Secretary, Expenditure, Ministry of Finance, enquiring whether I was willing to join him as Additional Secretary. Easwaran was a brilliant officer with a high reputation for probity, two years senior to me and belonged to the Gujarat cadre. I used to interact with him when I was Joint Secretary, Police. I had no hesitation in accepting his offer as I was keen to get back to Delhi as quickly as possible to join Indira and the children.

A few days after this, the State, which had been quiet and peaceful, erupted with student violence. The trouble started in Sambalpur University. A large number of Government buses were set on fire and I personally witnessed a burning bus in front of the State Secretariat in Bhubaneshwar. It was on the sixth day of the strike that I got a call from the Chief Secretary conveying to me the Chief Minister's decision to post me as State Home Secretary to take charge of the law and order situation. I asked him directly why he had never made any enquiries about me earlier, knowing fully well that I had been sidelined to work in an innocuous post for nearly three years. I also told him that I was not prepared to take up a new assignment in the State now as I was expecting a posting in Delhi in another three months' time and this may be communicated to the Chief Minister.

That evening I received another call from the Chief Secretary who said that the Chief Minister was willing to release me to go to the Centre on the receipt of appropriate orders. I replied that I would like to meet the Chief Minister personally and get his assurance before taking up the new job. I called on JB Patnaik the next day and I mentioned to him that I would not permit any illegal arrests or acts by the Police during the period I was Home Secretary. On receiving his assurance, I joined my new post in the first week of December 1980.

I decided to open a dialogue with the student leadership in Sambalpur. My message to them got me a favourable reply but they requested that I talk to them at Sambalpur. When I reached the circuit house after a long journey by car I got a further message that the talks should be held in the college premises. My knowledge of Oriya impressed them and the discussions lasted two hours. They were also impressed by the fact that I had come all the way to meet them and they appreciated my sincerity. By the time I returned to Bhubaneshwar the students had called off the statewide agitation. The trains started moving again. Illegal instructions issued to the IG Police, NN Swain, to thrash some of the students before they were released from police custody was countermanded by me after consulting the Chief Minister.

A day after my birthday I was sitting late in office when I got a call from Easwaran informing me that the Appointments Committee of the Cabinet had approved my posting to Delhi and formal orders were under issue. I still remember it was a full moon night when I received the good news. I was filled with happiness as I gazed out of the window, admiring the rose garden. I sent up a prayer of thanks to Ganapati, my favourite God. The next day I informed the Chief Minister and requested my immediate relief. On 15 March I was winging my way to Delhi.

13

Taking Charge

To be reunited with the family after a long separation was indeed bliss. I joined the Ministry of Finance as Additional Secretary, Expenditure. The Finance Ministry had its tentacles in the forty-odd Ministries and departments in the shape of financial advisors who advised their respective Secretaries and Heads of Departments. Within the financial powers delegated to the Ministries, the Secretary could accept or overrule the advice of the FA, but in matters beyond the delegated powers the files would be referred to the Secretary, Expenditure, for final orders. All matters referred to the Cabinet for approval by the Ministries had to be first approved by the Finance Ministry or the Finance Minister.

Easwaran spoke to me about the division of work between the Secretary and Additional Secretary. The Ministries and departments were equally shared by us, with the more important ones such as Defence, Industries and Commerce, which had large budgets, being retained by the Secretary. I had twenty FAs working under me in this arrangement and Easwaran, to my great astonishment, suggested that I should be vested with independent powers to deal with the proposals of these Ministries. He said that I need not route any files through him while referring the file to the Finance Minister, not even with regard to important policy matters. He was an amazing boss. I used to address him as 'Sir' while in office, but call him by his name outside.

I got a C-II Flat in Moti Bagh allotted for my residential accommodation and we soon shifted there from our one-room barsati in Anand Niketan. Indira and the children felt as if they had moved into a palace.

The Asian Games were being held in Delhi and I was the officer who would be handling the sanction of projects worth Rs 500 crore. These included the new sports stadia, renovation and repair of the old facilities, the Games Village and about seven overbridges on major roads to ease traffic congestion. It was one of the cleanest operations and was completed in time too. Indira and I attended the colourful opening ceremony using the gold passes given to me and it was indeed an impressive show. The Games, lasting ten days, passed off without a glitch thanks to the superb technical direction provided by Codanda Muthiah, the former decathlon champion of India.

International bids were invited by the Asian Games Organisation for the advertisement rights in the various stadia. Out of the bids received two were listed for further discussions—one in the USA and the other in Dubai. A high-level delegation was set up with the Director of the Asian Games as Chairman. A Joint Secretary from the Law Ministry and I represented Finance and after the visit, finalised the deal with the Dubai representative for 2.5 million dollars.

My next visit abroad that year was to Nepal. I was deputed by the Finance Ministry to attend a seminar on Indo-Nepal cooperation in development. It was held at the Soaltee Hotel in Katmandu. The same year I visited Geneva to attend a UN conference. LK Jha, ICS, who had kept a low profile after his retirement, was especially invited by the UN to attend this conference on simplifying the complex UN annual budget. However, as Jha was indisposed, I was asked by the Finance Secretary to attend in his place. It was my first experience of attending an international conference. Before leaving for Geneva I tried to acquaint myself with the budget format of the UN. Bulky documents were provided to me by the External Affairs Ministry; they were not reader friendly at all.

At the conference, presided over by the Under-Secretary General of the UN, the delegates were seated in alphabetical order and I found my place somewhere in the middle of the many financial experts gathered there. For the first time I donned the ear plugs to listen to the English translation of the babble of tongues, which make up a UN conference. In the beginning I was attentive to the various speakers who sounded impressively technical in their approach to the problem but as the conference progressed I realised that no practical solution was on offer. On the fourth day, when my turn came to speak, I told them how we had succeeded in demystifying the budget in India by bringing out three short summaries of the revenue and capital expenditures of the various receipts of the Government of India. I had brought three copies of these budget summary booklets with me, which I presented to the Chairman. I said that the UN budget should be recast using the latest accounting procedures and for this I suggested the setting up of an expert Committee to study the issue and make suitable recommendations for adoption by the UN.

My presentation received tremendous applause and as the conference progressed I found that the delegates started addressing me as 'Dr Somiah'. On the penultimate day of the conference, my suggestions were accepted for adoption and while the formation of the Committee was being discussed, the Chairman proposed my name for heading it. This would have meant a long-term perk for me, much sought after by the delegates, but I politely declined the honour as I was the alternate delegate from India. I suggested that LK Jha head the Committee. This was unanimously approved and Jha was, no doubt, very pleased.

Little did I know, then, that I would be personally involved in suggesting changes in the format of the UN budget, when, years later, I became Chairman of the UN Board of Audit. At that time I called for the recommendations made at the UN Secretariat by the LK Jha Committee. The records showed that about a dozen meetings had been held in various beautiful locations of the world but nothing concrete had come out of the deliberations of the Committee. This was not unusual as members treated these tours as pleasure junkets. To be fair to LK Jha, after chairing one session of the Committee, he had resigned owing to failing health.

In 1982, I was fortunate to see four natural wonders of the world—the Grand Canyon, the Niagara Falls, a close view of Everest and a distant view of the Mont Blanc in Chamonix. I also had a close aerial view of some of the tallest mountains of the Himalayan range—Lhotse, Makalu, Annapurna, Cho Oyo, Manaslu Himachuli and Kanchanjunga—during my Nepal visit that year.

The budget period is the busiest in the Finance Ministry. A large number of delegates representing industry, trade and commerce call on the Finance Ministry, pleading for a good deal for them in the budget. Two delegations from the Coorg Planters' Association and the United Planters' Association of South India (UPASI) met the Finance Ministry and for two successive years, when I was Additional Secretary, Finance, two major concessions were provided to them. The wealth tax and estate duty on plantations were abolished.

A delegation of Coorg teachers met me and said that they had been shabbily treated with regard to the fixation of seniority and protection of salary at the time Coorg merged with the State of Mysore. I pursued the matter and got them the necessary relief. Years later, this help was publicly acknowledged at a function held in Coorg to honour me when I was appointed the Comptroller and Auditor General of India.

My mother's seventy-fifth birthday was round the corner and I invited my sister, Rani, from Bengaluru to join us for the celebrations. A little earlier I had been promoted and posted as Special Secretary in the Department of Companies Affairs and so there were enough reasons to party. Indira baked a cake and in the evening we all drove over to Rathi's house near India Gate to cut another cake. It was a joyous family gathering.

A day later, when I returned home I found that my mother had caught a chill. The cold advanced to a chest cough and she was put on antibiotics. This gave her no relief and when she developed bronchitis we had to shift her to Safdarjung Hospital on 2 January 1983, much against her wishes. On reaching the hospital she refused to sit on the wheelchair and insisted on walking up to her ward. Her condition had deteriorated by the morning with what doctors diagnosed as galloping pneumonia. Rani and I were by her side when she passed away the next day.

14

Secretary, Government of India

Before I was promoted as Special Secretary, Department Company Affairs, I was appointed Secretary of the Department. That was when KS Bhatnagar retired. However, within a day the order was cancelled as Bhatnagar succeeded in getting a two-month extension. He was angling for the post of Comptroller and Auditor General and wanted to be in service while being considered for it. When I joined as Special Secretary, I called on him and also the Minister, Jagannath Kaushal. I also called on Ghulam Nabi Azad, Deputy Minister, Law, who occupied the room next to me. He was both charming and handsome and came into politics through the youth movement in the Congress. He made a claim that he had personally visited at least a couple of districts in each State and took pride in the fact that he had been to Coorg, too, and had met the good looking men and women of the place.

I utilised the two months of relative idleness, in reading up the Indian Companies Act, the Monopolies and Restrictive Trade Practices (MRTP) Act and so on. The IAS trains you to learn with every job and master it, before moving on to the next assignment. When a new mind applies itself to a task, it not only sees the routine but also a new approach to the problem. My judgment told me that the MRTP Act was a great hindrance to the rapid industrialisation of the country. The Act, conceived and enacted in 1969, stated that an industrialist with an asset of Rs 20 crore and above in plant and machinery, was considered a monopolist, irrespective of the market share of his product. For future expansion and setting up any industry he had to approach the Government for permission, in addition to applying for a licence to set up the industry under the Industrial Development and Regulation Act. Also, under the MRTP Act, the Secretary, Department Company Affairs, had to give the necessary clearance after hearing all his competitors who opposed his application.

I had the opportunity to voice my concern before the highest political level when Rajiv Gandhi succeeded Indira Gandhi as the Prime Minister of India. In his youthful zeal, Rajiv Gandhi initiated a process of personally interviewing the fifty-odd Secretaries of the various Ministries and departments to retain the best and to cut out the dead wood, sending them back to their respective States. In the process, my batchmates CR Vaidyanathan, Secretary, Health and R Gopalaswamy, Secretary, Urban Development, faced the axe. When I appeared before Rajiv Gandhi I found he was being assisted by Arun Singh, Member of Parliament (whom he later appointed as Minister of State, Defence Ministry). I personally knew Arun Singh as a member of the Managing Committee of the Asian Games. When the Prime Minister asked me if I had any new ideas on how to improve administration in my area of work, I straightaway asked him whether he had the political will to scrap the MRTP Act. Being new to his job, he blinked uncomprehendingly. But, Arun Singh, after hearing the reason for my suggestion, asked me whether I could suggest something less radical. I said that at least they could consider raising the limit of Rs 20 crore to Rs 200 crore, after giving allowance for inflation in the intervening period, since the enactment of the Act in 1969. After discussions it was agreed that the limit be raised to Rs 100 crore. This saved time and labour for all industrialists who trudged the corridors of my office seeking clearance under the MRTP Act.

I succeeded KS Bhatnagar as Secretary in the Department at the end of his extended period of service, but not before considerable drama. A day before he was to retire, I called on him and told him that his officers and staff wanted to give him a farewell party. He said he would talk about it later. On the final day I waited for some sign from him and was surprised to see him working late in the office. I thought he was taking time to collect his personal papers before finally leaving office. The next day sharp at 10 am I walked into the office building and proceeded towards the Secretary's room to take over my new position. The peon cautioned me that 'Saab' was still inside. I retreated to my old room, totally confused. Later I learnt that Bhatnagar was frantically ringing up his political connections for a further extension. He finally came to my room at 11.30 am to bid me goodbye.

One of the earliest visitors at my office was Mira Nair who won cinematic acclaim for her film *Salaam Bombay*. She had embarked on a film project titled *Kama Sutra* and was having difficulty in getting permission from the Archaeological Survey of India (ASI) to shoot some scenes. When I called my Personal Assistant to dictate a letter to be sent by her to the ASI, she surprised me by opening her portable typewriter and taking the dictation directly from me. She typed fast and accurately. Her impressive performance on the typewriter evoked my admiration as did the films she later produced and directed including *Monsoon Wedding*, which received worldwide critical acclaim.

Under the Companies Act, I also functioned as Chairman of the Company Law Board and was empowered to pass quasijudicial orders. In the MRTP hearings top lawyers such as Nani Palkhivala and Asoke Sen used to appear before me. Once, Asoke Sen was obviously unprepared when he was arguing. He started his arguments condescendingly, stating that as I was new to my job, he would take me along in reading out the plaint to me, before starting his arguments. I cut him short by stating that he could start his arguments straightaway. I told him that the least he could have expected from me as judge was that I would have read his plaint, especially when an eminent lawyer like him appeared before me. I could see him fumble and on realising that I had became aware of his unpreparedness, he quickly closed his brief, stating that he had just remembered an urgent appointment. With an understanding smile, I readily granted his request!

My old Ambassador car had done fifteen years service with me and I felt I should go in for a new car. Maruti Udyog, with Japanese collaboration, had recently introduced a car for Rs 50,000. It could seat four and it seemed to suit both the size of our family and our purse. I booked a car for early delivery. RC Bhargava, an IAS Officer, had been appointed Chairman and Managing Director of Maruti Udyog and I knew him well as he was a keen bridge player. After about eleven months of waiting I rang up Bhargava to enquire about the delivery of my car. He told me that the price of the car had increased by Rs 5,000 from the next financial year. However, as my delivery date was near he would try and push the allotment before the commencement of the next financial year. I told him not to do anything unusual in changing my delivery date. He followed my request and I got my car on 7 April 1984, at the higher price, a week after the commencement of the financial year. This was the car I used for twelve years and then gave to Pria in 1996. It was still in good running condition.

Top honchos of industry used to visit me as a matter of courtesy. Two interesting incidents happened during this time. Dhirubhai Ambani called on me, after Mukesh, his son, had earlier dropped in for fixing an appointment. I remember Dhirubhai as a charming personality, dressed in a spotless *dhoti kurta* (traditional Indian dress). He spent half-an-hour with me telling me about his humble beginnings and about his burning ambition to make India industrially strong. He then took leave and, after pretending to exit my room, entered it again as if on second thoughts, and offered me some Reliance shares out of his promoter's quota. I was taken by surprise but politely declined his offer. The canny man that he was, he was testing my level of integrity.

Another time, when the Chairman of Indian Explosives called on me and introduced himself as Baijal, I immediately recognised him. He had a grievance about his salary—in those days the salaries of all executive-level directors in a company had to have the approval of the Department of Company Affairs. His request to upgrade his salary was readily agreed upon by me and just as he was about to take leave, I asked him whether he remembered meeting me earlier. He was puzzled at my question. Then I told him that he and I had appeared for a job interview with the Imperial Chemical Industries (ICI) in Kolkata and while he stood first and got selected, I had stood third and just lost out on getting the job. The former company ICI had changed its name to Indian Explosives and in a span of thirty years Baijal had reached the top.

Mani Narayanswami, my batchmate who was Secretary, Textiles, called me one day saying that his friend Vijay Mallya wanted to meet me to sort out a problem. Mani escorted Vijay

Mallya personally to my room and the problem was sorted out. Vijay Mallya is now one of the leading industrial barons of India. Similarly, Raunaq Singh, Chairman, Apollo Tyres and a prominent industrialist of Northern India, came to my office once, escorted by two plainclothes guards. He fell foul of the Babbar Khalsa in the dispute between the Nirankaris and the Sikhs and was under a death threat. When I suggested politely that he tells his security guards to withdraw, he seemed insulted and within minutes staged a walkout! The arrogance of the man had to be seen to be believed.

On the day of the assassination of Indira Gandhi I left office a little early and returned to my flat in Moti Bagh, driving through deserted streets. The madness to attack the Sikhs in retaliation for the assassination had spread to Moti Bagh also. Soon, a sardarji on a two-wheeler with his wife were stopped by stick-wielding youths. Swinging their *lathis* (sticks), they knocked the turban off the sardarji's head and the hapless couple fell down. Seeing this unprovoked attack, I came down with my two young guests from Coorg. By the time we reached the scene the sardarji was found bleeding from a head wound and the woman had injuries on her hands. The boys stopped their attack on the couple when they saw us emerge with hockey sticks and cricket bats. They were double our number but cowards and retreated on seeing the determined look on our faces. It was a defining moment for me. I was happy that I had helped in saving at least two lives and I thanked the two lads for assisting me.

As Secretary, Department Company Affairs, I also had official dealings with the Institute of Chartered Accountants and the Institute of Company Secretaries. I attended the annual gathering of Chartered Accountants in Kovalam as their Chief Guest and addressed the annual gathering of Assocham

(Associated Chamber of Commerce and Industry) in Mumbai and the South India Chamber of Commerce in Chennai. At the former event I spoke about the evils of insider trading, which did not endear me to the crowd of industrialists assembled there.

After I had completed a little over sixteen months as Secretary, Department Company Affairs, which I was thoroughly enjoying, I planned a holiday with Indira and the children to Kolkata, Darjeeling and Sikkim in May 1984. I had been sanctioned fifteen days leave and I had made advance train bookings to and from Kolkata. It was at this stage that I received a call from the Cabinet Secretary, PK Kaul, that orders were being issued that very day for posting me as Secretary, Planning Commission, and that I would be taking over from KV Ramanathan. I was completely taken aback and demanded that I should have been consulted before this transfer. I also explained to Kaul that I had a quasijudicial role under the Acts that I administered and that I had about a dozen cases pending for issue of final orders. Finally, I mentioned to him that in another three days I would be off to Sikkim with my family and that I could take over the new job only after my return. He tried to bully me to comply with his orders but I resisted and in exasperation he dropped the telephone, cutting short our conversation.

A few minutes later I got a call from KV Ramanathan, a good friend of mine, asking me why I was dragging my feet to relieve him. Ramanathan, a brilliant and straightforward officer, fell foul of Rajiv Gandhi when he was Secretary, Chemicals and Fertilisers. He opposed illegal deals in awarding contracts for the construction of new fertiliser plants in the public sector. The Government was making an attempt to mollify him by posting him in a lucrative job abroad. Ramanathan was naturally keen to make a quick getaway from his present humiliating position and asked me whether I could help him in the matter. After some discussions it was agreed that when I complete my judicial work I would relieve Ramanathan and he on his part agreed to obtain the consent of my future boss in the Planning Commission to grant me ten days leave. With this pre-arranged agreed formula I joined as Secretary, Planning Commission.

We spent two days in Kolkata, two in Darjeeling and three in Sikkim. The rest went into travel time. We came back to the heat of Delhi, fully refreshed and the next day I took charge of my new job as Secretary, Planning Commission. The first person to be appointed as Secretary, Planning Commission, was Tarlok Singh, ICS. His tenure was a long one and people often joked—after Lok Sabha and Rajya Sabha comes Tarlok Sabha!

15

At the Planning Commission

Dr Manmohan Singh was the Deputy Chairman of the Planning Commission when I joined and Rajiv Gandhi was the ex-officio Chairman. Four eminent men were members of the Commission, with different subjects under their charge. I was the main coordinator and all files were routed through me for orders and approval. The job was totally different from the kind I held earlier and the vast secretariat housed in Yojana Bhawan, including various technical advisors, worked under my control and direction.

I joined the Commission at a crucial time when the seventh Five Year Plan for the period 1985-90 was under preparation and discussion. It was a complex maze of work and the Commission's busiest period. I worked on holidays and never left the office before 9 pm.

Within a few weeks, the first tentative draft of the seventh plan containing the broad outlines was placed before the Commission for approval.

In his first meeting of the Planning Commission, after we had completed our presentation, Rajiv Gandhi stated that he did not agree with our approach to the plan and wanted it to be recast completely. He shared his vision with us to lead India into the twenty-first century as a fully developed nation. He wanted us to plan for the construction of autobahns, airfields, speedy trains, shopping malls and entertainment centres of excellence, big housing complexes, modern hospitals and healthcare centres. He held forth in this way for the next half-an-hour and concluded his speech with a grin, suggesting that we should change our mindset in drafting the seventh Five Year Plan. We were shocked into silence. Dr Manmohan Singh called an internal meeting of the Commission to discuss the matter further. The broad consensus that emerged was that the Prime Minister was urban-centric without any knowledge of the socially and financially backward condition of the vast population living in the rural areas. It was decided that in the next meeting we would try and educate the Prime Minister about the hard realities of the widespread poverty prevailing in the country.

In the next meeting of the Planning Commission, the soft-spoken Dr Singh deliberated at length on the negative economic indicators prevalent in the country, which could not be ignored for providing relief in any future plan. The Prime Minister was not impressed and made some hurtful derogatory remarks about Dr Singh's presentation. He then turned to the other members for comments but none of them had the courage to speak up. He finally turned to me and said sarcastically, 'Let us hear what the Secretary has to say about the approach to the plan.'

In response I mentioned that during the thirty-year period of the last six plans we had achieved an economic growth rate of two to three per cent annually (which the economists derided as the Hindu rate of growth). We had now chalked out a plan of five per cent growth annually. In the first chapter of the draft plan, we had foreseen a similar growth pattern for the next fifteen years. This was difficult to achieve given the past experience.

I went on to say that even if we achieve this ambitious projection, the country could in no way match the West. Our efforts would relieve intense poverty in the rural sector and would provide for better drinking water facilities in the rural area, better healthcare and education for the poorer sections of the society and good growth in the industrial sector. I also mentioned that if the intention was to reach the Western standard of living for the entire population of India, there were not enough energy sources in the entire world to achieve it. High standards of living required high energy consumption per capita. After this the meeting ended without any specific direction from the Prime Minister.

A few days later the Prime Minister shared his thoughts with journalists, calling us a 'bunch of jokers' who were bereft of any modern ideas of development. When this news made headlines in the newspapers, Dr Singh, emerging out of an urgent meeting with the other members, called me to his office. He looked distraught and terribly upset with the Prime Minister's remarks. He told me that he was tendering his resignation as he seems to have lost the confidence of the Prime Minister. I sat with him for nearly an hour and told him not to take the extreme step and blamed the Prime Minister's ignorance for this behaviour. I further advised that since the Prime Minister was young and inexperienced, it was our duty to educate him rather than abandon him. I was finally able to convince him not to act hastily and that was my good deed for the day.

Within six months, we finalised the draft plan with the Prime Minister's approval. His suggestions were taken into account by increasing the provision for the development of national highways, improvement of airports and urban infrastructure. By this time the Prime Minister had learnt the magnitude of rural distress in the country through his frequent visits to rural areas. The plan finally approved for presentation before the National

Development Council (NDC) contained all the key elements directed against poverty and hunger, as originally suggested by us.

The Chief Ministers of all States were members of the NDC with the Prime Minister as its Chairman. Dr Manmohan Singh, Deputy Chairman of the Planning Commission, VP Singh, Finance Minister and PV Narasimha Rao, the seniormost Cabinet Minister, were its other members from the Centre. The draft Central plan was circulated to all the States and their Chief Ministers were invited to a two-day session of the NDC for giving the final stamp of approval to the seventh Five Year Plan. The meeting was held in the main conference hall of Vigyan Bhawan where simultaneous translation and interpretation facilities were available.

It was a tradition for the Chief Ministers to address the gathering either in Hindi or English, except for MG Ramachandran, Chief Minister of Tamil Nadu, who gave his address in Tamil. Special arrangements were made for the simultaneous interpretation of the speech in Hindi and English. NT Rama Rao, the newly-elected Chief Minister from Andhra Pradesh, was a Telugu fanatic and I took the extra precaution to ascertain from the Chief Secretary, Andhra Pradesh, whether Rama Rao would address the NDC in Telugu. Shravan Kumar, a batchmate of mine, who was Chief Secretary, Hyderabad, assured me in writing that Rama Rao would address us in English. As confirmation he sent three copies of his printed speech in English.

The meeting of the NDC started with the welcome address delivered by Dr Manmohan Singh, followed by the Prime Minister's inaugural address. The Chief Ministers in the hall were seated alphabetically in the order of the States they represented. On the dais were the Prime Minister, flanked by Narasimha Rao, VP Singh and Dr Singh. Behind them were seated the Cabinet Secretary, Secretary, Finance, the Principal Secretary to the

Prime Minister and I. After the inaugural address by the Prime Minister, the Chief Minister of Andhra Pradesh was invited to speak. Surprisingly, Rama Rao started speaking in Telugu. To my unspoken query, directed at Shravan Kumar, seated next to the Chief Minister, I got a mere shrug. I acted quickly to retrieve the situation by sending two copies of his written speech in English to the booths manned by the English and Hindi interpreters. They immediately started making their commentary, according to the written text of the speech given to them.

Within a few minutes Narasimha Rao, who knew Telugu, gestured to me that what was coming through on his earphone did not match what Rama Rao was speaking. He briefed the Prime Minister about this. I realised then that Rama Rao had abandoned the prepared written speech and was speaking extempore in Telugu. I got a scribbled note from the Prime Minister through Sarla Grewal, the Principal Secretary to the Prime Minister, that the interpreters in English and Hindi should be suspended immediately. I scribbled back pointing out that if that was done, there would be protests from the assembled Chief Ministers and that it was better to allow the charade to continue. He understood my concern and instead ordered that at the end of Rama Rao's speech the interpreters be placed under suspension for their grave error. I skipped this order, too, in spite of repeated prodding from Sarla Grewal. The next day, when I met the Prime Minister and explained to him the reason for the confusion, he and I shared a laugh. Shravan Kumar was highly apologetic for the wrong advice that he had provided me. After two days of deliberating, the NDC finally approved the seventh Five Year Plan.

There were repeated complaints made to the Planning Commission that out of every rupee released by the Planning Commission for the implementation of the Central scheme by the States, only a portion of it reached the targeted beneficiary.

I decided to undertake a countrywide survey about this complaint and I entrusted the survey to reputed economic surveyors. Two districts from each of the twelve major States were earmarked for survey. The results confirmed our worst fears that allowing for twenty per cent as the cost of administrative overheads, fifty per cent of the assistance was siphoned off by corrupt intermediaries. It was on the basis of this survey that Rajiv Gandhi made his oft-quoted public remark that the poor got only thirty per cent of the amount released by the Centre for poverty alleviation schemes in the States.

In the seventh plan, for the first time, we earmarked Government assistance for welfare schemes to be routed through some reputed Non-Government Organisations (NGOs). This was done after detailed discussions that the Deputy Chairman and I had with Bunker Roy who had spearheaded a successful development model in Tilonia in Rajasthan. In Tamil Nadu, the Government took the help of NGOs in implementing the family welfare measures, including birth control, very successfully. Another first for the seventh plan was the inclusion of a highly imaginative environmental programme to clean up the Ganga River. In the plans that followed, higher allocations were made for bettering the environment in different areas but analysis revealed that the implementation had been poor in many cases, including the Ganga Action Plan to maintain the purity of its waters.

A yearly exercise is done in the Planning Commission to finalise the annual plan of the various Ministries. Before the formulation of the plan for the next year, a review is done of the current year's progress in plan expenditure to assess the requirement of funds for the next year. These review meetings are conducted with the Secretary, Planning Commission and the official heads of the different Ministries and departments. In the review meeting of the Railway Ministry, attended by the Chairman, Railway Board, there was a difference of Rs 100 crore in the assessment made by them and the sum arrived at in the Planning Commission. The review meeting could not bridge the gap in spite of protracted negotiations and the special request made by the Chairman.

That evening I received a telephone call from Madhavrao Scindia, Minister, Railways, inviting my wife and me for dinner. I had briefly known him before he became a Minister and I accepted his invitation under the impression that he was inviting us to attend a general party that he was hosting. When we arrived at his residence the next evening, we found to our surprise that we were the only invitees in a sit-down dinner. After a liberal lacing of pre-dinner Scotch whisky, we were served the best of French wines with our meal. Both the Minister and his gracious wife were at their charming best and my wife and I returned home a little bemused by their lavish hospitality.

During and after dinner I thought the Minister would raise the issue about the shortfall in the plan assistance provided to the Railways. There was not a word about that. I appreciated the Minister's diplomatic finesse when the Chairman, Railway Board, rang me up the next day and I assured him that we would increase the plan assistance by Rs 50 crore. Half-an-hour later, the Minister was on the line thanking me for this and it was my turn to thank him for the excellent dinner he had hosted for us. Madhavrao Scindia proved to be the best Minister the Railways had for a long time. He had the knack of combining business with princely hospitality and charm.

We once had an interesting visitor to the Planning Commission. He was Mengistu Haile Mariam, the dictator and strongman of Ethiopia who had toppled the Government headed by King Haile Selassie. He was on an official visit to India and when he met the Prime Minister he expressed a desire to have an interaction with the Planning Commission. The full Commission met him to brief him about the planning process in India and the central role played by the Planning Commission in coordinating the development activities in the country. Being left-oriented he expressed a desire to set up a Planning Commission in Ethiopia. When we met him he was clad in a natty blue safari suit and did not at all look the tyrant that he became later.

In the historic Punjab Accord, which brought temporary peace to the State, it was agreed that the Union Territory of Chandigarh would be transferred to Punjab and, in return, Punjab agreed to share the waters of the Sutlej River with Haryana and Delhi. The Yamuna link canal was to be fully financed by the Centre. The Planning Commission was placed in charge of the project for release of Central assistance. The Ministry of Irrigation and Power established a special construction unit headed by a Chief Engineer. Work on the project, which had started briskly, came to a sudden halt when it reached a village that was an Akali stronghold. The Prime Minister asked RD Pradhan, the Home Secretary, to use the good offices of the Planning Commission to sort out the problem. I summoned the Chief Engineer and after studying the contour maps of the village, suggested to him to make a diversion to the alignment of the canal so that it is routed through the adjoining Government forest land. The protest of the villagers who were objecting to their land being acquired soon died down. The knowledge that I had acquired years ago in survey and settlement came in handy to solve this problem. The IAS is indeed multidimensional in its work culture.

I had completed two years in the Planning Commission and after the hectic activities there, I was looking forward to enjoying the fruits of my labour for the next one year. I wanted some peace and quiet but the stars overruled my plan. After attending a routine Secretary Committee's meeting with PK Kaul, Cabinet Secretary, I was about to leave his office, when he asked me to stay on. Once the others had left the room he looked at me quizzically and asked me whether I had any special influence with the Prime Minister. I replied laughing that the Prime Minister, not long ago, had called us a 'bunch of jokers'! PK Kaul then revealed to me that to fill up the vacancy of Secretary, Home Ministry, on the retirement of Pradhan, he had suggested the names of three officers to the Prime Minister. These three officers were Reggie Khosla, a batchmate of mine and Mehra, both from the UP cadre of the IAS, along with Ramachandran of the Kerala cadre. All three had earlier worked as Chief Secretaries in their States. The Prime Minister ignored his recommendation and chose me instead to be the Home Secretary, said Kaul, much to my astonishment.

I took leave of the Planning Commission to join the Home Ministry on 1 June 1986 as Special Secretary and having worked as an understudy for a month became Home Secretary, Government of India.

16

Decisive Role

Buta Singh was the Home Minister when I joined the Ministry. He appeared to be friendly and well intentioned. Arun Nehru was the Minister of State, who wielded enormous power in the Ministry, being a close confidant of the Prime Minister. He was, however, held up in Srinagar as he had suffered a mild heart attack while touring J&K. The doctors had advised complete rest for him for a month as he was not in a position to take the air journey back to Delhi. Though resting he was attending to the urgent work of the Ministry, issuing orders on the telephone. He was receiving the many IB reports issued daily, keeping himself abreast of all important political developments in the country.

A week after I had joined the Ministry, Buta Singh told me to ask the IB not to send its daily reports to Arun Nehru. He was evasive when I asked him the reason for this decision. Back in my office I called for the official orders issued under the Rules of Business of the Ministry, allocating the work of the Ministry between the Minister and the Minister of State. On reading the allocation order it became clear to me that Arun Nehru was handling the more important files of the Ministry and the role of the Home Minister in administering the Ministry was negligible. I also concluded that stoppage of sending the daily IB reports to Arun Nehru required official amendment to the order describing his charge in the Ministry. When I conveyed this to the Home Minister he tried to browbeat me, stating that the Prime Minister had approved of this measure. I held out and told him I would be meeting the Prime Minister in the evening and will bring to his notice that informal orders would not be correct or advisable. Buta Singh glared at me as I withdrew from his office.

In the evening, after discussion with the Prime Minister, it was decided to issue an official amendment to the allocation of the work order, divesting the Minister of State of most of the powers enjoyed by him. The IB stopped sending its daily reports to Arun Nehru in Srinagar. A couple of days later I received an irate call from Arun Nehru asking for an explanation for the stoppage of the reports. I explained that it was being done to spare him extra strain and wished him a speedy recovery. He only quietened down on being informed that the proposal had the approval of the Prime Minister. A week later Arun Nehru returned to Delhi by a special flight in a Border Security Force (BSF) plane and I was driven up to the landing strip to receive him. This was my first call on him and I was looking forward to meeting him. I greeted him with a 'Namaste' and, as he descended from the stairs, I extended my hand for a formal handshake. He ignored my proffered hand and without saying a word to me he got into his car and drove off!

The next day he attended office and rang me up on the Rax telephone, asking me to come over to his room. When I entered, he was pacing up and down in an agitated manner. He questioned me at length about how the revised orders allocating the work between him and the Home Minister got issued and whether the orders had the approval of the Prime Minister. I diplomatically told him that the Prime Minister appeared concerned about his health and the revised orders were issued in his own interest to lighten his workload. He gave me a snort of disbelief and asked me to follow him as he started walking out of his office.

The Home Minister's office was next door and he led me inside the room. On seeing Arun Nehru enter, Buta Singh shot up from his seat and in the most obsequious manner received him with folded hands, addressing him as 'Sir' all the time. It was the most astonishing sight that I witnessed that day with Arun Nehru and Buta Singh. I soon retired from the room, allowing the two Ministers to settle their quarrel in privacy.

The next day Arun Nehru came to office to address the annual conference of the State Director Generals (DGs) of Police. I accompanied him to the conference and while sitting next to me he whispered that this was the last conference he was attending in the Home Ministry as he would be sending in his resignation as Minister that day. That was the last time I saw him. Later he joined VP Singh's Ministry for a short while. The estrangement between him and Rajiv Gandhi started after the Bofors deal surfaced and there was widespread speculation about their role in it.

The Bofors payoff scandal held the attention of the nation for a very long time. I got to know some pieces of authentic information of the Bofors deal from persons who were closely involved with the purchase of the Swedish howitzers. I met Arun Singh, the former Minister of State in the Defence Ministry, by chance on a flight from Hyderabad to Delhi. When I asked him why he had resigned from the Defence Ministry, he told me he had no other option but to do so when the Prime Minister did not support his decision to invite the Chairman of Bofors for a discussion in Delhi to clarify certain aspects of the case.

NN Vohra, the then Additional Secretary, Defence, who worked with Arun Singh, confirmed this story to me later. When I called on General Krishnaswamy Sundarji in Coonoor, where he had settled after retirement, he mentioned to me that after the scandal of alleged high-level payoff was highlighted in the Indian press, he had addressed a secret note directly to the Prime Minister suggesting the cancellation of the entire deal with Bofors. But his note was returned to him personally through SK Bhatnagar, Secretary, Defence, without any action being taken. Bhatnagar, a batchmate of mine, confirmed this to me and lamented that this fact was maliciously used by the CBI to involve him in a case of conspiracy, along with the other accused, including Rajiv Gandhi and was jointly prosecuted in the Bofors payoff case. After years of trial the case ended in the acquittal of all the accused. Bhatnagar had died long before the judgment, a disillusioned but honest man. He had shared a few secrets with me that unravelled the Bofors case but they necessarily have to remain a secret. As a footnote to the story on Bofors I would add the fact that on one occasion I played tennis with Ottavio Quattrochi, the Italian businessman involved in the scam, on the lawn tennis court of Delhi Gymkhana Club. I was introduced to him by Subhas Mehta with whom I used to play tennis often at the club.

Pradhan, my predecessor as Union Home Secretary, had worked very hard to bring peace to the troubled lands of Punjab, Assam and Mizoram by getting Accords signed during his tenure. The Mizoram Accord was signed with Lal Denga late in the evening on his last day of duty and as his successor I was present during the signing ceremony. The Punjab and Assam Accords ran into difficulty while being implemented but I started with a clean slate as regards the implementation of the Mizoram Accord. All the terms of the Accord were strictly adhered to by both parties. Lal Denga and his underground rebels resurfaced and surrendered their arms. Efforts were made to effectively resettle the rebels. The Congress Government in power voluntarily resigned, paving the way for elections that were held without any untoward incident. Lal Denga was sworn in as the Chief Minister. Mizoram is even now a haven of peace in the midst of the turbulent North Eastern States.

While implementing the Accord, Lal Denga visited me twice and during his second visit, while we were having tea, I noticed his palm with a shortened lifeline. He told me that he knew he had not many years to live and that knowledge had impelled him to restart the dialogue with the Government to bring peace to Mizoram during his lifetime. He fulfilled his wish by providing a peaceful and stable Government for the full term of his office. His untimely death a few years after he relinquished office robbed the nation of a charismatic figure who recognised the future written in his palm.

When I took over as the Home Secretary, a few incidents alerted me that probably my office was bugged. I had my office electronically swept and, sure enough, both my telephones were found to be bugged. I knew it was the handiwork of HA Barari, who had joined the IPS the same year that I entered the IAS. I had met him earlier in Mount Abu during my training period. He was the Director in charge of the IB. I called him to my room and gave him a good tongue-lashing for their audacity to bug the Home Secretary. He feigned ignorance and denied the charge but it was a warning to him not to act funny with me.

Barari was due to retire in three months' time and I started making enquiries about whom to appoint as his successor. Barari mentioned that he had two Additional Directors to assist him, the seniormost being Prasun Mukherjee, an IPS officer belonging to the West Bengal cadre and MK Narayanan, of the

Tamil Nadu cadre. Barari said that even though Narayanan had superior ability, in the interest of maintaining seniority he would recommend the name of Mukherjee. I elicited the opinion of the other top Police Officers heading the BSF and CRP and all were unanimous in endorsing the advice given to me by Barari.

The Director's post is a very crucial one in the Home Ministry as the actions taken in the Ministry were largely guided by the intelligence provided to us by the IB on all significant events, including political, taking place in our vast country. I was obviously keen on filling the post with the best man available. After discussion with Buta Singh, it was decided to appoint MK Narayanan after shifting Mukherjee from the IB to the Home Ministry on promotion as Special Secretary, Home. It took me a week to get the approval of the Secretary, Expenditure, for the creation of this extra post. I then moved the file officially for getting the approval of the Home Minister and the Prime Minister for both the appointments. Even after a week, the file had not moved from the Home Minister and I asked him the reason for the delay. He mentioned to me that he had not been able to meet the Prime Minister to have a prior discussion with him in the matter. When I heard this I requested Buta Singh to turn back and look at the picture hanging behind him on the wall. It was a picture of Sardar Patel, the first Home Minister of Independent India. Pointing to it, I told Buta Singh that he should never forget he was sitting on the august chair once occupied by Sardar Patel who would have made his own choice in such a matter without consulting anyone and, even if the Prime Minister did not approve of his proposal, he would fight for getting it. I also told him that if anything went wrong in the Home Ministry, it was he who would be held responsible and that was all the more reason to make his own selection to fill up this post. I added that if he had any reservations about appointing MK Narayanan as Director, I would withdraw the file and submit it again with a revised proposal.

Buta Singh knew he was cornered and he quickly signed the file and gave it to me. We received the Prime Minister's approval within two days. Both Narayanan and Mukherjee were happy as was the IPS fraternity since, for the first time, they got a foothold at the highest level into the Home Ministry. Narayanan was known to me as a junior in Loyola College but my decision would have been the same even if I had not known him. He turned out to be outstanding in his job and ably assisted me in sorting out several complex issues. He lay low after retirement but about three years ago he was appointed as the National Security Advisor succeeding JN Dixit who had an untimely demise. He was deeply involved in crafting the nuclear deal with the USA and in discussions with China to sort out the border dispute between the two countries.

Hardly three months into my job as Home Secretary and, on 2 October, I received a frantic call from the Home Minister early in the morning. He was screaming his head off, saying that there was an attempt on the life of Rajiv Gandhi when he came to Rajghat to pay annual homage to Mahatma Gandhi. I calmed him down and rushed to my office to handle the aftermath of the failed assassination attempt. My enquiries from the IB revealed that it was gross failure on the part of Kaul, DIG, Security, of the Delhi Police, in screening the area before the visit of the dignitaries to Rajghat that day. Despite an alert issued by the IB, based on a RAW report that there may be an assassination attempt by a person hiding in the shrubbery, the DIG, instead of personally screening the area, had put up an alert on his noticeboard for his subordinates to take action. Kaul was highly connected—he was the son of Sheila Kaul, a cousin of Rajiv Gandhi. I drafted the order suspending him from service for gross negligence of duty. I took the draft order to the Home Minister and at first he was unwilling to approve it, but finally I obtained his consent.

The Director Intelligence Bureau (DIB) kept me personally informed of the detailed sequence of events at Rajghat that morning. The President and his entourage were the first to arrive and they spent fifteen minutes there. Next came the Prime Minister and his entourage and, as he was passing near an archway covered with thick foliage, a pistol shot was heard. Instantly the security personnel with him surrounded the Prime Minister to provide him a human shield and he was quickly escorted out of Rajghat. The Delhi Police arrested a sardarji with a countrymade pistol in his possession. The assassination attempt failed mainly because of the poor weaponry and marksmanship of the assassin.

As the Prime Minister was busy with other engagements, neither Buta Singh nor I could meet him until late in the evening that day. I went in my official car to pick up Buta Singh from his residence and, as he got into the car to proceed to the Prime Minister's residence, I found him holding a *japamala* (a beaded necklace) and chanting a prayer. During the journey I suggested to Buta Singh that we both should offer to step down from our respective jobs when we meet the Prime Minister as we had failed to provide foolproof security to him. Buta Singh asked whether it was necessary to do so and I reiterated my advice to him.

At the Prime Minister's residence, the DIB was waiting to join us. We met the Prime Minister in the conference room where he was seated at the head of the table; Buta Singh, the DIB and I sat to his left. The Prime Minister told us that the DIB had already briefed him about the arrest made at Rajghat after the assassination attempt and of the Delhi Police's negligence in properly screening the area to make it sterile. He congratulated the Home Minister for the prompt action taken by him to place the DIG, Security, under suspension. Buta Singh, apprehensive till then about the outcome of the meeting with the Prime Minister, perked up, accepting the congratulations of the Prime Minister. While the conversation was on I whispered to Buta Singh to offer his resignation but he ignored me until I myself opened up, owning moral responsibility for failing to provide security to the Prime Minister. I offered to step down from my post as Home Secretary and Buta Singh joined in the chorus about failing in our responsibility. The Prime Minister said it was not necessary as the person directly responsible for the security failure had been proceeded against for disciplinary action. Buta Singh was very happy at the outcome and during our journey back he thanked me for the good advice that I had given him. He called me *Bada Bhai* (Big Brother); he would occasionally address me in the same fashion.

There is a humorous sequel to this story. Rajiv Gandhi, while describing this incident to his Cabinet colleagues, exhibited a wry sense of humour. He mentioned that, immediately after the shots from the assailant were heard, the local Police surrounded the canopy from all sides and started firing at the assailant who was hiding at the top of the canopy, but not a single shot hit the assailant who finally stood up with his hands up, to surrender, when the Police firing abated. With a twinkle in his eyes, the Prime Minister said that, fortunately, the assailant was not at ground level, in which event, the policeman would have killed each other by their aimless firing, leaving the assailant unscathed! Turning to me, Rajiv Gandhi said, 'Mr Home Secretary, I think the Delhi Police need better shooting practice lest they kill each other.' There was spontaneous laughter all round.

With the assassination of Sant Harcharan Longowal by the hardline Sikhs, the Punjab Accord, so finely crafted, collapsed. Terrorism raised its ugly head in Punjab, aided and abetted by the Inter Services Intelligence (ISI) of Pakistan. To tackle the situation, a top class Police Officer belonging to the Maharashtra cadre was sent to Punjab a few months before I took over as Home Secretary. He was Julius Ribeiro, a batchmate and personal friend of mine (he was earlier DIG in the CRP when I was the Joint Secretary, Home) who had both an imposing personality and reputation. He decided to lead by example and the first thing he did was to employ Sikh policemen in the team of his personal security, a practice that cost the life of Prime Minister Indira Gandhi. Within a few days of my assumption of office as Home Secretary, he called on me to brief me about the latest developments in Punjab. I posed the question to him then whether it was not prudent to have his personal guards drawn from a Central Police organisation and his brave answer still echoes in my mind. He said that if he had to lead the Police in Punjab he had to first trust them.

A month later there was a serious attempt to kill him and his wife when they were camping at the IPS mess in Amritsar, which was located in a protected area of the Punjab Police Lines. When Julius met me after this incident, I suggested two measures to strengthen his personal protection. I recommended that he has a personal security officer of SP rank who would be in overall charge of his security and that he take a senior officer as his deputy to help him fight the growing menace of terrorism in Punjab. The second suggestion was taken up for implementation first and Julius left the task of selecting a suitable officer for the post on me, but he lay down one condition—the officer chosen should be a Jat Sikh.

I made my enquiries and finally chose KPS Gill, an IPS Officer of the Assam cadre. He had a very good record of service and was reported to have handled the growing Assam agitation well, when he was serving in the State. He was in Delhi on deputation and was functioning as the IG, Administration, in the office of the DG, CRP. I decided to assess him personally and following the discussion that I had with the DG, he appeared before me ostensibly to discuss the pending administrative issues of the CRP.

I chose teatime to interview the officer as I could spend more time with him over a cup of tea. An impressive looking tall sardarji gave me a smart salute as he entered my room. When I asked him about his opinion on how to tackle terrorism in Punjab he was sanguine. He felt that the situation could be brought under control by firm measures, both political and administrative. I was impressed with the officer's personality and his overall record. Without mentioning the main reason why I had called him over for discussion, I thanked him for coming to my office and bade him goodbye.

When Julius next called on me a week later I mentioned KPS Gill to him. His response surprised me. He laughed and said that though Gill may be a very good officer, he was given to heavy drinking after sunset and he would be useless to help him in any way after 7 pm. I was sorry to hear this and asked Julius to suggest someone else. He met me again a week later and said that he was unable to find any other Jat Sikh as good as KPS Gill. He approved his name after stating in good humour that he was capable of taking care of himself after 7 pm.

Gill's selection for a Punjab posting proved to be a masterstroke in the long run. When Julius Ribeiro was promoted and appointed as an Advisor to the Governor of Punjab, Gill succeeded him as DG, Police. He set up a scorching pace against terrorists, using unorthodox methods in eliminating them. He, however, fell a victim to his weakness for excessive drinking and got himself involved in a very unsavoury incident. At an evening party hosted by a senior IAS Officer in Chandigarh, Gill, in an inebriated condition, patted the bottom of a senior lady IAS Officer who objected to his boorish behaviour. She raised a shindy about the incident and, in spite of the best efforts of the host to make Gill apologise to the lady, Gill refused. The next day she made a written complaint to the Governor, which was enquired into by Ribeiro. The press had got hold of the news and since everyone loves a scandal, adverse reports about Gill's misconduct were being published. As Gill was tackling the terrorist menace effectively, I spoke to the Governor to end the controversy by making Gill apologise to the lady. The Governor was unsuccessful in his efforts to make Gill apologise in spite of the adverse findings of the Advisor who had held an enquiry into the matter. The lady, getting no redress from the Governor to her complaint, filed a criminal case against Gill in the court alleging that he had molested her under the influence of liquor. The matter had turned grave and when Gill next called on me officially, I told him to settle the matter out of court. Before he left my office, he promised to apologise, but he never kept his promise. He completely avoided meeting me thereafter and he started to call on the Home Minister whenever he visited Delhi. The criminal case against him was fought by him tenaciously for more than eighteen years and the Supreme Court finally gave its verdict, accepting the charge of molestation made against him and imposed a heavy fine of Rs 2 lakh on him to be paid as compensation to the lady officer. She, in turn, requested the court to give the money to charity as she was satisfied that the accused had been held guilty by the highest court in the land and her stand had been fully vindicated.

I ran into KPS Gill many years after I had demitted office as Home Secretary. As the Comptroller and Auditor General I was travelling to Chennai from Delhi in 1994 and KPS Gill was seated next to me in the plane. He had retired from service and had recently been elected the President of the Indian Hockey Federation and was making his first visit to Chennai in that capacity. He has been a miserable failure in the job of reviving the fortunes of hockey in India, in contrast to his phenomenal success in eliminating terrorism in Punjab, for which he will always be remembered by a grateful nation.

When I assumed charge as Home Secretary, a very able IPS Officer, Ved Marwah, was the Commissioner of Police in Delhi. He called on me and we had a detailed discussion about the law and order situation in the capital. He mentioned that he was uncomfortable with the Home Minister as he used to request him to give prize postings of important police stations in Delhi to some of his favourites, who were known to be corrupt officers. He wanted my advice on how he should handle such requests, which he found difficult to implement. I told him clearly that he should firmly resist them and to explain to the Minister that, as he was responsible for maintaining law and order in a politically sensitive area such as Delhi, he has to ensure that good officers are posted to important charges. He asked me whether he has my support in resisting the illegal requests from the Minister and I told him that he had my fullest support. He appeared to be considerably relieved on hearing this and said he would follow my advice.

Within three months of this conversation, when I was with the Home Minister, he casually mentioned to me that it would be better if Ved Marwah is transferred. An IPS Officer of the Punjab cadre could be brought in his place, so that there could be better liaison between Punjab and Delhi in coordinating anti-terrorism activities. I replied to the Home Minister that Ved Marwah is one of the finest officers we have in the country and he has already established an anti-terrorist cell in Delhi and that the cell is in close touch with a similar one in Punjab. I also told him that this measure was recently introduced at my initiative after discussions with the DG, Police, Punjab. The Home Minister was visibly unhappy with my reply and he ended our conversation by saying we would discuss this later.

Within a month an opportunity arose for the Home Minister to raise this issue again. We had made elaborate security arrangements in Delhi for receiving Ryzhkov, the Prime Minister of USSR, on his official visit to Delhi. He was received with much fanfare at Palam Airport by Rajiv Gandhi and his Cabinet colleagues. It was planned that his motorcade would travel to India Gate from where it would drive along Rajpath and after cresting Raisina Hill, where the North and South Blocks are located, would enter the south sunken road on its way to Rashtrapati Bhawan where he would be residing. It was also planned that Rajiv Gandhi would accompany Ryzhkov, travelling in the same car, as an extra gesture of warm friendship between the two countries.

Ved Marwah was present at the airport to supervise the security arrangements and, when he was leaving after seeing off the VIP motorcade, he was accosted by Natwar Singh, Minister of State in the Ministry of External Affairs. The Minister said that his official car had gone missing in the snarl of traffic at the airport. He requested Ved Marwah to give him a lift in his car and to drop him off at his office in South Block to attend to urgent work connected with Ryzhkov's visit. The gentleman that he was, Ved Marwah willingly agreed. Instead of going straight back to his office located at the end of Tilak Marg, Ved signalled to his driver and escort jeep with armed guards to proceed to South Block. He was impeded in his progress by the crush of traffic but finally arrived by South Avenue to enter the road from the middle to proceed to South Block to the right.

A traffic policeman posted at the junction signalled the vehicles to stop but, on seeing the Police Commissioner in the lead car, permitted the vehicles to enter.

As they turned to the right, Ved was horrified to see Ryzhkov's motorcade enter the road from the South Block side. He immediately stopped his vehicle and so did the jeep following him. The Russian security guards accompanying Ryzhkov were alarmed to see two vehicles ahead that were partially blocking the narrow road and they drew their weapons in readiness. As the motorcade passed Ved's car, Rajiv Gandhi recognised him and signalled to him in anger, his eyes betraying his outrage. The motorcade from there had unhindered progress to Rashtrapati Bhawan and Ved reached his office after dropping Natwar Singh at South Block.

Near noon I received a call from Buta Singh. He ordered me to place Ved under suspension immediately stating that the Prime Minister had ordered it. He could not suppress his glee. When I asked him what was Ved's misconduct, he did not reply, but again reiterated that I should immediately come to Parliament House with the draft suspension order for his formal approval. I rang up the Director, IB, who briefed me that the IB security-spotter placed near the entrance of the road had filed a telephone report about the obstruction caused to the VIP motorcade by the vehicle of the Police Commissioner, Delhi. I sent out an alert for Ved to immediately get in touch with me and within half-an-hour he reported to me the details of the incident and stated that but for Natwar Singh he would have been nowhere near the motorcade. I rang up Natwar and he confirmed the incident.

When Buta Singh rang me up again from Parliament House at 2 pm that day, asking why I had not met him with the draft suspension order, I narrated to him the details of the incident, adding that Ved was not at fault and his version of the incident was corroborated by Natwar Singh. Buta Singh was obviously frothing in the mouth with anger at my seeming insolence in not obeying his order. He shouted at me, using Punjabi slang, that if I did not appear before him in half-an-hour's time with the draft suspension I will have to bear the full consequences of not obeying the Prime Minister's and his orders. Saying that he banged the telephone and that is the last I heard from him that day. He was catching a 4.30 pm flight to Chennai and it was indeed fortunate that I did not have him breathing down my neck.

I was glad I had gained some time to retrieve the situation for Ved. I rang him up and asked him not to report for duty the next day and be on a day's casual leave until I could personally explain the situation to the Prime Minister and he accordingly proceeded on leave. As the Prime Minister was extremely busy that day with the VIP visit I could not meet him. The President was hosting a banquet that evening for Ryzhkov and I knew that the Cabinet Secretary and the Principal Secretary to the Prime Minister would be there. I rang up both of them and, after giving them a gist of the story, I requested them to tell the Prime Minister that I would be meeting him the next day to brief him about the Ved Marwah episode. The message was conveyed to him and the next day, I explained the position to him in detail, highlighting that I had the story confirmed from Natwar Singh. The previous day I had requested Natwar Singh to also brief the Prime Minister, but strangely enough, he did not have the decency or courtesy to come to the rescue of an officer who had got into needless trouble in trying to help him. The Prime Minister, I believe, later sent for Ved and, on hearing his explanation, stayed his hasty verbal order to suspend him. Ved, after a very distinguished service in the Police, retired from service and, a few years later, was appointed Governor of Mizoram. When I wrote to him congratulating him, I got his reply acknowledging, with gratitude, the help that I had extended to him.

After his return from Chennai, Buta Singh did not send for me or speak to me for a week. I had transmitted the latest developments of Ved's case to him. After a week, everything fell into place and it was business as usual.

I knew Afsar and Akbar Khaleli, grandsons of Sir Mirza Ismail, the former Diwan of Mysore State; they were my juniors in Loyola College. Akbar joined the IFS and was the Indian Ambassador in Tehran where he met me with a personal problem and sought my help when I was Home Secretary. His wife, Shakire, whom he had left behind in Bengaluru during his posting, had suddenly disappeared and was not traceable for more than a year. Her house was in the possession of a Swami with whom she was on 'friendly' terms. In the criminal case filed by his daughters, investigation had not solved the mystery of her disappearance though the Swami, along with others, had been questioned at length. He requested me to have the matter reinvestigated by a Central agency. I mentioned to him that his suggestion was not a feasible option but I could ring up the Home Secretary, Karnataka, to get the matter reinvestigated. It was a happy coincidence that NA Muthanna (Lalu) was the State Home Secretary and, after I had spoken to him, Akbar met him at Bengaluru along with his daughters.

Shakire belonged to the Ispahani family and she had inherited large properties in Bengaluru. She was personally very rich, too. I met her once in New Delhi when she called on us, along with

Afsar and his wife Farkhunde. Indira and I took them out for dinner at the popular Fujiya restaurant and after the meal, while I was lighting up a cigar, she extracted a slim black Turkish cigar from a leather case and asked me for a light. She was a modern and attractive woman, who appeared to be without any inhibitions.

Muthanna, the Home Secretary, entrusted the reinvestigation of the case to the Corps of Detectives (COD) and within six months they cracked the case. Her body was found in a sealed wooden coffin, buried underneath the staircase of her house. Investigation revealed that the Swami had got a pit dug under the staircase, while getting the house renovated a fortnight before Shakire's disappearance. Her disappearance made headlines in Bengaluru and one of the 'grave-diggers', suspecting the worst, started blackmailing the Swami. It was from him that the COD got their first lead and breakthrough. When the coffin was dug and opened they found the body decomposed. There were big scratch marks on the sides of the coffin inside, indicating that the death took place inside the sealed coffin and there was a fierce struggle to get out. Chemical analysis of the viscera indicated sedation by sleeping pills. The Swami had obviously buried her alive after giving her sleeping pills. After years of trial and appeal, the High Court of Karnataka finally sentenced the Swami to life imprisonment. He is still in jail but has appealed to the Supreme Court against the sentence.

17

Across the Border

When the Prime Minister of Pakistan, Muhammad Khan Junejo, visited India for talks, the venue was fixed at the Windsor Manor Hotel, Bengaluru. I made a special trip to Bengaluru to check the security there. The most important subject of the spreading terrorism in Punjab was discussed during these talks and Rajiv Gandhi expressed our concern about the covert help being given to the terrorists by Pakistan. It was decided that the Home Secretary of India would lead a delegation to Pakistan to hold talks with his counterpart in Pakistan to identify the necessary measures to be taken by both the countries to counter the menace. When this decision was communicated to me by the Prime Minister's Office, I was not happy. I rang up AP Venkateswaran, the Foreign Secretary and shared with him my reservations about the proposal and suggested to him that since the Foreign Office was well versed in diplomacy, he should head the delegation with assistance from senior officers of the Home Ministry. Within an hour, ND Tiwari, Foreign Minister, rang me up and said that I should head the delegation. At my suggestion it was decided that he would depute one of his senior officers dealing with Pakistan to assist me. It was also agreed that since there was heavy illegal movement of narcotics from Pakistan to India, narcotics control would also be discussed with the Pakistan authorities.

I met the Prime Minister before proceeding to Pakistan and, on the appointed day, I flew with my four-member delegation to Islamabad in a BSF plane. I had a brief tour of the new capital of Pakistan and after lunch with our High Commissioner in Pakistan, SK Singh, proceeded to Lahore with him as the fifth member of my team. I was formally received with a guard of honour by the Pakistan Rangers (the counterpart of our BSF) and by Mehmoud, Pakistan's Interior Secretary, whom I would be meeting officially the next day. The press briefly interviewed me; I made the correct diplomatic noises and my arrival in Lahore was also covered by the television. I had arrived in Lahore formally dressed in a black *bandhgala* (formal jacket) but what surprised our hosts was the dark brown woollen cap that I wore. I had picked up this impressive cap from the Jama Masjid area a long time ago.

We were driven straight to Hilton hotel where our entire delegation was housed. We had been warned that our rooms would be bugged by the ISI and not to have any open conversation about the impending talks. The next day we were driven over to the conference venue and ranged against us across a long table was Mehmoud, assisted by a senior officer of Pakistan's Foreign Ministry, the Director General of the Pakistan Rangers, another General probably working in the ISI and the Head of the Narcotics Control Board. Our delegation had a similar composition except that we had no representation from the IB; our fifth member was SK Singh.

The discussion had a formal opening with introductions and a welcome speech by the Secretary, Interior Ministry. After a brief response in diplomatic language, I said that I was not a trained diplomat and many of the things I had to say to them may not sound pleasant to their hearing. I spoke for half-an-hour, setting out the circumstantial evidence we had of Pakistan helping the terrorists in Punjab, the cover provided by the Pakistan Rangers for the illegal border crossings of terrorists from Pakistan to India, details of the existing training camps on the border set up by the ISI and the confessions of the captured terrorists recorded on video. The DG, BSF, supplemented my statement and Srinivasan, Joint Secretary, External Affairs Ministry, presented further evidence of Pakistan's complicity. In response, Mehmoud and his delegation flatly denied any complicity in the matter.

At the end of their statements, I laughed aloud and said that in that case, we from India would have to do something dramatic to make them admit their guilt. After making that loaded statement I stopped talking, pretending I was searching for my pocket leather cigar case. I took my own time to pull a cigar out. I then took some more time lighting it, before continuing. All the while there was great expectancy of what I would say next. I said in a loud voice that in order to make them believe this, we would have to march across the border and catch them 'with their pants down', training the terrorists in the camps set up by them. There was hushed silence and I quickly forestalled their angry retort by adding that I never expected them to confess about their involvement. I, however, expected that we will both work out joint measures to contain the menace of terrorism. This brought the discussions back on track and it was agreed that the chiefs of the border forces and the representatives of the Foreign Ministers may meet separately to identify the joint measures to be taken. With this agreed formula we adjourned for lunch.

After lunch, the issue of narcotics control was taken up for discussion. I was astonished to learn that one person out of every nine in Pakistan imbibed drugs, which were flowing in freely from Afghanistan where the poppy plant was grown widely without any control. I mentioned that the terrorists infiltrating into India were the main carriers and if they were stopped from crossing the border there would be effective control of the movement of narcotics. It was, therefore, decided that the two representatives of the Narcotics Control Board of both the countries may join the earlier sub-group formed during the discussions in the morning to work out a joint strategy to control the drug menace.

In any big conference the secret of success is to appoint sub-groups to work out the basics of the issues discussed. Having done just that, I decided to spend the next day sightseeing in and around Lahore. We drove down to Taxila (original name Taksha Shila) to see the famous ruins of the oldest library in the world built during Emperor Harsha's time. That was also the place where a Greek colony was set up with Seleucus as the Greek Governor left behind by Alexander before retreating from India. Seleucus was an able general and the ruins of the colony where he lived with his soldiers showed skills of good town planning with straight roads and proper drainage in place. I gazed at the surrounding mountains with the thought that Alexander had also gazed at them a long time ago. The origin of the Kodavas of Coorg is a mystery as our customs, manners and physical features are entirely different as compared to the people living in the South. There is a belief among the Kodavas that a breakaway group of Greek soldiers wandered down to the South and settled in Coorg, cohabited with the local women and became our ancestors. Wandering round the ruins of the Greek Colony at Taxila, I imagined I had come to the home of my ancestors.

In Lahore I visited many beautiful gardens including those surrounding Emperor Jehangir's tomb. I took a drive past the Lahore Gymkhana Club where I had played bridge thirty years earlier. I walked down the famous Anarkali Bazar, with SK Singh. At first he was hesitant to accompany me but when I told him that he will never have the diplomatic freedom to walk the place alone, he quickly agreed. He thoroughly enjoyed the experience.

I had instructed Srinivasan to sit with his counterpart and draft a joint statement to be issued by Mehmoud and me before our departure from Lahore that evening. The statement had been drafted well, mentioning that the BSF and Pakistan would conduct joint patrols in identified sensitive areas of the border and hold frequent flag meetings to coordinate their activities. I had instructed Srinivasan that condemnation of terrorism in Punjab should figure prominently in the joint statement, but in the draft presented to me this key element was missing. There was only a general condemnation of terrorist activities without being area-specific. I raised this issue with Mehmoud when we met at lunch and requested him to get the statement redrafted accordingly. After lunch he rang me up to say that he had consulted his fellow delegates who had advised him not to agree to my proposal. I pointed out to him that Pakistan did not deny the existence of terrorism in Punjab affecting the civilian population and, having agreed to joint measures to tackle the menace, should have no hesitation to condemn terrorist activities in Punjab. I added that such a positive statement from Pakistan could only support their stand that they were not aiding the terrorists. At 4 pm Srinivasan informed me that Mehmoud had not agreed to my suggestion. I then sent word to Mehmoud that there would be no joint statement and I would be flying back home that evening to report to our Prime Minister that our talks had failed.

My threat worked and the amended statement was jointly signed by Mehmoud and me. It was also agreed that the statement would be simultaneously released from Lahore and Delhi to the press at 7 pm, local time Delhi. Mehmoud saw me off at the airport and he gave me an affectionate hug.

I landed at Palam Airport at 6.30 pm and was received by Parthasarathy, Joint Secretary, External Publicity of the External Affairs Ministry, who had arranged a press conference for me to address on my arrival. I was alerted by him that, apart from the national press reporters, there were international reporters also present at the conference. After reading out the joint statement, I faced a barrage of questions to which I responded in a straightforward manner, sounding neither pessimistic nor too optimistic about Pakistan's response to the successful implementation of the agreement. I said that we have to wait and watch and that the future was not ours to see. Doordarshan also covered the conference and I figured prominently in the 9 pm news bulletin, which has a national coverage. Some of my friends in Orissa rang me up the next day that, while watching the broadcast, they noticed the thick smoke that was curling up from the ashtray where I had kept my lit cigar! *Time* and *Newsweek* carried small write-ups about my visit to Pakistan in their next issue.

The day after my arrival I called on the Prime Minister accompanied by SK Singh and gave him a detailed account of the talks. He was tickled when I told him about my rhetorical threat to 'catch them with their pants down' and he summoned half-a-dozen of his Cabinet colleagues to listen to the story, which I repeated before them, much to their amusement. VP Singh, Finance Minister and Natwar Singh, Minister of State, External Affairs Ministry, were also present.

The Prime Minister wished to have my assessment as to the likely outcome of the talks and the joint statement. I gave him my frank opinion that the outcome would be negligible on both, the control of terrorism and narcotics control, given the well-known fact that the ISI was deeply involved in the nefarious activities. Drugs earned them a handsome personal income as well as extra money required for the training of the terrorists and for equipping them with weapons, explosives and ready cash. My prediction came true for I had read the mind of Zia-ul-Haq, President of Pakistan, correctly. He was a smart operator who, while making the right noises about maintaining friendship with India, was bleeding it to death with terrorism and the export of drugs across his country's borders. Zia was an alumnus of St Stephen's College before Partition. During his visit he did all the right things, going to his alma mater in Delhi and offering a *chaddar* (holy cloth) at Ajmer Sharif. He met an untimely death in a plane crash. I was still the Home Secretary when this happened and our Government as a precaution alerted the border guards to be vigilant.

18

Fighting Terrorism

The Fifth Pay Commission made known its recommendation about the enhancement of Police pay scales and I convened a meeting of all the Central Police Chiefs to ascertain their reaction. None of them was happy with the recommendation. That is the normal reaction of all Government servants and has to be discounted. After detailed discussions, I picked up two issues for further examination in consultation with the Ministry of Finance, namely, the pay scale of DGs of Police in the States and the pay scales applicable to the Delhi Police. The Central Cabinet had appointed a Cabinet Committee headed by the Finance Minister to look into genuine grievances and to correct the anomalies, if any, that may arise in applying the broad spectrum of the new scales to replace the old ones.

I personally appeared before the Cabinet Committee with a written memorandum. There were a few other Secretaries, too, to redress the anomalies occurring in their Ministries, with their own memoranda. Having summarily dismissed the plea of two Ministries, the Finance Minister, VP Singh, took up my memorandum for examination. After reading it cursorily he tried to repeat his act of dismissal by calling out to the next Secretary to speak. I intervened in a loud voice stating that I had not come as a supplicant before him but was holding the responsible position of Home Secretary dealing with complex law and order issues including terrorism in the country and I could not be brushed aside, before being given a hearing. I also added that in case I was not heard, I would take the battle up to the Cabinet level to obtain redress.

My forceful words shook him and he tried to mollify me by saying, 'Somiah Saab, why are you getting angry?' He heard my case and after that he ordered the Finance Secretary to examine the issues raised in the memorandum and put it up to him for orders. MK Narayanan, DIB, whom I had taken with me to assist me in the matter, was a witness to this and the news was soon out in the Police circles that the Home Secretary had confronted the Finance Minister to get better pay scales for them. Suffice it to say that the Cabinet finally approved the enhancement of the pay scales applicable to the DGs of the State Police and to the Delhi Police in general.

After my return from Pakistan, AP Venkateswaran, Foreign Secretary, made an official visit to Pakistan to discuss bilateral matters, including Siachen. A little after his return, Rajiv Gandhi decided to hold his first press conference after becoming the Prime Minister. He had by then completed his visits to the USSR and the USA, which were hailed in the national press as having been highly successful and he wished to take advantage of that while meeting the media.

When a dignitary such as the Prime Minister holds a press conference there is considerable amount of behind-the-scene activities. The Cabinet Secretary, the Foreign Secretary, the Commerce Secretary, the Finance Secretary and the Home Secretary spent days with the Prime Minister, coaching him about the right answers to be given at the conference.

The conference was held in the main hall of Vigyan Bhawan and both the national and international press was well represented. The Prime Minister answered all the questions hurled at him with confidence. The Cabinet Secretary, the Foreign Secretary and I were in the left-hand corner of the hall and we were happy that the Prime Minister had done well in his first press conference.

Our happiness, however, was shortlived. The reporter of the Urdu paper *Jung* rose to ask the last question. He queried the Prime Minister whether it was true that he had accepted an invitation to visit Pakistan, as announced by the Indian Foreign Secretary when he visited Pakistan recently. It was a simple question, but the Prime Minister's answer was strangely off-key. He paused a little before announcing that we will have a new Foreign Secretary; after saying that he made a quick exit.

We were all shocked by his answer and I remember Venkateswaran, who was sitting next to me, say 'paithyam' in Tamil, meaning madness. On hearing this strange announcement by the Prime Minister, the reporters started heading towards us to question the Foreign Secretary. I quickly herded Venkateswaran outside and whisked him away from Vigyan Bhawan in my official car. As Home Secretary I had the privilege of having a telephone and wireless fitted in my car for quick communication. My personal security officer could summon my car immediately after the Prime Minister had left and Venkateswaran and I made a quick getaway. We drove straight to South Block and I escorted Venkateswaran to his office room. He was also surprised at the strange behaviour of the Prime Minister. After discussion, he decided that he had no other option but to resign from the post and also from the service, which he did immediately. I later learnt that the Prime Minister had offered him an ambassadorship in Europe but

Venkateswaran stuck to his decision. He had a brilliant career and all his peers spoke well of him. Everyone was shocked at the behaviour of the Prime Minister. Venkat and his wife are now settled in Bengaluru. He is intellectually very active and he is the Founder Member and Chairman of the Asia Centre in Bengaluru. I consider it an honour to be a Founder Member of the Centre, along with him.

News coming from Punjab was not good. Terrorism acts had increased and the terrorists were openly targetting the Hindus, pulling them out of buses and trains and massacring them. They were trying their best to break the deep bond of friendship between the Hindus and the Sikhs and wanted to provoke retaliatory action from the Hindus. They failed miserably in this attempt and this was one of the reasons we could finally win our battle against the terrorists. We were particularly vigilant in Delhi where not long ago anti-Sikh riots had taken place following the assassination of Prime Minister Indira Gandhi.

It is against this backdrop that I received a flash message from the IB that Virk, DIG of the CRP, had been fired upon by terrorists from inside the Golden Temple on his rounds of the perimeter wall of the temple. He had a miraculous escape, with the bullet grazing his chin and had been hospitalised with a minor wound. Details of the incident that followed the flash message indicated that Virk had objected to a wall being constructed, when he was shot at and injured.

When I rang up Siddharth Shanker Ray, Governor, to learn more about the incident, he told me that under advice from KPS Gill, DG, Police, they were preparing a strong Police force to enter the Golden Temple to apprehend the culprits. Punjab was under President's Rule, with the Government headed by the Akali leader Surjit Singh Barnala having resigned earlier for the non-implementation of the Punjab Accord. I firmly advised the Governor not to take any hasty action as we had confidential information that a large number of armed terrorists had taken control inside the temple. After Operation Blue Star, we had introduced the practice of checking of all visitors by the Police. They had, however, successfully hoodwinked us to move in arms and ammunition concealed in the transport vehicles entering the temple carrying provisions for the *langars* (free kitchens) functioning inside. When the Governor insisted that it was essential to take the steps that he had mentioned to keep up the morale of the Police forces as suggested by KPS Gill, I literally ordered him, placing an embargo on any unilateral action taken without consulting the Centre.

PG Halarnkar, DG, CRP (I had especially chosen him to head the CRP when he was Commissioner, Police, Bengaluru) and I were the first to brief the Prime Minister about the serious incident at the Golden Temple that day. It was decided to discuss this further later in the evening in a meeting where the Home Minister and Director, IB, would also be present. Siddharth Shanker Ray flew down to Delhi along with KPS Gill to attend this meeting and they reiterated their earlier advice to mount a Police operation immediately to enter the temple and apprehend the culprits holed up within. The DIB and I argued against this, citing the bloody aftermath of Operation Blue Star. We advocated the deployment of the National Security Guard (NSG), a specialised force trained to handle such situations, raised after Operation Blue Star.

Our view prevailed and a company of the force was flown into Amritsar in the special planes attached with the force and by midnight they took up vantage positions on high-rise buildings round the temple. By morning loudspeakers were mounted around the temple and appeals were broadcast urging the terrorists inside to surrender, indicating that the temple was surrounded by the NSG. By evening the close relatives of the terrorists, some of whose names we knew, were made to join in the appeal, urging the terrorists to surrender.

The terrorists were spread across various locations in the temple. They were expecting a charge from the armed Police on the ground as had happened with the Army charge during Operation Blue Star. They were bewildered by the new technique adopted by us. They tried to regroup within the temple, using the cover of darkness, but the NSG, after giving them due warning, targetted them as they tried to change positions. The NSG had trained sharpshooters with specialised guns and night vision and they killed one or two terrorists when they tried to shift positions. The terrorists found themselves trapped as they could not move even to ease themselves or to eat. On the third day they raised the white flag of surrender. They were instructed to walk out of the Golden Temple with their hands up, leaving their arms behind. The British Broadcasting Corporation (BBC) and Doordarshan had taken their positions along with the national and foreign press reporters on vantage points round the temple. Within the temple there were also innocent pilgrims who had been held hostage and the motley crowd that came out had to be carefully screened. In the process of screening, one of the terrorists, who was wanted in connection with a recent shootout in Delhi, bit a cyanide capsule and died when identified. He had organised a bomb blast in the residence of a Jain family when they were celebrating a birthday, resulting in many casualties.

The surrender of the terrorists was not smooth as some of the hardcore terrorists had sneaked into the holy Harmindar

Sahib in the middle of the lake inside the temple complex. We had given strict instructions to the NSG not to shoot at the Golden Temple and taking advantage of that about a dozen terrorists took asylum in Harmindar Sahib and the siege of the temple continued.

In the meantime, P Chidambaram, Minister of State, Home, had convened a meeting of all the editors of the national dailies to brief them about the progress of operations, which we had termed Black Thunder. Some foreign correspondents, including Mark Tully, were present at the meeting. On the fifth day, the terrorists emerged with their hands up and were taken into custody. Finally, it was hunger that brought about their surrender.

On taking possession of the precincts of the Golden Temple, the Police found to their horror that the Harmindar Sahib had been badly desecrated. The terrorists who took shelter there, not finding any place to ease themselves, had filled the holy urns made of gold and silver with their shit and urine. When I got this news, after conferring with Chidambaram, we decided to send the press photographers to record the desecration done by the terrorists. We took this extraordinary measure to guard ourselves against any charges of desecration of the holy temple, which may be engineered by Sikh organisations such as the Babbar Khalsa, which were inimical to the Government. The national and the foreign media were highly appreciative of the manner in which we flushed out the terrorists from the temple without much loss to life or property.

While everyone thought the operation was over, I was concerned about the residual resentment with the Sikhs about the force used on their shrine. I rang up the Governor after about a week of the completion of Operation Black Thunder and requested him to visit the Golden Temple to show our respect for the Sikh religion. He was, however, reluctant to visit the temple on security considerations. I then thought of requesting Buta Singh but I remembered that he had been barred entry into the temple. I decided to undertake the pilgrimage myself and, on Buta Singh's advice, I sounded the Prime Minister, who supported the proposal.

I sent word to the Governor and KPS Gill about my proposed visit to Amritsar to go to the temple so that they could make the necessary security arrangements. I flew to Amritsar accompanied by Indira, Pria, Anand and Ammu, the wife of the DIB. At the reception in Amritsar the DGP was conspicuous by his absence but the IG, CRP, who received me, had made all the security arrangements. We entered the temple precincts early in the morning to avoid the rush of pilgrims and while we were being conducted around we were shown some of the bullet marks on the walls relating to the recent encounter. We had covered our heads at the temple and after doing a round of the holy tank, we entered the Harmindar Sahib. All of us took our seats on the *durries* (floor coverings) spread before the Granth Sahib and listened to the ongoing *kirtan* (chanting of hymns) for an hour in silence. This was my second visit to the temple, the first having been made in the company of my parents and sisters nearly thirty years earlier. We had not intimated the press but in the Punjab papers the next day, there were banner headlines of my visit along with my wife and children. This gesture received high praise from the local press and, two months later, I even got an appreciative letter from an unknown Sikh in Canada.

19

Different States

As Cabinet Secretary, BG Deshmukh started a new trend of high-level discussions on security-related matters. He chaired the meeting of the core group every Wednesday at 3 pm. The group comprised the Chief of the Army Staff, the Defence Secretary, the Home Secretary, the Director, IB and the Director, RAW and any other person to be co-opted. The core group had no set agenda but it was an open-house discussion on matters relating to security, both internal and external. We had very extensive discussions on Punjab, J&K, the North East and the growing menace of Naxalism in the first three or four meetings.

Army Chief General Krishnaswamy Sundarji was a very articulate member of the group. He raised the issue of the Defence budget not being adequate to cater to the twin threats of Pakistan and China on the western and northern borders. If both countries decided to go to war, he pointed out, our Defence forces would prove to be woefully inadequate. We asked Sundarji to quantify the monetary assistance required to make the Army and allied forces strong enough to withstand these threats. A detailed presentation was made by General CN Somanna (my cousin), Director of Military Operations. We invited the Finance Secretary and the Navy and Air Force Chiefs to be present as well. The Financial Advisor of Defence, a Secretary-level officer, also made a presentation.

During the course of four meetings, we were convinced that the full preparedness to meet the twin threats would require doubling the current Defence budget and that the country could not afford that luxury without a very deep cut in developmental expenditure, as analysed by the Finance Secretary. In the fifth meeting it was concluded that the only way open to us was to keep the border issue with China on the backburner and to improve our relationship with China by concentrating on other issues such as bilateral trade, cultural exchange and cooperation in the field of economic development. For this new approach to succeed it was necessary that our Prime Minister visits China and opens a new chapter of negotiations. The Chinese response was friendly and the Prime Minister's visit was a diplomatic success.

As Home Secretary I visited many States, the chief among them were Assam, Tamil Nadu and Gujarat. Indira accompanied me on these visits. We stayed at the Raj Bhawan in Chennai. The Governor was Bhishma Narain Singh, whom I used to know as a Minister in Indira Gandhi's Cabinet. We had a surprise visitor at the Raj Bhawan—Natwar Singh joined us for dinner. He had resigned from service and was a Minister of State in the External Affairs Ministry. That brings me to the odd fact that the 1953 batch had that year captured administrative power in North and South Blocks housing the important Ministries of Home, Finance, Defence and External Affairs. Venkataramanan and Bhatnagar were Secretaries of the Finance and Defence Ministries while I was Home Secretary and Natwar was Minister in the External Affairs Ministry.

Our next memorable visit was to Goa. We had timed it to coincide with the carnival, a colourful hangover of the Portuguese rule. The call of the mountains has always been strong in me. I told the Director General, Indo-Tibetan Border Police, that I would like to visit their mountaineering training centre in Auli from where I had planned to go to Kedarnath, the ancient Shiva temple. After a strenuous five-hour trek we reached a bend in the pathway from where we could see the temple. We called for a brief halt there to enjoy the scenery. I lit my cigar and was enjoying both the puff and the scenic view when suddenly a thought struck me that before entering the temple I must give up something that I like very much. I looked at Indira seated next to me and I told myself that I cannot give her up. I looked next at my cigar and without any hesitation I threw it into the gorge below. The year was 1987 and I was a long-standing smoker for the past thirty-three years. I gave up smoking that day never to smoke again. It was as if the Gods had ordained me to give up smoking for my own good. Strangely enough I suffered no withdrawal symptoms. I am writing this in June 2007, twenty years after that day in Kedarnath. I am just back at home after two bouts of stay and treatment in the intensive care units of Chinmayananda and Manipal hospitals for collapsed lungs and breathing difficulty in April and May this year. If I had not given up smoking on that day, I would have been dead by now.

Trouble was brewing in North Bengal with the demand for Gorkhaland raised by Subhas Ghising, an ex-Army Gurkha non-commissioned officer. Gurkhas from Nepal had settled in large numbers in the Darjeeling District and in parts of Siliguri.

They were ignored and neglected under the communist rule as they did not join the communist cadres, though they formed the bulk of the population of the area. The Gurkhas under the leadership of Ghising were demanding the establishment of a separate State in the area populated by them. The IB reported heightened tension and unrest in the area. The simmering trouble blew up into open violence when a procession of the Communist Party of India (Marxist) better known as CPI (M) was prevented in the Mirik area. The CPI (M), which controlled the labour in the tea estates, retaliated with attacks on the shops owned by the Gurkhas. The reaction of the Gurkhas was swift and in the growing violence the CPI (M) cadres sustained many injuries and casualties. The State Government tried to control the situation by rushing armed constabulary and, following an incident of firing by them, the situation went out of control.

The Gurkha National Liberation Front (GNLF) under Ghising went on the rampage, attacking Government offices, public transport and the assets of the tea companies. When this news reached me I rang up the Chief Secretary and asked him to advise his Government to hold talks with Ghising to meet their demands. I also assured him that the Centre was firm that there would be no concession on Ghising's demand for statehood. When this message was communicated to Jyoti Basu, the Chief Minister of West Bengal, his response was that the Gurkhas should be asked to get back to Nepal and there could be no talks with him. Sporadic violence continued. On request we supplied extra strength of CRP to deal with the situation and also to hold a bye-election that was due in the Kurseong area. Ghising decided to boycott the elections and he issued an appeal to the local people not to cast their votes. His hold over the electorate became clear to us when the boycott was a complete success.

This jolted all of us to action. I told the Home Minister and the Prime Minister that it was essential to invite Ghising for talks since the State Government was refusing to talk to him. They both agreed to my suggestion that I meet the Chief Minister of West Bengal to take his consent for the talks to be initiated by me. I made a trip to Kolkata for this purpose. The Chief Minister was adamant as he was suspicious of the Centre's moves. I tried to allay his fears by assuring him that the main demand of the GNLF to have a separate State called 'Gorkhaland' carved out of West Bengal would not be conceded but this did not satisfy him and I came back to Delhi empty-handed. Shortly after this, violence flared up in the Darjeeling area and the Home Secretary and the Chief Secretary rang me up for the deployment of extra Central forces. I was annoyed enough by this time to ask them to go and climb a tree.

This had the desired effect and Jyoti Basu rang up the Home Minister and agreed that we could hold talks with Ghising. I extended an invitation to Ghising to come and meet me—this was conveyed to him through the IB operatives in Darjeeling and he responded on the condition that the talks would be on a one-on-one basis. My talks with Ghising lasted for four months during which time we met ten times in Delhi. Ghising was a shifty customer to talk to, as he would never maintain eye-to-eye contact but I allowed him to talk most of the time. He narrated at length the discrimination that they faced at the hands of the State Government since they were branded as foreigners and not Indian citizens, though they were settled in the Darjeeling area since the time of the British. He was especially bitter about the lack of suitable employment for the Gurkhas, except as recruits in the Army. He also mentioned the growing disenchantment they had with the local communist cadres who tried to terrorise them when they refused to join them. He wanted a separate State for the Gurkhas as they spoke a different language and they wanted recognition for their language 'Gurkhali', which he said was different from Nepali. I listened to him patiently, expressing sympathy for their cause for economic improvement, but from the very beginning made it clear to him that there cannot be a break-up of West Bengal. He returned to the same theme repeatedly but being patiently firm against statehood I told him if I have to sell the idea for the West Bengal Government's consideration, he has to abandon this claim and instead ask for self-governance in certain areas of development in the places dominated by the Gurkhas. I wore him out by the time we met for the seventh time. In the last three meetings I involved the Chief Secretary of West Bengal in the discussions and finally the idea of an autonomous hill council to be administered by the councillors headed by Ghising chosen in a special election to be conducted in the hill areas of Darjeeling, Kurseong, Kalimpong and part of Siliguri emerged. Separately I had assured Ghising that the Chairman of the council would be given the special status of a Cabinet Minister but for this, he should agree to take a senior officer of the West Bengal IAS cadre as the Chief Executive and Secretary of the council. The council would be fully funded by the State Government and would have autonomous powers in some specified areas of development. I asked the Chief Secretary to brief his Chief Minister while I briefed the Home Minister and the Prime Minister.

The Chief Minister was pleased with the outcome of the talks but was wary of giving Cabinet Minister's status to Ghising. I made another trip to Kolkata and met Jyoti Basu and explained to him that it was a package deal to make Ghising agree to take a senior officer of West Bengal to function as Secretary and Chief Executive of the council. It would be an ex-officio status and would not give Ghising access to Cabinet meetings. The Chief Minister finally agreed to the package.

A date was fixed for the tripartite signing of the agreement at the Writer's Building in Kolkata. The Home Minister Buta Singh and I along with Indira flew down in the BSF plane. We were received by the Chief Secretary and the DGP and we were escorted through the streets of Kolkata with sirens blaring and traffic was stopped for our smooth passage (I was unhappy that this was done to the inconvenience of the public). In the presence of Buta Singh, Jyoti Basu and Ghising, the Chief Secretary of West Bengal and I signed the tripartite Accord. This brought much-needed peace to the area and it got the appellation of the 'Darjeeling Accord' by the media. The West Bengal assembly enacted the establishment of the Darjeeling Hill Council and Ghising and the persons he nominated were elected to the council. Peace was restored in the area.

Three years later there was a serious attempt to eliminate Ghising but he had a miraculous escape. The unity of the GNLF, however, was permanently shattered. Though there was peace in the area, proper development suffered. I visited Darjeeling nearly twenty years after the Peace Accord, in April 2006 and heard that while Ghising was honest, the councillors were corrupt. Ghising's effectiveness was also greatly diminished as he could not move about freely in the area fearing assassination. In April 2006, when I called on him at his office at Lal Kothi, I was astonished to see the scale of security he had been provided. A full platoon of armed constabulary was guarding the office in pill boxes and behind sand bags and he had a convoy of five cars. I learnt that his timing of travel was kept secret and he used to choose different cars to travel in. I was received by him with much affection and was offered traditional silk scarves as a welcome gesture. I spent an hour with him in his office, which was full of pictures of Durga, Shiva and Parvati. The largest picture decorating his office was that of Sai Baba. He mentioned to me that, disgusted with the corrupt practices of his councillors, he had recently commanded all of them to resign and they had obeyed his writ. He was currently negotiating with the Central Government to accord constitutional status to the Darjeeling Hill Council at a par with Hill Councils of the North East and he would permit elections in the area controlled by him only after his demand was met. He enquired about my family and when I told him that I had three grandchildren he asked his Personal Secretary to get some sweets for them. When I finally took leave of him, he gave me a large sealed container of éclairs to be enjoyed by my grandchildren. I found that Ghising had aged considerably.

On his request I visited the newly-constructed Jubilee Park, along with Indira, in the evening after visiting the Mountaineering Institute set up by Tenzing Norgay. We were taken around the institute by its Director and saw the pictures of famous mountaineers of Everest in the museum. We stayed at the Darjeeling Club from where we got a superb view of the Kanchenjunga gleaming in the morning sun. On our way out we went past Ghoom, the highest located railway station of India and paid our homage to the statue of the Unknown Soldier, which was situated near the loop of the railway track of the Darjeeling toy train.

20

Difficult Decisions

During the period I was Home Secretary, the Babri Masjid issue was emerging. It had been dormant for many years after the initial trouble in 1947 when the idols of Ram, Sita and Lakshman were surreptitiously installed in the premises of the mosque, which had remained derelict and unused by the Muslims for a long time prior to it. Babar, the first Mughal Emperor, had built this mosque in the sixteenth century after he had allegedly destroyed an earlier Ram temple located at the site. Hindus laid claim to this site as Ram Janma Bhoomi and had initiated a case in the local court years before we gained Independence and it is probably the longest pending civil case. Immediately after Independence, news reached the Home Ministry under Sardar Patel that the Hindus had installed the idols in the mosque, creating unrest in the local Muslim population. Sardar Patel was clear in his approach to this sensitive issue—he ordered the immediate removal of the idols. He was strongly supported in this move by Pandit Jawaharlal Nehru who requested the Home Minister on file to ring up the Uttar Pradesh Chief Minister, GB Pant, to implement the directive without delay.

GB Pant is reported to have been not too happy about this directive but he nevertheless had this order transmitted to the District Collector for implementation. The District Collector,

Nair, ICS, took his time to implement the order, allowing the Hindus to obtain a stay order from the local magistrate. The magistrate also ordered that the main entrance should stay locked and only a priest was allowed access to do the daily rituals. The character of the derelict mosque was permanently altered to that of a temple. The local Muslims accepted the situation as a fait accompli but hotly contested the Hindu claim to the site pending in the court. This was the situation when the contentious issue got raked up after Rajiv Gandhi took over as Prime Minister.

The Bharatiya Janta Party spearheaded the movement for the building of a new temple in the area. The Akhila Bharatiya Vidya Parishad (led by VP Singhal), the Bajrang Dal and the Sadhu Samaj gave vocal support to this demand. Some of these organisations met me to lay emphasis to their claim. My suggestion to them to await the verdict of the courts did not please them. I advised the Prime Minister that with the huge majority that he commanded in the Parliament he should have a resolution passed that all religious structures existing at the time of Independence would be protected by the State from vandalism or destruction but Rajiv Gandhi did not have the necessary courage to uphold publicly the secular nature of our polity. The mounting frenzy of the Hindu fundamentalists, not having been nipped in the bud, resulted in the eventual destruction of Babri Masjid years later in December 1992, leading to widespread communal riots in the country. Surprisingly, a month after I had left the Home Ministry, I learnt that a *shilanyas puja* (prayer offered before starting the construction work of any building) was performed at the site.

In 1985, the Supreme Court of India had decided in favour of Shah Bano, an elderly and unknown Muslim divorcee, the daughter of a head constable, who had been fighting for seven years in the lower courts for Rs 500 as maintenance from her husband to whom she had been married for forty-three years and who had divorced her to marry again. The maintenance grant she asked for was under the relevant provisions of the Criminal Procedure Code, which had stood the test of time and was applicable to all citizens of India irrespective of caste, creed or religion. The Supreme Court finally ruled in her favour. Muslim fundamentalists, including the Shahi Imam of Jama Masjid, started ranting against the judgment, stating that Muslim women can be governed only by the Shariat, which prescribed that on divorce a Muslim woman was entitled to only the return of *mehr* (a gift given by the husband to the wife in Muslim marriages) and the payment of maintenance during *iddat* (three months).

Rajiv Gandhi was initially inclined to resist this demand; he asked his Cabinet colleague Arif Khan to defend the secular stand in the Parliament, which was in session. This request was made to Arif Khan by Rajiv Gandhi when I was present in the Prime Minister's chamber. Arif Khan made a brilliant speech quoting various laws in many Muslim countries, which provided for payment of maintenance to divorced Muslim women. Yielding to the pressure of the Muslim fundamentalists Rajiv Gandhi quickly reversed his position and asked another of his Muslim Cabinet colleagues, Ansari, to speak in Parliament demolishing the points made by Arif Khan. In May 1986, the Muslim Woman (protection of rights on divorce) Act got enacted in Parliament, nullifying the Supreme Court judgment. I later learnt from Buta Singh that Muslims had to be appeased as elections were to be held shortly in Kerala where Congress depended on the Muslim vote to win.

Rajiv Gandhi was a signatory to the Punjab Accord. One of the main provisions of this Accord was the transfer of Chandigarh to Punjab. The Home Ministry did all the preparatory work including the financial and legal matters necessary to effect the transfer. Rajiv Gandhi changed his mind midway and stalled the transfer, keeping in mind the likely repercussions it would have for the Congress Party that was facing the elections to the State Assembly being held in Haryana shortly. Nevertheless, the Congress lost badly at the hands of Devi Lal who became the Chief Minister. Chandigarh remains a Union Territory of India.

I was getting sick of my work and the long hours I used to keep in office and I felt that I needed a change. I applied for three weeks' leave stating that I was visiting Egypt and Greece on a holiday. The Home Minister appeared surprised at my request and told me that he could not spare my services for such a long time as Punjab was still on the boil and it was unthinkable to have the Home Ministry unmanned. I told him that I was getting physically and mentally exhausted and I needed a change badly. He was finally persuaded to agree to my request but told me that I had to seek the permission of the Prime Minister. When I met the Prime Minister the next day and mentioned my visit to Egypt and Greece, he was also reluctant to let me go but finally agreed when I told him about his own recent holiday in Lakshadweep. 'You have me there,' he said, with a smile.

On the law and order front everything was quiet during the three weeks I was absent from the Home Ministry. Things were, however, getting hot in Sri Lanka. The External Affairs Ministry had worked on the Sri Lankan peace package in consultation with the IB and RAW who had contacts with V Prabhakaran, the leader of the LTTE. He was secretly flown to Delhi and kept in a safe house for conducting the peace negotiations; he was also given Rs 50 lakh to help rehabilitate the militants. I came to know this from IB sources, though I was not privy to the secret negotiations that were being carried out to bring peace to Sri Lanka. The LTTE and the Sri Lankan Government were at loggerheads, leading to the collapse of the peace process and the retreat of the Indian Peace Keeping Forces from Sri Lanka. The forces incurred heavy losses from the booby traps and guerilla warfare unleashed by the LTTE. The relations between the LTTE and Rajiv Gandhi became embittered after this and Prabhakaran got Rajiv Gandhi assassinated by a suicide bomber, years later, at Sri Perambadur in Tamil Nadu.

Salman Rushdie burst upon the literary scene with his much acclaimed book *Midnight's Children*. His controversial book *Satanic Verses*, however, led him to be reviled by Muslim communities from all over the world for writing derogatively about the holy Quran. Some copies of the book reached the Indian bookstores and Muslims here began to agitate. Buta Singh rang me up and told me to check whether we could ban the book in India. I told him that if a copy of the book is provided to me, I could have the matter examined. The next day I received a call from Khurshid Alam Khan, Member of Parliament (who much later became the Governor of Karnataka), that he would like to meet me with a copy of the book. It took me two days to read it. The book could be more aptly called *Satanical Verses* as it gave a prejudiced account of the Prophet. In the eyes of the Muslims anything derogatory said of the Prophet was blasphemy. I read *Satanic Verses* and came to the conclusion that the book needs to be banned in the interest of maintaining law and order in the country.

After taking legal opinion the book was banned in India and Pakistan followed suit a few days later. Some in the media criticised this action but the national press was generally supportive.

Now let me narrate a lighter incident in which I was involved. Agreeing to the request of my wife and children that we have an evening out together at the newly-opened restaurant, Sona Rupa, at Connaught Place, we piled into our Maruti 800 and drove to the restaurant. On our way back after a tasty meal, seeing no traffic at a road junction, I jumped the red light. A policeman, hiding a few yards away, stopped me. While agreeing to pay the fine, I casually asked the sub-inspector why he was laying traps at night when there was hardly any traffic. His nonchalant answer was that he could catch people like me more easily at this time and fulfil his monthly target. My children were dumbfounded by this response. When I was driving away they asked why I had not revealed my official identity to escape the fine. I told them that no man, however high his position, is above the law. The Delhi Police, to this day, is unaware that it had booked the Union Home Secretary in a traffic offence.

21

Several Encounters

In the course of my work I used to meet the Prime Minister at least three times a week and during one of these visits I found Amitabh Bachchan waiting to meet the Prime Minister. I smiled at him in recognition and he smiled back. He was then a Member of Parliament from Allahabad but his brush with politics was shortlived. On another occasion, when I was waiting to meet the Prime Minister in his antechamber, the Prime Minister came out of his room escorting Mother Teresa. He introduced me to her and told her that I was the best person to consult to sort out her problem. The Prime Minister went back to his office while I sat next to Mother Teresa and learnt from her that one of the nuns assisting her in Kolkata was a foreign national whose visa for stay in India had not been extended though its extension was sought in time. As visa extension was done by the Home Ministry, I requested her to come to my office and I escorted her, along with her companion nun, in my car. On enquiry I found that the nun had stayed in India for five years and further extension of the visa had been denied by the visa section of the Home Ministry. After a discussion with Mother Teresa it was agreed to grant a final extension of the visa for one more year. She blessed me and left my office. Later I received a thank you note from her. I was fortunate to meet her and be of some help to such a noble soul, who was so full of love and compassion. I consider meeting her as one of my richest experiences.

I had an encounter of a different kind when I was the Home Secretary. During my tenure, R Venkataraman got sworn in as the President of India succeeding Zail Singh and a little later Shankar Dayal Sharma was sworn in as the Vice-President. The Home Secretary has an important role to play at these formal functions. He reads out, in Hindi, the letter of appointment issued by the Election Commissioner and following this the oath of office is administered to the dignitary by the Chief Justice of India. At the swearing-in function of the Vice-President I noticed that in the enclosure earmarked to seat the personal guests of the Vice-President designate, there was an impressive personality with a long beard, wearing a saffron robe. After the ceremony was over and we were all walking over to have tea with the President and the Vice-President in the adjoining room, the saffron-clad person was next to me. I smiled at him and he introduced himself, stating that his name was Vachaspati, an astrologer who resides in the USA and is the personal astrologer of the Vice-President. He asked me whether I was the Home Secretary and when I answered in the affirmative he said he would like to meet me again. I told him he could come to my office at 4 pm and asked him what the problem was. He replied that after looking at my face he felt I would have an interesting future and he wanted to read my future. When I did not react to his statement he asked me whether I believed in astrology. I replied that while I did believe in astrology, I had no desire to know my future. My remark was overheard by Minister Vasant Sathe who was walking behind me. He thumped me on the back and said that all of them were waiting to get an appointment with Vachaspati while, surprisingly, I was refusing a session with him. In reply I mentioned to the Minister that he could now seek an appointment with Vachaspati in the slot vacated by me! Vachaspati expressed his surprise at my reluctance to meet him and moved away from me to be near the new Vice-President.

Ramakrishna Hegde was the Chief Minister of Karnataka and with his growing reputation as a very able political administrator people started talking about him as being capable of being a good Prime Minister. He was at the zenith of his power when a foolish thing he did led to his downfall. The Parliament was in session in Delhi when one fine morning the national daily *The Indian Express* prominently published a taped conversation between HD Deve Gowda and Chandrasekhar, both belonging to the Janata Party, plotting the downfall of Hegde. This news prompted Madhu Dandavate of the Janata Party and a Member of Parliament to ask a starred question, seeking information whether the Central Government was responsible for tapping the inter-city telephone call between Deve Gowda and Chandrasekhar. The Parliament Secretariat forwarded the question to be answered by the Ministry of Communications.

The Secretary, Communications, rang me up on the Rax telephone and sought guidance as to the answer to be given since the Home Ministry was the nodal Ministry for authorising the tapping of telephones under the one-and-a-half-century-old Indian Telegraph Act. The question was sent to me for advice and my enquiries through the IB revealed that the Karnataka State Inspector General (IG) had authorised the tapping at Bengaluru. I obtained a copy of the top secret order issued by him to the telephone authorities.

Keeping that copy in the file, I recorded a note saying that since the Centre had not done the tapping we could file an innocuous reply stating that we had not authorised the tapping. It was a safe answer to give as the question was specific and it was not the Centre's policy to reveal everything. The file went up to the Prime Minister through the Home Minister for approval.

In the Cabinet Committee on Political Affairs (CCPA) meeting held that evening, this matter came up for discussion where orally I reiterated my advice. There was an animated discussion and Narasimha Rao held the view that it was politically expedient to embarrass Hegde and the Opposition by revealing that Hegde, the Chief Minister of Karnataka and a political colleague of Deve Gowda and Chandrashekhar, had authorised the tapping of their telephonic conversations. This view finally found acceptance and I handed over the file to the Secretary, Communications, to draft a suitable reply for his Minister to answer the question in Parliament the next day. While I was leaving the room, the Prime Minister called me over to his side and told me in a low voice that a copy of the Karnataka IG's telegram authorising the telephone tapping should be released immediately to *The Times of India* to further embarrass the Opposition. I told him that it was illegal to do so under the Official Secrets Act as the communication was top secret and he should desist from such an action. Rajiv Gandhi was not happy with my reply and stared at me in anger. I held his gaze and excused myself from his presence, wishing him good night. I had barely reached my office when there was a call from the Prime Minister's Office to send them a copy of the top secret order and I told the caller that the relevant file had been handed over by me to the Secretary, Communications.

The next day the morning edition of *The Times of India* carried banner headlines stating that it was the Chief Minister of Karnataka who had the telephones tapped, giving all the details of the telephone numbers kept under observation. When Madhu Dandavate read the news, he absented himself from Parliament, hoping that his question may not be answered in his absence.

Contrary to the established practice of skipping answers to questions asked by members who were absent, the Minister, Communications, answered the question, including supplementary ones. All the sordid details were reported in the national press the next day and Hegde had no option but to resign. He soon faded away from the political scene.

Zail Singh became the President of India with the support of Indira Gandhi and he was reported to have remarked that he was prepared to sweep the floor she treads on. He repaid the debt to her after her assassination by making Rajiv Gandhi the Prime Minister even before he was elected as the leader of the Congress Party, thus scotching the ambition of Pranab Mukherjee who was actively lobbying for the post. Instead of being grateful to Zail Singh for this action, Rajiv Gandhi started ignoring him after he became the Prime Minister. It is normal for a Prime Minister to call on the President and brief him of the Government's policies from time-to-time. It is also normal for the Prime Minister to approve all the proposals sent by the President's Secretariat for the President to travel to friendly countries in response to their invitations. For reasons that were not clear, Rajiv Gandhi failed to accord the necessary courtesies to the President as Head of State and a serious rift developed between them, by the time I took over as the Home Secretary. Ominous news was trickling from the Rashtrapati Bhawan that in his frustration Zail Singh was even considering dismissing the Prime Minister under a mistaken and shallow interpretation of the Constitution that a Prime Minister remained in office at the pleasure of the President. We also learnt that the press, inimical to the Congress Party, was fishing in troubled waters, especially *The Indian Express* whose editor S Mulgaonkar was noticed to be repeatedly visiting Rashtrapati Bhawan to meet the President. When I confidentially asked Varadan, Secretary to the President, he said that all was not well in the Rashtrapati Bhawan, as some papers were moving directly between his Deputy Secretary and the President without him being consulted. He also mentioned that the President was having closed-door meetings with a number of legal luminaries.

I brought all this verbally to the notice of the Home Minister and the Prime Minister. Collating the information received by us it was clear to me that the President was determined to dismiss the Prime Minister on the wrong premise that he had the power to do so. Soon we got confirmation that the draft dismissal order had been kept ready for the dismissal of the Prime Minister. On hearing this Buta Singh called on the President and had a long and friendly chat with him. The President mentioned that he was angry with the Prime Minister. Buta Singh responded by stating that he would request the Prime Minister to call on the President to clear any misunderstanding between them. The President's reply was that it was too late. When Buta Singh returned and reported this conversation, we knew for certain that the President was about to dismiss the Prime Minister. It was then decided that the Vice-President would meet Zail Singh and make him aware that the Prime Minister had secret intelligence about the President's likely action and in retaliation the Prime Minister was preparing to start impeachment proceedings against the President in case he took the unconstitutional step of dismissing the Prime Minister. When Venkataraman, the Vice-President, called on the President, the latter told him that the walls in the Rashtrapati Bhawan seem to have ears and led him outside to hold their discussion. Venkataraman suitably advised him and requested him not to precipitate a constitutional crisis in the country.

As Zail Singh's term as President was coming to an end, the Election Commission was making preparations for the election of his successor. Venkataraman was the consensus choice as candidate but there was an Opposition candidate whose name I forget now. There were two other candidates who were joining the fray for the publicity it brought them. Once the candidate's name was finalised, he was provided with personal security so that no harm came to him during the election. This was a precaution we took to ensure that the election was not countermanded with an untimely death of a candidate. It was reported by the IB that one of the candidates who was contesting the election seeking publicity was a heart patient. We offered him a stay in Government accommodation to be under proper medical treatment during the election period. He accepted the offer and hence received the best medical attention.

RVS Peri Sastri, the Chief Election Commissioner, rang me up informally and gave three different dates to hold the Presidential election for us to decide on the final date. All the MPs of the Lok Sabha and Rajya Sabha, together with the MLAs of the State Legislatures, were to vote to choose the President and countrywide arrangements were to be made by me as Home Secretary to ensure a peaceful poll at all the stations, to be held on a single day. The returning officers were the Speaker of the Lok Sabha and the Speakers of the State Legislatures where polling was held, as appointed for the Presidential election by the Election Commissioner. I consulted the Home Minister and the Prime Minister to finalise the date of the election and communicated it to the Election Commissioner; this was done informally over the telephone. Within a couple of days the Election Commissioner issued the gazette notification officially announcing the date for holding the election; copies of the notification were dispatched to all the States.

When I thought that everything had fallen into place, I got a call from the Prime Minister's Office mentioning that the Prime Minister had second thoughts about the date of the election and whether I could sound the Election Commissioner about this. I replied that since the Election Commissioner had already notified the date and all the States had been informed, he had no authority to change it. I asked the reason for the change and was told that TN Seshan, the Security Advisor in charge of the Prime Minister's security, had suggested a new date as he, being an astrologer, felt it was more propitious. I laughed and told him that Seshan had better confine his activities to safeguard the Prime Minister and not be his astrological advisor. When I was asked to at least sound the Election Commissioner about changing the date, I told him to advise the Prime Minister that no change in date was possible now. This was a telephonic conversation that took place at nine in the night when I was still in office, as was the usual practice.

The next day at 7 am I got a call from the Election Commissioner at my residence enquiring whether I had not consulted the Prime Minister before communicating to him the date for holding elections. I told him that I had his consent to the proposed date and asked him in return why he was making this enquiry. He told me that the previous night he had been woken up by a call from the Prime Minister's Office, communicating the Prime Minister's desire to postpone the election date by a couple of days. He said that he had explained that legally it was not open to him to change the date as desired by the Prime Minister. The response to this was an offer of Governorship to Peri Sastri if he acceded to the Prime Minister's request, indeed a devilish attempt to seduce a constitutional authority to do an illegal act. Peri Sastri firmly refused the inducement but he was distressed that such an offer was made to him. Despite all these backroom manoeuvres, the election was held on the prescribed date and went off smoothly with Venkataraman winning hands down. Peri Sastri slipped into retirement, quietly upholding the best of traditions in maintaining his integrity.

At the swearing-in ceremony of the President, the Home Secretary has to read out the long appointment letter issued by the Election Commission in Hindi, appointing the President. After this, the Chief Justice swears in the President, the old and the new Presidents exchanging places on the dais. My knowledge of reading the Hindi script was limited and I did many hard days of practice reading until I was letter perfect in both intonation and delivery. I read it out so well that General Sundarji, Chief of Army Staff, who was present at the ceremony, complimented me and so did many of the Ministers present. Little did they know how hard I had rehearsed!

Disquieting news about serious unrest in the Police forces of Gujarat was trickling in through the IB reports. This was like the unrest in the Police forces of Uttar Pradesh, which I had to tackle years earlier when I was a Joint Secretary in the Home Ministry. I summoned the Home Secretary, Gujarat, Vittal (who later retired as the Central Vigilance Commissioner). His more detailed account of the mounting unrest convinced me that we had to take preventive action against the Police union leaders. While I advised the Home Secretary to continue his dialogue with them to contain the situation, I simultaneously worked out a contingency plan, in consultation with the Defence Ministry, for the local Army command in Gujarat to secure the Police armouries throughout the State. Our advance planning was just in time as a week later the Ahmedabad Police in uniform ransacked and torched the office and press of a prominent Gujarati daily, which carried an article listing the recent and past misdeeds of the city Police. The same day I prepared a Cabinet note for the consideration of the Cabinet Committee on Political Affairs. I recommended the disarming of the Gujarat Police by the local Army Command and the arrest of the arsonists as well as taking into custody the leaders of the Police union. On my suggestion, the Home Minister summoned the Chief Minister of Gujarat, Amar Singh Choudhary, to be present at the CCPA meeting being held that night. I had also alerted the Defence Ministry to alert the local Army Command to be in readiness for a midnight takeover of the Police armouries and the Army had the necessary time to reach all the district headquarters to take coordinated action to take over the armouries.

The Chief Minister and Home Secretary of Gujarat were present at the CCPA meeting, which was held at 7 pm under the chairmanship of PV Narasimha Rao, Minister, Human Resource Development, in the absence of the Prime Minister who was indisposed. I briefly summarised the prevailing situation in Gujarat, about the Police unrest there and the proposed Army action that was kept ready to crackdown against the Police armouries at the stroke of midnight. I thought that with the Chief Minister of Gujarat agreeing to the proposed action, the decision of the CCPA in support of the proposed action would be quickly forthcoming. Of course, I had not taken into account the dithering attitude of Narasimha Rao, whose weakness was revealed that night. He was unable to take a decision, any decision, for that matter. The discussion lasted two hours with Narasimha Rao asking a hundred questions about the likely repercussions of our action. But, he just would not take a decision. Even if he had taken a decision against the proposed action, we would have been relieved. It is this dithering indecisiveness that led to the destruction of the Babri Masjid years later when he was the Prime Minister. I whispered to Buta Singh, Home Minister, to make a suggestion that we consult the Prime Minister, Rajiv Gandhi and his suggestion was gladly accepted by Narasimha Rao. All of us landed at the Prime Minister's house and after I had once again summarised the position to him, the Prime Minister turned to Narasimha Rao and asked him why there was a problem in arriving at a decision when both the Home Secretary (meaning me) and the Chief Minister of Gujarat were in favour of the proposed action. Narsaimha Rao readily concurred and the meeting with the Prime Minister lasted barely fifteen minutes.

On return to my office I gave the go-ahead signal to the Defence Ministry, after dispatching both the Chief Minister and the Home Secretary by plane to reach Ahmedabad in time for the action to follow. I stayed in office till 3 am and was happy to receive confirmation from the Army Command in Ahmedabad that all the Police armouries in the State had been taken over peacefully by the Army units. With the help of the CRP, the union leaders were also picked up simultaneously at midnight from their houses and taken into custody. Within a week the situation was brought under control.

Some Chief Ministers and Governors of States used to drop in to my room for informal discussions after they had met the Home Minister whose office was located down the corridor. Among the Governors, General Krishna Rao and his successor Jag Mohan Malhotra, both briefed me about the growing fundamentalism among the Muslim population in the Kashmir valley. They blamed the various *madrasas* (Islamic schools) that were functioning as a breeding ground for fundamentalism and poisoning young minds.

Following this briefing, I sent a message to Farooq Abdullah, Chief Minister, J&K, saying that I wanted to call on him when he was in Delhi next. A week later, he surprised me by coming to my room unannounced after he had visited the Home Minister. He sauntered in casually and as I got up to greet him he stood with his arms spread out, admiring the room. My office was large and its walls were oak-panelled, giving it a majestic look. I had a large half-circular-shaped oak table covered by glass with eight deep-cushioned chairs. There were three sofa settees with a centre table with flowers in one corner and a mini-conference table with chairs in the opposite corner. A large balcony faced South Block and the room was very tastefully curtained. It was also centrally air-conditioned. There was a big attached bathroom for my personal use. The Chief Minister, with a friendly grin, said that his room was not half as grand.

In the course of our conversation I told the Chief Minister about our concern regarding the functioning of the *madrasas*. He went back making a lot of promises which, unfortunately, he never fulfilled. For a long time, gentle Sufism had penetrated the fabric of the Muslim faith. This was sought to be replaced by a more bigoted approach to religion, a handiwork of ISI Pakistan to foster secessionist activities.

Veerabhadra Singh, Chief Minister, Himachal Pradesh, also paid me a surprise visit once. The request he made, however, surprised me even more. His political opponent in the Congress Party was Ram Lal who was the timber mafia king of Himachal. It was the same Ram Lal who later, as Governor of Andhra Pradesh, had illegally dismissed the Rama Rao Government. Ram Lal had spread various false rumours about the Chief

Minister of Himachal being corrupt. The honest man that he was, Veerabhadra Singh was troubled by these false charges and wanted to be clear of them. But the request he made to me was politically suicidal in nature. He told me that he would be suggesting to the Centre that a CBI enquiry be held into the false charges. I advised him against any such move as the CBI was under political control and was not independent in its functioning. I told him that his request may boomerang on him if his political opponents had the ear of the Centre and were able to manipulate an adverse finding from the CBI. I have yet to meet a more honest and naïve Chief Minister. He accepted my advice and when we met again when I was the Comptroller and Auditor General of India, he recalled my advice to him.

Mohan Khatre of the Maharashtra cadre was Director, CBI, when I was the Home Secretary. It was rumoured that he had effectively put a lid on the CBI enquiry on the Bofors payout. I used to meet him quite often as the criminal investigation wing of the CBI fell under the jurisdiction of the Home Ministry. He was a name-dropper, but he kept his distance from me when he realised that I was not impressed. He was due to retire in a couple of months and there were rumours that he may be appointed as Governor of a major State. I invited him for a discussion about choosing his successor and he said that his deputy, Radhakrishna Nair, Additional Director, CBI, was a competent officer and could succeed him. I made my own independent enquiries, which confirmed his advice. I then walked across to the room of Secretary, Department of Personnel, to consult her. My batchmate Pratibha Trivedi was the Secretary and she, too, was of the opinion that Nair would be a good choice for the post of Director, CBI. I asked her to initiate the proposal on the file and after obtaining her Minister's approval, pass the file to me. This would be endorsed by me and the Home Minister, before the proposal was sent for the Prime Minister's approval, which came readily. A fortnight before Khatre was to retire, the gazette notification appointing Nair as Director, CBI, was issued.

A week later, Mohan Khatre dropped in to my office late at night and after discussing a case, mentioned to me casually that the Prime Minister had sent word to him to continue in office for a year more. In view of this he requested me to cancel the notification appointing his successor as Director, CBI. I told him that not only was it not possible to do so, it was also not advisable to do so as unsavoury motives may be ascribed to his being granted an extension. I also told him that he had done well in his job and it would be graceful to retire rather than hanker after an extension.

Khatre did not appear too pleased with my advice and withdrew from my office. The next day I got a call from Gopi Arora requesting me to process the case for a year's extension for Khatre. He also asked for the appointment of Nair as Special Director, CBI, not upsetting his promotion but only making a change in his official designation. I was informed that the Prime Minister had desired that a year's extension be granted to Khatre. I told Gopi Arora that it was not possible to restart the file without mentioning the reason for doing so. I also suggested to him to advise the Prime Minister not to pursue the matter.

By the evening I got a note signed by Gopi Arora saying that the Prime Minister wanted revised orders to be issued granting extension in service to Khatre for one year. Orders were issued in compliance with the Prime Minister's desire. On receipt of the revised orders Nair rang me up and wished to meet me. He was an honest and high-spirited officer who, after meeting me, went on a month's leave and then resigned from service prematurely. There was public concern and justified criticism of the extension granted to Khatre but he did not appear concerned. On the other hand he took revenge on me for not agreeing to his extension, but that is another story. Khatre had to end his service in ignominy as, towards the end of his career, he got mired in a scandal involving his son and himself in a fraudulent financial deal with Reliance Industries.

Just before I took over as Home Secretary during the regime of my predecessor Pradhan, orders were placed for the supply of 2,500 pistols from a Czech public sector undertaking. This was to be done after observing all the formalities of test firing the pistols of rival firms and by inviting quotations by sealed tenders. In earlier purchases of pistols for supply to the paramilitary forces, the test firing used to be done by the Army. In this case, however, it was done by a joint test firing team of the paramilitary forces and supervised by a Committee consisting of the DG, BSF and the DG, CRP. In the file it was seen that the revised procedure was followed under the specific orders of Arun Nehru, Minister of State in the Home Ministry. He wrote on the file that the Army took a long time to give their advice after test firing the pistols and hence the tests may be done in-house to avoid delay. The Czech pistols came through the tests as best suited and after negotiating the price with the firm on the basis of the lowest tenders received, orders were placed for the supply of the pistols. The first batch of a thousand pistols arrived about six months after I took over.

On test firing a large percentage of defects emerged. I ordered on the file that the entire lot may be returned to the firm for suitable replacement. The second batch of pistols arrived three months later and they were also found defective on test firing. I called for a meeting with the DG, BSF and the DG, CRP, to discuss the method followed by them in certifying these pistols.

They informed me that their test firing was done on the Army pattern and even the Special Protection Group (SPG) employed for the protection of the Prime Minister was armed with these pistols, which were chosen by them after independent test firing checks. But, I was not satisfied with their reply as adverse press reports started appearing hinting of malpractices in the purchase of these pistols.

The Opposition had raised the issue in Parliament and Buta Singh was particularly happy to put Arun Nehru (who had authorised the purchase) on the spot even though he had left the Ministry. I summoned the local agent of the supplying firm and asked him to arrange for the return of the advance payment made to his principals. A representative of the firm met me and apologised for the supply of defective pistols and mentioned that in view of the large orders received by them for the supply of these pistols from a large number of purchasers, they had sub-contracted the manufacture of the pistols to a sister firm in Czechoslovakia. I insisted on the refund of the advance.

After he left, I rang up DR Tiwari, Joint Secretary, External Affairs Ministry. I wanted to discuss this matter with him urgently as I had learnt that his area of work covered Czechoslovakia. I told him that we were already facing the flak of the Opposition about the Bofors gun deal and I did not want the purchase of the Czech pistols to figure as another scandal. I suggested to him that as the supplier of pistols was a Government-owned company, it may be possible for the Czech Government, with whom we had good relations, to persuade the supplier of defective pistols to return the advance payment made to them while placing the order. After summoning the Ambassador of Czechoslovakia to the External Affairs Ministry, Tiwari reported to me that they had agreed to refund the advance and take back the defective pistols. The money was refunded to us by bank draft within a fortnight of our diplomatic approach. A day after this Buta Singh, in reply to a starred question about the defective supply of the pistols, made a unilateral commitment to entrust the case to the CBI for enquiry. He made this commitment without consulting me and even before I could brief him about the refund of the advance payment. After his return from Parliament I chided him for making a hasty announcement without consulting me. When I told him that every penny of the advance had been recovered from the suppliers, instead of feeling happy he started asking me how I could have asked for the refund without taking his permission. I was irritated by his arrogance and told him that the money involved was not his but that of the Government and I did not need anyone's permission or approval for safeguarding the Government's interest. He was not at all happy about the refund as he thought that he would put Arun Nehru on the mat by ordering a CBI enquiry against him.

As a follow-up to the Home Minister's announcement in Parliament, the CBI took charge of the file relating to the purchase of pistols but not before a Xerox copy of the notings in the file was prepared and kept in a sealed cover in the Ministry. I did this knowing full well the dubious ways of the CBI to twist facts under political pressure. A couple of months later I demitted office as Home Secretary and took charge as the Central Vigilance Commissioner. I got a call from Khatre that he would be sending a DIG-level officer from the CBI to take my evidence in the enquiry being held by the CBI and requested my cooperation. I readily agreed and gave the necessary evidence about the defective supply of pistols during my tenure as Home Secretary. I also insisted on recording about the refund of the advance payment and about the unnatural behaviour of the Home Minister in showing dismay rather than happiness when I informed him of the refund. When the DIG reminded me that I was speaking against the Home Minister I told him that his duty was to record the evidence as was given and not be afraid of anyone. He left after taking my signature on the evidence recorded.

The next morning I was astonished to see banner headlines in *The Indian Express* that the CBI had examined the Central Vigilance Commissioner in the Police pistol case, almost implying that I was a suspect in the case. I rang up the Director, CBI, and gave him a mouthful. One of the newspapers even carried a cartoon showing Buta Singh and Arun Nehru taking potshots at each other using pistols, with Somiah the former Home Secretary caught in the middle, trying to avoid the bullets. Khatre had his revenge after all. The CBI enquiry fizzled out after some time.

During my tenure as Home Secretary, the three Union Territories of Mizoram, Goa and Arunachal Pradesh attained statehood with suitable amendments to the Constitution of India and with the concurrence of the Central and State legislature. The Pay Commission had announced the revised pay scales applicable to the various services in the Government of India. With considerable difficulty I obtained the concurrence of the Finance Ministry and of the Cabinet to give a better deal to the Delhi Police and for upgrading the pay scale of the Director General of Police in the States. The IPS and the Delhi Police were appreciative of my efforts in this regard, especially as hardly any other change was made in implementing the Pay Commission's recommendations in dealing with the other services.

I had a successful tenure as Home Secretary and the national press was also very supportive, except in the case of *The Indian Express* where Arun Shourie was the editor. When *The Indian*

Express was facing serious labour unrest I had instructed the Commissioner of Police, Delhi, to provide necessary protection to the building and assets, even though the paper was generally critical of the Government. The labour based their protest by picketing the office and printing press located on Bahadur Shah Zafar Marg. Their picketing was successful as even the few loyal workers were prevented from attending work, a legitimate labour tactic, as long as physical violence was not involved.

On the fifth or sixth day of the strike, Arun Shourie, who was holed up in his office, rang me up at 8 pm and started talking in a raised voice. He said that the Delhi Police was incapable of maintaining law and order in the city. I asked him to tell me where they had been remiss and he told me that the Police was not helping the loyal workers to break the pickets set up by the striking workers. I told him about the instructions I had given to the Police to intervene only if any violence was committed and reminded Arun Shourie that peaceful picketing by the striking workers could not be interfered with by the Police. Arun Shourie raised his voice a couple of decibels and threatened that I would be reported upon adversely in the next issue of the paper and that I should not underestimate the power of the media. I told him that he could do his worst if he thought fit and I was not bothered with his threats. I ended the conversation by disconnecting the phone.

There was a stray incident of communal disharmony in my home district, Kodagu. It started as a case of eveteasing of a Coorg girl by the youth belonging to the Moplah community, which led to violence and arson in the market area of Virajpet. The next day a wayside temple was found desecrated and the clashes continued between the two communities resulting in the death of two Moplahs, one of them having suffered gunshot wounds. With a massive show of force, the district administration brought the situation under control and peace returned to the area.

The Moplahs of Malabar in Kerala have lived in peace for centuries in Coorg and they were the main traders of the produce of Coorg—coffee, oranges and spices. They also traded in fish, bringing fish to Coorg from the nearby seaports of Kerala. I was happy that peace had returned to Coorg by the deft handling of the situation by the local administration. A month later we were surprised to receive a letter from the Chief Minister, Kerala, addressed to the Home Minister about the incident and suggesting that gun culture in Coorg had to be curbed. This was to be done by withdrawing the concession under the Indian Arms Act granted to the Kodavas, which permitted them to own guns without a licence under the Arms Act.

The section dealing with the Arms Act was in charge of a Malayali section officer and he gleefully supported the proposal, with endorsements from the senior officers, when the file landed on my desk. In the Arms Act enacted by the British Government in India, the Indian princes and the Kodavas of Coorg owning Jamma land were both exempted from the provisions of the Arms Act. Indira Gandhi, while abolishing the payment of Privy Purses to the princes whose territories were ceded to India at the time of Independence, got the concession of exemption under the Arms Act enjoyed by them also abolished. This fact was also mentioned in the letter of the Chief Minister of Kerala who wanted the similar exemption granted to the Kodavas abolished. I recorded an appropriate note in the file explaining the rationale why this concession was granted to the Kodavas in the first place and also the fact that possession of a gun (which is worshipped) is as sacred to the Kodava inhabitants of Coorg, as it was sacred for a Sikh to possess a *kirpan* (sword). Buta Singh readily agreed with me and a suitable reply was sent to the Chief Minister of Kerala. The age-old custom and right of the Kodavas was thus safeguarded.

The order of the Supreme Court confirming the death sentence of Satwant Singh and Kehar Singh, responsible for the assassination of Indira Gandhi, was announced and soon mercy petitions were addressed by them to the President. These were received in the Home Ministry from the President's Office. They were quickly processed and presidential consent was received for their rejection. Within a week both of them were hanged at Tihar Jail.

Indira and I visited Dimapur in Nagaland on the invitation of the DG, Assam Rifles. We had an interesting two-day stay there and the insurgency situation was reviewed by me during the visit. Our next trip along with Pria and Anand was a visit to the Andaman and Nicobar Islands. Such holidays were necessary as the kind of job I held was full of stress.

As Home Secretary I was chairing the official Committee to select not more than about a hundred names for awards of State honours to be announced on Republic Day. We used to receive over two thousand recommendations from State Governments and private organisations and some even shamelessly recommended themselves. Lobbying was intense, especially at the political level. In the two years that I was Chairman of the Committee, we chose excellent persons for receiving the award including Viswanathan Anand, the chess champion who later became the world champion, the film actor, Shabana Azmi, the great guru of Odissi dance, Kelu Charan Mohapatro, Dr Manmohan Singh, the present Prime Minister and Dr Mohan Das, the noted orthopaedist of Chennai.

I was also the Chairman of the Committee to select candidates for the President's medal for distinguished service and for gallantry to policemen of the States and the paramilitary forces, on Republic Day. These two Committees, which I chaired, kept me busy for over a fortnight with frequent meetings in December.

My last engagement in the Home Ministry was in response to an invitation extended to me by the Foreign Secretary to address a gathering of Indian Ambassadors of Asian countries on terrorism in India. It also included Pakistan's role and the active support being extended by Pakistan to terrorist activities in India. On the appointed day, a Deputy Secretary from the External Affairs Ministry came to the Home Ministry to escort me to the venue of the meeting. The card that announced her arrival carried the name 'Ponnappa'. When she came in, assuming that she was from Coorg, I greeted her in the Coorg language and asked her family name. She smiled and said that she was a non-Coorg married to a Coorg named Ponnappa. We came across her next when, in 2003, Indira and I, along with some friends, were passing through Bangkok on our way to Angkor Vat in Cambodia. She was the Indian Ambassador in Thailand at that time.

Indeed, the job of Home Secretary, Government of India, is one of the most taxing jobs. One has to be alert round-the-clock. Everything bad happening in the country—law and order, natural calamities such as floods, droughts and cyclones, or sensitive information about insurgencies and terrorists—lands on his table in the shape of Intelligence reports. The voluminous information received daily has to be read, digested, analysed and immediate action initiated.

A nightmare for the Home Secretary is whether, in his quick reading of the Intelligence reports, he has missed out on any important nuance requiring urgent action. My successor Kalyanakrishnan was sacked from his job when he missed out reading just two lines of the Intelligence report where there was a hint that an attempt would be made to kidnap the daughter of Syed Mufti Mohammed, the Home Minister. When the kidnapping did take place, without any preventive action being taken, the Home Secretary was shown the door. I always felt I was sitting on a powder keg, which could blow up in my face at any time.

At my farewell party, alluding to a sardarji joke, I compared myself to a sardarji who, while accidentally falling from the top of the Empire State building, was asked midway how he was. The sardarji bravely replied, 'So far so good.' I was serious when narrating this, but it did raise a laugh from the Minister (himself a sardarji) and my colleagues.

22

Central Vigilance Commissioner

I did not know in July 1988 that my tenure in the Home Ministry was about to end. I was looking forward to my retirement from service a few months later in March 1989 and was not expecting any change till then, especially when I was doing so well on the job. As the 'Que Sera' song goes, 'The future is not ours to see'.

I was in office late at night drafting a statement for the Prime Minister to deliver in Parliament the next day when I had a surprise visitor. Manish Bahl, a Madhya Pradesh cadre IAS Officer, dropped into my room at about 8.30 pm and informed me that the file relating to the extension of tenure for the Central Vigilance Commissioner (CVC) UC Agarwal (an officer of the Orissa cadre and a year senior to me) had come back from the Prime Minister who had not approved the extension. I had not sought this information and I just nodded in acknowledgement, hoping that he would leave, as I was busy. Manish, however, had other ideas. He said he was on the lookout for a suitable person for the post of CVC and he had discussed the matter with his Minister, Chidambaram. Both of them thought I had the right credentials for the post but Chidambaram felt that I may have a higher ambition of becoming a Governor after being a successful Home Secretary.

I listened to him with disbelief as an offer was being made to me unasked about a very good post-retirement benefit.

I told Manish that I did not nurture at any time the thought of being a Governor of a State as I felt that there was too much pressure of a political nature from the Centre on the Governors, which forced them more often than not to commit constitutional blunders. Home Minister Buta Singh had offered me a governorship, which I had declined telling him I was not a pliant person. I told him that I had seen him in action giving telephonic instructions to the State Governors who were willing to do his bidding out of gratitude. I thanked Manish for his offer but I said that I could give my consent only after consulting my wife. I also told him that I was extremely busy and would not like to be disturbed just then.

I came home and Indira and I discussed the offer after dinner. She was at first of the view that since I was doing extremely well as Home Secretary, I should not step down from the post just then. She also thought that rumours may surface that I was being shunted out of the post to an unglamorous one such as the CVC, whose work was shrouded in anonymity. I told her that in nine months I would be retiring at a time when Pria and Anand would not have completed their college education and it was necessary for us to be in Delhi until they finished college. I added that I was not the type who would lobby for a post-retirement job and here was a good offer being made to us that we should accept for the children's sake. It did not take me long to convince her and the next day I informed Manish that I would accept his and Chidambaram's offer of being considered for the post of CVC.

Later in the day I mentioned this to Buta Singh who was not at all happy with my decision to leave the Home Ministry. Within a week orders were out posting me as CVC and my successor was also named—Kalyanakrishnan, who was functioning at that time as Chief Secretary, Uttar Pradesh. I had taught Kalyanakrishnan Chemistry in Loyola when I was lecturer there. Probably for the first time a student was succeeding his teacher in a prestigious post in the Government of India, an occurrence that is unlikely to repeat itself.

The orders were out at the end of July, but my relief from the Home Ministry was being stalled by the Home Minister as he wanted me to complete some of the pending urgent work. He was also peeved that he had not been consulted about choosing my successor and Chidambaram, acting within the southern network, had chosen a fellow Tamilian as my successor. In the second week of August I got a call from Kalyanakrishnan that he was ready to move to Delhi and wished to know my convenience for handing over charge. When I mentioned this to Buta Singh he said that he would not relieve me quickly as he wanted my continued advice. I told Kalyanakrishnan that he could take some leave and visit his hometown; it would be best for him to do so now as he could not get away after taking charge as Home Secretary. He thanked me for my advice as he had not taken leave for a long time and he went home for forty-five days.

The handing over of charge to him finally took place in the first week of October that year. Sure enough, rumours were floating that I was resisting being shunted out of the Home Ministry and my wife's apprehensions in this regard were right! When I called on the Prime Minister to take leave of him he commended me for the sound advice he received from me (not that he followed it) and wished me well in my new job. Thus ended one of the most taxing and, at the same time, interesting assignments I held during my entire career.

23

Keeping an Eye

Following the Santhanam Committee's recommendation for setting up the institution of the Central Vigilance Commissioner to act as an advisor to the Government on matters dealing with corruption at the official level (not the political level), the Government appointed the first Central Vigilance Commissioner. The post was created in the late seventies by a Government order notified in the gazette. The appointment was to be made by a warrant signed by the President. The tenure would be three years, extendable by two more years. The Central Vigilance Commissioner would be an independent authority subordinate to none, with the necessary powers to deal with cases of official corruption at all levels. It would be mandatory for the Government to accept the Central Vigilance Commissioner's advice on the punishment to be awarded. If this advice was not implemented, the Central Vigilance Commissioner had the authority to inform Parliament about the breach in his annual report to Parliament. His jurisdiction covered the officers of nationalised banks and the Central public sector undertakings. The Defence services and the judiciary, however, did not come under his purview. The first Central Vigilance Commissioner was Nittoor Srinivasa Rao, a High Court Judge of Karnataka, who later retired as the Chief

Justice of the High Court. His successor was Subimal Dutt who retired as the Foreign Secretary. I think I was the fifth person appointed to this post.

I had to oversee a technical wing headed by an officer of the rank of Superintending Engineer to examine civil construction projects. I also had under me about half-a-dozen enquiring officers to conduct departmental enquiries against persons with corruption charges. The recommendations of the CBI in regard to the findings in these cases were subject to my scrutiny.

I moved to my new office, which was located in an official bungalow (once occupied by Morarji Desai when he was the Finance Minister) on Ashoka Road near India Gate. The office seemed drab in comparison to the grandeur of the oak-panelled room of the Home Secretary in North Block. The pace of work was also leisurely and a complete contrast to my earlier job of continuous high pressure activity. Against this background I decided on a more active role for myself by visiting the Central public sector undertakings located in the four corners of the country. During my tenure of eighteen months, I visited about forty undertakings and interacted with their officers by carrying the important message to them in, what I believe was, a dual role of the Central Vigilance Commissioner—that of Shiva and Vishnu—a punisher of evil and at the same time a protector of the good. I conveyed to them the message that if anyone thinks that he/she has been falsely implicated in any case they could meet me personally and explain his/her case to me.

In this way I was able to help a large number of persons who were otherwise honest, the most prominent among them being E Sreedharan, the no-nonsense straightforward Railway officer who constructed the Konkan Railway in record time and who is now doing such a wonderful job with the Delhi Metro. I am one of his ardent admirers as he singlehandedly withstood the corrupt suggestions of his Minister when he was constructing the Konkan Railway.

I was escorted by V Krishnamurthy, Chairman, Steel Authority of India, in his company plane to visit their headquarters in Ranchi and address the senior officers there. Later, the same plane ferried Indira and I from Delhi, along with Geethakrishnan, Finance Secretary and his wife Renu, when we visited the Bhilai Steel Factory. After this we drove on to Malanchkhand, visiting the copper mines and then on to the Kanha wildlife game sanctuary where we stayed for two nights. This sanctuary, which is the largest in India, has well preserved teak forests. We were fortunate to see wild dogs called *dhol* as well as the famous *barasinghas* (antlers with twelve curved horns) and a leopard crossing the road right in front of our jeep. The game warden greeted us excitedly the next morning, promising us a sight that we would never forget in our lives. After breakfast we mounted two elephants and ambled across to the place where the tigress and her cub were feeding on the huge boar they had killed the previous night. Very few people would have seen a wildlife scene as dramatic as we saw that morning. After half-an-hour, the tigers lay down to rest and the cub turned on its back, lifting its paws up in the air. This sight is vividly etched in my memory. During my tours in India, I also had the good fortune to visit other game sanctuaries such as those located in the Corbett Park, Kaziranga, Mudumalai, Bandipur, Siriska, Ranthambore, Nagarahole and Simlipal. I enjoyed seeing the variety of fauna and flora here.

I had an interesting visit to Nalco, a public sector mining and manufacturing plant located in Koraput District in Orissa. In the course of my tours I also visited the super thermal power station at Singrauli in Uttar Pradesh. On the way I stopped at Varanasi, visiting its famous university and from there went on by road to the Kali temple at Vindhyachal before reaching Singrauli. At the temple, the priest tied a yellow sacred thread on my right hand, asking me not to remove it as it would bring me luck. He also mentioned that on the day the sacred thread broke on its own, with wear and tear, I would get good news. The thread broke a year later and, sure enough, on the same day I got an astonishing offer of a job that propelled me to unexpected heights in my career.

My office was shifted to the Indira Gandhi Memorial Trust by the Government and I relocated myself in Kota House on Mansingh Road. Within three months I retired from the IAS in March 1989. However, I continued as CVC on a re-employment basis. When I retired from the service, my children were still studying—Pria was in her second year in college and Anand had just joined Economics Honours in Shri Ram College of Commerce.

On the day the sacred thread frayed, I got a call from Vinod Pande, Cabinet Secretary, to say that the Prime Minister had decided to appoint me as the Comptroller and Auditor General. He wanted my consent for processing the case further and to obtain the President's approval. I was stunned by this offer and asked why my cadre-mate, TU Vijayashekaran, had not been appointed though his name had the approval of the Finance Minister. Vinod Pande did not expect this reply from me and said, 'Sir, I am offering you a sweet which you are refusing to accept and I am indeed surprised at your negative response.' I told him that I was confused at the offer as I had already congratulated him personally in advance and I required a day's time to think it over. He told me that the offer being made to me was known only to the Prime Minister and the Finance Minister and he would wait for my reply, provided I did not discuss this matter with any of my official friends. I readily agreed to this. After the telephone conversation ended, I sat for an hour thoroughly dazed at the turn of events so accurately predicted by the priest in Vindhyachal a year ago. In the rat race of Delhi, considerable lobbying is done by officers to get into such high profile posts and here I was being considered for the post without any effort being made by me!

To resolve the dilemma raging within me, I turned to my wife for advice, asking her to come to my office urgently. Her response amazed me. She asked if I was being sacked from my job as had happened to many senior officers with the change of the political regime. Later she said that if I was being considered for the post in the shape of a rival proposal, not to accept it. However, if it was an alternate to a rejected proposal, I should have no hesitation in accepting the job. She asked me whether the proposal to appoint Vijayashekaran had been rejected. I told her that I was not sure as the Cabinet Secretary had mentioned to me that some difficulties had cropped up in considering Vijayashekaran for the post. Indira advised me to first ascertain the correct position from the Cabinet Secretary before responding to his offer.

The next day I called Vinod Pande and on my specific query to him about Vijayashekaran, he clarified that the proposal to appoint Vijayashekaran as Comptroller and Auditor General had been rejected by the President of India. While rejecting the proposal, the President had mentioned that though Vijayashekaran had an excellent service record, he had no experience in handling financial matters, not having held any finance post in his career. On this clarification I agreed to be appointed as Comptroller and Auditor General. I also asked Vinod Pande to convey my thanks and personal regards to the Prime Minister. After four days the Cabinet Secretary informed me that the President had approved my appointment and that the news would be released to the media soon. I requested him to keep Vijayashekaran informed of the developments so that he was not shocked by the news. Vijayashekaran met me in my office to congratulate me. He said he had no hard feelings against me as Vinod Pande had informed him of all the details of my appointment. He further told me that he was to succeed me as Central Vigilance Commissioner.

24

A Constitutional Authority

I was sworn in as the Comptroller and Auditor General of India by the President on 15 March 1990, four days after my fifty-ninth birthday. My tenure was for six years and the swearing-in ceremony, attended by my friends and well-wishers, was held in the yellow room of the Rashtrapati Bhawan. The Vice-President, the Prime Minister and some Ministers were present at the function. Some prominent Coorgs of Delhi were also present and it was a proud and joyous moment for all of us. The best photograph that I have of the occasion is the one taken with Indira, Pria and Anand proudly standing beside me.

As I drove up to my office on Bahadurshah Zafar Marg that day, I felt happy that at last I was taking up a job where there was none to oversee my work and I would function independently. My constitutional position was such that I was not subordinate even to the Prime Minister or the President. If I had to proceed on leave, I had only to keep the President informed. Ambedkar, while framing the Constitution of India, had ensured complete independence for the Comptroller and Auditor General. Even the expenditure for his office is charged to the Government of India and does not require any legislative approval. In the UK the Comptroller and Auditor General was an officer of the Parliament and was subject to its control.

I was sworn in as the Comptroller and Auditor General of India by the President on 15 March 1990, four days after my fifty-ninth birthday.

At the swearing-in ceremony at Rashtrapati Bhawan with Indira, Pria and Anand.

Another unique feature of the Indian Constitution is that the Comptroller and Auditor General is responsible for the audit of all Government accounts—whether they relate to the Central Government or the Governments of the States and Union Territories. The mandate of the Comptroller and Auditor General's audit covered all the Central and State Government public sector undertakings and all local bodies substantially financed by the Government. It included the audit of receipts and systems audit of programmes and projects of the Government to ascertain the value derived from the implementation of the projects, apart from the transaction audit. In the USA, which is a federation with constituent units, the Auditor General, being an officer of the Senate, was responsible for auditing the accounts only of the Federal Government. Each State in the USA has its own Auditor General. Even most of the advanced States do not permit Government receipts to be audited by the Auditor General. This is a unique function assigned to the Comptroller and Auditor General of India.

The official reach of the Comptroller and Auditor General in India is enormous, with offices in every State and Union Territory. The officer and staff strength is over six to seven thousand. At one time the Comptroller and Auditor General was responsible for maintaining the accounts of both the Central and State Governments but, about thirty years ago, the maintenance and management of Central accounts had been taken over by the Central Government and placed under a Comptroller General of Civil Accounts. The format of the Government accounts is as prescribed by the Comptroller and Auditor General to maintain uniformity and no change can be made in the format without his consent. In pay and rank he enjoys the same privileges as a judge of the Supreme Court.

This is much more than the privileges given to the highest civil servant and the Defence chiefs. To ensure his independence, the Comptroller and Auditor General cannot be removed by the executive once appointed. He can only be removed by impeachment by Parliament, as applicable to a judge of the Supreme Court.

The first Auditor General of Independent India was Narahari Rao, a Kannadiga and I was the second from Karnataka to be appointed the Comptroller and Auditor General of India. In the main conference room of the Comptroller and Auditor General's office, the portraits of all past Auditors General, starting from the British period, adorn its walls and they all look a solemn lot. To break the monotony, I remembered to smile when I sat for my portrait before I demitted office!

When I took over as the eighth Comptroller and Auditor General of India a number of States had a history of delayed finalisation of the annual accounts, which, in turn, delayed the laying of annual audit reports before the State legislatures. This was remedied by the time I demitted office and I consider it a major achievement. The follow-up action on the audit findings was also in heavy arrears, including the examination of the audit reports by the Public Accounts Committee of the State legislatures. To suggest remedies for this ticklish question, which impinged on the independence of the State legislature, I appointed a high-level Committee. I was able to persuade one of the retired Secretary-Generals of the Lok Sabha to head this Committee.

The Committee headed by SL Shakder gave its report a year before I demitted office and considerable progress was made in cleaning up this area as well. An all-India Auditor General's conference was organised within a year of my entering office. It was inaugurated by the President of India and new ground was covered to make audit an ally to foster good governance. My first tour outside Delhi was to Shimla where, after a detailed inspection of the Indian Audits and Accounts Service (IA&AS) training institute located there, a number of improvements were introduced in the training of the IA&AS probationers. I earmarked funds for supplying individual computers to the probationers and computer training was made compulsory for the probationers for the first time. The other training academies of the IAS and Central Services introduced compulsory computer training for their probationers much later. Computer orientation of the IA&AS and of the audit staff in the staff training institutes was a major achievement during my tenure. Such expertise in our officers and staff helped when we entered the international arena of the audit of the United Nations.

Even after being elevated to the rank of Secretary to the Government of India, I had not shifted residence from my three-bedroom flat in Moti Bagh to a bungalow. I thought this was not necessary as my retirement was round the corner. Now, with a six-year tenure as Comptroller and Auditor General, we decided to move. We were shown three bungalows and finally chose the one with more than an acre of gardens, on Kushak Road. We had a happy stay in the house for nearly six years during which time we developed the gardens in the front and on the side of the house.

In a separate plot near the servants' quarters we even developed a vegetable garden. Peacocks would visit our lawns early morning in winter. The garden was a riot of colour. We fell in love with the house and this prompted me to write a letter to the Prime Minister suggesting that the house be earmarked as the permanent residence of the Comptroller and Auditor General. This suggestion was accepted and I consider this as one of my minor achievements.

Within a month of my appointment as Comptroller and Auditor General, I received an invitation to visit China. The invitation was accepted but at my request it was postponed to the next year, as I wished to gain some experience before I made the trip. My first visit abroad as Comptroller and Auditor General was to London, in October 1990, to attend the Commonwealth meeting of the Supreme Audit Institutions (SAIs). It was a forty-six-nation conference held in the luxurious premises of Lancaster House, adjoining Hyde Park. My interventions at the conference and the suggestions I made were well received. I met Sir John Bourne, the Comptroller and Auditor General of the UK and many other Comptrollers and Auditor Generals from Asia and Africa.

At the conference I learnt that the UK Comptroller and Auditor General was a member of the three-member UN Audit Board and that the Asian slot in the membership held by the Comptroller and Auditor General of the Philippines was falling vacant in two years time. The idea that we should try for the vacant slot occurred to me then and on my return to India I wrote a letter to the Prime Minister, Narasimha Rao, who was also the Foreign Minister, that I needed the support of the External Affairs Ministry in my bid to become a member of the UN Board of Audit.

In my letter I pointed out that with more than a hundred years of experience behind us, we were second to none in the field of Government audit and that it was indeed surprising that we had never before attempted to audit the UN. The Prime Minister's reply was prompt, assuring me the support of the External Affairs Ministry. He concluded his letter by stating that he had directed the Foreign Secretary, JN Dixit, to meet me and discuss the matter further. With his help a detailed plan to lobby for the post to get international support was worked out. This included writing to all our Ambassadors.

The membership of the UN Board of Audit was an elective post with all the members of the UN General Assembly taking part in the election to be held by the Assembly. In addition, I wrote individual letters to the members of the SAIs to prevail upon their Governments to support my candidature.

After the conference in London, I flew to Washington to visit my office there. The auditors stationed in Washington audited the accounts of the India supply mission and the Indian embassies located in North and South America. A month before the elections, in November 1992, I went to New York to host a dinner for the permanent representatives to the UN and to enable them to acquaint themselves with the candidate they would be voting for. The attendance at the dinner was more than seventy per cent, thanks to the efforts put in by our own UN Mission. Following this good turnout, Pakistan, which was considering offering itself as a candidate for the elections, withdrew its candidature. In the elections held in the UN General Assembly I was elected unopposed, providing for the first time an opportunity for Indian audit to enter the arena of international audit. It was a great turning point in our audit experience.

My next trip abroad that year was to Korea to attend the annual meeting of the governing board of the Asian Organisation of Supreme Audit Institutions (ASOSAI), being held in Seoul. Here we called on the President of Korea who served us delicious ginseng tea. My contribution at the ASOSAI meeting was considerable and my popularity increased after my first speech where I paid a compliment to the country. I mentioned that the word 'Korea' had five alphabets—K stood for knowledge, O for organisation, E for enterprise (at this stage the Auditor General of Australia interrupted me, saying that I had forgotten the alphabet 'R', I bade him to have a little patience) and

A for ability. The alphabet R stood for roll and if you roll all the attributes together you have the word 'Korea'. This speech was made at the opening session of the meet, which was covered by the local press and my speech was not only applauded but also widely quoted in the newspapers the next day.

At the meeting I also proposed that the next meeting of the ASOSAI general body be held in India in 1993. I reminded the governing board that the birth of ASOSAI was in India, the first meeting having been held in New Delhi in 1979 and it was high time the body revisited its birthplace. The invitation was accepted unanimously. When I returned to Delhi we had two-year lead time to prepare for holding the international conference.

On 22 May 1991 we were woken up early in the morning by our friend Chandramouli to say that Rajiv Gandhi had been assassinated. It was indeed shocking news and the next day we rang up our friends and relatives to cancel the garden dinner party that Indira and I had planned for our twenty-fifth wedding anniversary. We mourned the loss of a young man who died before reaching his full potential.

I chose Kerala as the first State to visit after taking over as Comptroller and Auditor General. My senior officers advised me against it, saying that my predecessor TN Chaturvedi had avoided visiting the State after hearing that his own predecessor Gian Prakash had been *gheraoed* (encircled) and humiliated by the unruly staff of the local AG. Kerala had been under communist rule for years with labour unions on the warpath and the resulting indiscipline had spread to Government offices. Despite this advice I visited the offices located in Trivandrum and my visit went off well, with the staff receiving me with garlands. On their invitation, I addressed the staff of the combined offices, assuring them of my support for their legitimate demands, adding that intimidation and indiscipline would not be tolerated. I told them of my plans to enter the field of international audit and urged them to take to computer training as books of accounts in international organisations were computerised and there were no paper books of accounts to audit. It turned out to be a very harmonious and successful visit.

Within a year of my appointment as Comptroller and Auditor General, I underwent a heart operation. I had been playing tennis every morning and there was no warning that I had a heart problem. I used to visit the Wellington Hospital every year for a physical check-up and this time when I went there, I was put on a treadmill test for the first time. It was detected that I had ischaemia and I was advised to have an angiogram done. The next day I got myself admitted to the Escorts Heart Institute and Research Centre. Dr Naresh Trehan advised that I should undergo a bypass operation as three of my arteries were blocked to the extent of eighty, ninety and hundred per cent. Indira wanted me to take a second opinion so I sent the angiogram to Dr Khaleelullah, the physician consultant to the President of India. He felt that a heart operation may not be necessary and the problem could be adequately tackled by stenting. I told Indira that I was in favour of the operation as stenting would only be an intermediate step and I wanted to lead an active life.

It was decided that I would get myself admitted to Escorts for the operation on 12 March, a day after my birthday. Indira used to celebrate my birthday in grand style every year, inviting my relatives and friends for a high tea with cocktails. At the birthday bash, my friends came to know for the first time that I was entering the hospital the next day and they could not believe that I could be so jolly and unconcerned in a situation like that. In response I offered them another round of drinks and asked them to drink to my health. Indira, too, put up a brave and smiling front and I admired her for it.

The Government offered to bear the expenses of my operation abroad either in the UK or the USA. I was also told that I could take my wife along for the operation. However, I declined the offer, as I felt that it would be better for Indira to be with friends and well-wishers while I underwent the operation.

I felt no fear as the doctor appeared with a syringe to sedate me. I silently chanted the prayers in Sanskrit taught to me by my father and soon I was unconscious. It is a fact that I have no fear of death. I got up the next morning feeling much better. My recovery was fast and after a month I started getting files home after rejoining duty. On the forty-fifth day I cycled up to the Gymkhana Club and resumed playing tennis. Khushwant Singh, who also played tennis at the club in the mornings and who used to attend the club under Police escort as he was under threat by the 'Khalistanis', envied my carefree morning bicycle ride. A year after my operation I took the arduous trek to the Vaishnodevi temple in Jammu. From Katra I took a pony for the journey up. On the way down, the Accountant General, Jammu (who was my escort) and I wore our tennis shoes and did a slow jog downhill for more than half the way to Katra.

I will now take you back to a major event in my life that took place three months before my operation, in December 1990. Coorgs, with their long association with the Defence services, are highly enthused when a Coorg attains the rank of a General in the Army. He is felicitated, feted and honoured at a function in Coorg. When I became a Secretary to the Government of India, it did not cause even a ripple in Coorg. When I was appointed as the Comptroller and Auditor General of India, the world 'General' in my designation stood out and I received messages of congratulations from hundreds of people from Coorg including some I did not know. Soon after that I received a written invitation from KM Bopiah, the youngest brother of Field Marshal Cariappa, to attend a joint function in Coorg organised by all the Kodava Samajas to honour me.

This function was held in the building of the lower Kodava Samaja, Madikeri, where I was received with traditional Coorg music. I was conducted to the dais where, to my surprise, was seated Field Marshall Cariappa in full Coorg attire. Though he was not too well and was under treatment at the Air Force hospital, Bengaluru, he had graciously agreed to preside over the function. I felt deeply touched by his presence and there was a lump in my throat as I bowed before him and touched his feet, the common Coorg salutation accorded to elders. I introduced my wife and children to him and after the introduction they were seated right opposite us in the front row. There was an extraordinarily loving gesture made by Field Marshall Cariappa before delivering his presidential address. He called out to Pria and Anand by name to come to the dais and when they walked up he gave each of them a bouquet of flowers fresh from his garden. I thanked him for his gracious presence at the function. That was the last time I saw him for he passed away within six months.

25

Interesting Times

We visited China in September 1991. The dates for this visit were fixed in such a way that on the last day we could witness the opening of the Asian Games in Beijing. Indira accompanied me and so did Rathi and Vinay who came at their own cost. Before I set out for China, I met the Prime Minister, VP Singh, on his request. He mentioned to me that they had received no response to their invitation to the Prime Minister of China, Li Peng, to visit India following the earlier visit made by Rajiv Gandhi to China a few years ago. The Prime Minister desired that in case I had an opportunity to meet Prime Minister Li Peng, I should reiterate India's invitation.

The Auditor General of China received me at the airport and we were escorted to the hotel located near Tiananmen Square. This was the same hotel from where the internationally famous video was taken of a lone Chinese boldly blocking the advance of a Chinese Army tank with its turret gun pointing at him.

After a day's sightseeing, I was told that Li Peng would be happy to receive me and I was escorted to his office by the Auditor General and Ranganathan, the Indian Ambassador to China. I remember I had to walk down a long red-carpeted corridor to reach the Prime Minister's room. As the door to his office opened, I was surprised to see Li Peng waiting to receive me. He gave me

Being welcomed by Li Peng, Prime Minister of China, at his office in Beijing, 1991.

The atmosphere was friendly and I took the opportunity to remind Li Peng of the standing invitation extended by our Prime Minister to visit India.

a warm handshake and made solicitous enquiries about my stay in Beijing. He mentioned that China had recently set up an audit organisation in China and he requested Indian assistance to train its auditors. I said that we would be only too happy to assist and the training could be done by organising bilateral visits of the auditors between India and China. Li Peng suggested that both the Auditors General could have a Memorandum of Understanding about the training schedule and the costs involved. I proposed that the training would be imparted by us free of cost as a goodwill gesture and the auditors during their bilateral visits could bear their own costs of travel and lodging. I also invited the Auditor General of China to visit India to sign this memorandum.

The atmosphere was friendly and I took the opportunity to remind Li Peng of the standing invitation extended by our Prime Minister to visit India. I spoke about the historical ties that India and China had developed over centuries despite the formidable physical barrier of the Himalayas. I also reminded him about Fa-Hien and Huen Tsang, the famous Chinese travellers who visited India on foot centuries ago crossing the Himalayas and India's export of Buddhism to mainland China. I mentioned that there had been a period of strained relationship between the two countries but we should put that behind us to concentrate on development and the eradication of poverty.

When I had finished talking, Li Peng warmly reciprocated my sentiments and said, 'Please tell your Prime Minister that I will visit India shortly and the date of the visit could be finalised by mutual consultation.' Ranganathan shot off a message conveying the good news to our Foreign Secretary and on my return to India the Prime Minister rang me up to thank me. Six months later Li Peng visited India and so did the Auditor General of China with whom I signed the Memorandum of Understanding agreed upon in principle in Beijing.

During my visit to China, Ranganathan brought to my notice a petty case of theft by a senior Cabinet Minister from India while leaving the hotel in Beijing. The hotel reported the loss of a Ming vase and a Chinese carpet from the suite occupied by the Minister and had included the cost of the stolen items while submitting their bill to the embassy for payment. Ranganathan sought my advice, especially as he was apprehensive of an audit objection being raised. I told him to settle the bill in full promptly and to save India's honour. It is the same Minister who had constructed twenty cow sheds in the compound of his official residence in Delhi (the local municipal regulations prohibit maintenance of cattle in New Delhi).

With Deng Xiaoping in power in China, Mao Tse Tung's legacy was being downplayed and I could not get an official visit arranged to his grand mausoleum in Tiananmen Square. My Personal Assistant, Jagannathan and I paid a private visit to Mao's mausoleum. The Great Helmsman, as he was called, transformed China in a manner that no one could have predicted.

On our last day in China we witnessed the opening ceremony of the Asian Games from the VIP enclosure. What caught the fancy of everyone was when the Chinese women, in their rich and traditional colourful dresses, made precision landing within the stadium from an aeroplane.

From Beijing we flew to Tokyo where we stayed at Hotel Otani. Shiv Shankar Menon was at that time a senior officer in our embassy in Tokyo and the Indian Ambassador Arjun Asrani had assigned him the task of chaperoning us. Food in Japan, as also in China, did not suit our tastebuds and, especially for a vegetarian, the choice was limited. Jagannathan was a vegetarian and he could only eat the sticky Japanese rice and to make it palatable he added a lot of chili powder. The poor chap suffered from stomach cramps on the return journey. The Ambassador had arranged for our return journey from Osaka to Tokyo by road so that we could do some sightseeing on the way. I recollect now that the most important thing we saw on the journey was the statue of a Golden Buddha seated in a lotus position. From Japan, Indira and I flew back to India, halting for two days in Bangkok. Here we spent our time sightseeing. We visited the Palace, whose main attraction was the Jade Buddha, which we saw with reverence and awe. On the whole it was an interesting visit to the Far East and to China, the land of an ancient civilisation.

Vietnam is one of the most interesting countries I have ever visited. In Ho Chi Minh City, the capital of Vietnam, it was difficult to believe that the country had been at war with the USA a few years ago, a war in which a million Vietnamese had been killed, fighting for their independence. I paid my homage by placing a wreath at the mausoleum containing the preserved body of the legendary Ho Chi Minh.

I went to Mumbai to meet the scientists at the Bhabha Atomic Research Centre. Chidambaram was in charge of the Centre and he took me around. Later, I visited Mahabaleshwar and saw the ancient Shiva temple there. My next visit was to Bengaluru to interact with the scientists of the Indian Space Research Organisation (ISRO) headed by Dr Krishnaswamy Kasturirangan. Space satellites were being manufactured here. I drove down to Hasan where I visited the satellite tracking centre. My visits to Sriharikota (where satellites are launched) and to Thumba (where the satellite engine tests were done) completed my tour of ISRO's facilities in the country.

The reason why I visited so many scientific establishments is because there is a connection between science and audit. Due to the tight budgetary position, the allocation of funds for undertaking scientific activities and research was very little. That, I felt, was all the more reason why audit should guard against wasteful expenditure. The result of the audit of scientific establishments was to be presented to Parliament in a separate volume and my visit was mainly to convey the audit message of good governance in their financial activities.

A few days after my return to Delhi, Dr Arunachallam, Scientific Advisor to the Defence Ministry, called on me and suggested that we have a seminar between his scientists and the audit officers. He felt that scientists working in his organisation should have a good understanding of the audit approach in order to minimise adverse audit comments. I thought it was an excellent idea and told him that I would be sending my deputy to discuss the details of organising the seminar.

The following month I visited Hyderabad to inaugurate the seminar. It was a big gathering of scientists working in different scientific establishments of the Defence Ministry, the largest of them being the Defence Research and Development Organisation (DRDO). After the inauguration, there was a sit-down lunch with their top scientists and it was here that I met Dr Abdul Kalam. On his invitation, I paid a visit to the missile centre that he was heading. He took me around the centre and explained the great progress that India had made in developing rocketry and missile technology with no outside help. He told me about his Rameshwaram background and his unsuccessful attempt to join the airforce, after which he joined the DRDO. He had a brief spell with the National Aeronautics and Space Administration (NASA), USA, and that was what spurred his interest in rocketry and missile technology. Our interaction was warm and friendly.

We were destined to meet again three years later. When Dr Arunachalam retired, Dr Kalam succeeded him as Scientific Advisor to the Defence Minister. Later, he became the Scientific

Advisor to the Prime Minister. One morning, I received a call from him, asking for an appointment. He introduced himself as the person I had met in Hyderabad. I was a little puzzled at his request but I readily agreed to meet him. He came in with a shy smile and after the initial conversation, said that he wanted my advice on an important matter. He fished out a letter from his pocket and asked me to read it. It was from the Governor of Tamil Nadu, ex-officio Chancellor of Tamil Nadu University, inviting Dr Kalam to join the University as its Vice-Chancellor.

Dr Kalam sought my advice on whether he should accept the offer. He remembered my telling him that I was a graduate of the University when we had first met. I was deeply touched by his gesture and the faith he reposed in me. Here was a very talented but simple man and I thought he would do well as a Vice-Chancellor. However, keeping in view the highly politicised and corrupt atmosphere prevailing in the University, I advised him not to accept the job as he would be a thorough misfit. I also urged him to continue his scientific pursuits in rocketry and missile technology as his contribution in this field would be much more than in an academic job. He heard me out patiently and left. He acted on my advice and refused the job. A few years later he was the surprise choice for the post of the President of India. Indeed, he was one of the most loved and greatest Presidents that India has had.

About two years after I assumed office as Comptroller and Auditor General, I got a call from the Private Secretary to the Chief Minister of Karnataka, saying that the Chief Minister Deve Gowda was visiting Delhi and would like to meet me. It was agreed that we would meet the next day at 10 am in my office. That night I got another call from the Private Secretary asking me that as the Chief Minister had an appointment with Pranab Mukherjee for the same time as my appointment, could the meeting be postponed to the afternoon? I told him that since I was receiving a delegation from the Auditor General of France, I would not be able to meet the Chief Minister in the afternoon. As the Chief Minister was returning to Bengaluru the next day by the night flight, I offered to call on the Chief Minister at 9 am.

I arrived sharp at 9 am and found two gentlemen already seated there, waiting to meet the Chief Minister. One was a reporter from *Ananda Bazar Patrika* and the other a *jyotish* (astrologer) dressed in a *dhoti* and *angavastram* (attire worn during festivals and auspicious events). They were curious to know who I was. I parried the questions of the journalist and only revealed that I was a resident of Delhi waiting to meet the Chief Minister.

All this while there was no sign of the Chief Minister. I was annoyed at the delay and after waiting for half-an-hour quietly slipped out of the sitting room and drove back to my office. Soon after reaching the office, I got a call from the Personal Secretary apologising frantically. I gave him a bit of my mind and asked him to tell the Chief Minister that he must learn to stick to the appointed time for his meetings.

That evening Indira and I caught the flight to Bengaluru. In my absence, Deve Gowda, in order to make amends, visited my residence with a bouquet of flowers. The bouquet was received by Rahul, my nephew, who was staying with us at that time. To this day, I have no idea why the Chief Minister wanted to meet me.

26

Checks and Balances

I was elected to become a member of the United Nations Board of Audit and my term was for three years, June 1993 to June 1996. I became the Chairman of the Board for a year on 1 January 1995. The Auditor Generals of the UK and Ghana were the other two members. The work of the UN audit was divided among its members and for three years India was on the Board. We audited the accounts of the UN headquarters in New York and seven other UN agencies round the world, including the UN High Commissioner for Refugees (UNHCR) in Rome, UN Habitat in Nairobi and UN University in Tokyo. The UK was responsible for the audit of the UN agencies. These were mainly in Europe and Ghana for the audit of expenditure on UN Peace Keeping Forces round the world. The total expenditure audited was five billion dollars and the cost of the annual audit was 3.6 million dollars equally shared by India, the UK and Ghana.

Every year I sent twenty teams of auditors, in two spells of two months each, to audit the organisation under my charge. Each team consisted of two members. It was headed by an IA&AS Officer and assisted by a senior audit officer. The selection of the teams was purely on merit and only those persons who had excellent knowledge of computer operations were chosen. The computer training of officers and staff initiated by me paid rich dividends. Computer orientation was especially checked at the interview stage and this spurred more officers and staff members to become computer literate.

A senior IA&AS Officer was posted at the UN office in New York as Director of Audit. His job was to supervise the work of the auditors worldwide, to receive their comments and fashion them to draft audit reports that were placed before the Board of Audit for its approval. There were three such Directors of Audit in the UN office in New York, each representing the three countries that had Auditor Generals on the Board. They coordinated the work among themselves to liaise with the UN organisations and to obtain their comments on the draft audit reports before putting them up to the UN Board of Audit. The final audit reports of the UN and its other agencies were finalised in the final meeting of the Board that lasted about a week. This meeting was held in New York.

Though I travelled all the way to New York for my first meeting of the UN Board of Audit, I could not attend it. While playing tennis the previous day I had missed the ball and, unable to control the down swing of the racquet, I had hit myself on the shin bone. I retired early that night but woke up a little past midnight with a severe pain in the leg and fever. The hotel doctor asked me to get into the bath tub filled with ice-cold water. This brought my body temperature down but the pain and swelling did not abate. I was advised complete bed rest. The clinical tests revealed that I was suffering from an acute septic condition caused by the wound on my skin and I was prescribed a very high dosage of antiseptic pills. I was bedridden in the hotel for ten days and my departure from New York back to Delhi was delayed. I kept in touch with Indira over the phone but in true Hindi film style she began to wonder whether I was actually ill or just faking it in order to have a good time abroad! On the eleventh day I was well enough to travel and was sent home in an Air-India plane. Indira was shocked to see my condition and I assured her that the worst was over. I did become all right, but even now I have a slight limp in my right leg.

As a member of the UN Board of Audit my visits to New York were frequent and I had an office in the UN building. Indira used to accompany me often on these trips. The Indian audit team excelled itself in tackling the audit of the UN. Since only the best of my officers were selected to head the audit teams, their output was extraordinarily good. After reading our audit report, which contained detailed recommendations for the better implementation of the computerisation programme under way in UN offices, Joseph Connor, UN Under Secretary General (who was earlier Chairman of PricewaterhouseCoopers), was particularly impressed with the detailed knowledge my team had on computers.

I received a letter from Bowsher, Auditor General of the USA who was also the Chairman of the International Organisation of Supreme Audit Institutions (INTOSAI), to head a Sub-Committee of the organisation. I was given the task to find out how best computer auditing techniques could be introduced in the various SAIs of the world. Probably Connors had spoken to Bowsher about our excellence in the computer field. I felt greatly honoured to receive this invitation. The letter from the Chairman gave me the power to choose my own Committee members; the only condition was that one-third of them should be the representatives from less developed countries in the field of audit.

I accepted the invitation and soon the Committee was notified with the membership of the Auditor Generals of the UK, Germany, France, Ecuador, Saudi Arabia, Canada, Japan, Sweden and the Pacific island of Kiribati. After two years, the Committee had prepared a directory of all the SAIs about their state of preparedness to introduce computer auditing. A training manual for all the SAIs, prescribing the syllabus for basic, intermediate and advanced training capsules for the auditors to familiarise themselves with computer auditing techniques was also made available along with a manual on computer security, including the fight against possible virus attacks. A half-yearly journal titled 'Into-IT' that contained interesting house articles on computer auditing was published and circulated.

Our output was hailed as phenomenal and it eventually led to India being honoured with the coveted Jörg Kandutsch Award, given for excellence in international cooperation in the field of audit. This is a prize established by the German SAI. It is announced once in three years at the world conference of INTOSAI. The award given to us was announced in 1998 in the Santiago (Chile) meeting of INTOSAI, after I had demitted office as the Comptroller and Auditor General, but the citation read out during the award ceremony mentioned my name. Vijay Shunglu, my successor, who received the award, was good enough to get a bronze replica of the award prepared for me. It now hangs proudly in my office room as does the original in the Comptroller and Auditor General's office room in Delhi.

I attended the world conference of INTOSAI held in Washington in October 1992 and was asked to chair the session on the computerisation of the activities of SAI. The conference was attended by the SAIs of one hundred and sixty countries and, as a result, I got instant recognition as a prominent and active member of INTOSAI. The next world conference of INTOSAI was held in Cairo in October 1995 where I was unanimously elected the Vice-Chairman.

In response to the invitation that I had extended to the member countries of the Asian Organisation of Supreme Audit Institutions (ASOSAI) in Seoul, delegates from forty-one countries attended the general body meeting of the organisation held in Delhi in November 1993. It was inaugurated by the Vice-President of India and the Finance Minister, Dr Manmohan Singh, addressed the gathering as the Chief Guest. The delegates, numbering nearly hundred, were entertained after the official discussions of the day with cultural shows and dinners. The venue of the conference was Ashok Hotel and a lavish dinner was hosted by me on the last day. At the Delhi conference I was elected the Chairman of ASOSAI for the next three years from November 1993 onwards.

As Chairman of ASOSAI, I automatically became a member of the Governing Board of INTOSAI, which met once a year in different locations of the world. I attended two meetings, one held in Vienna and the other in South Africa. It was a repeat visit for me in Vienna, where I had gone twenty years ago as a tourist along with Indira. The President of Austria was a personal friend of Bowsher and we were invited for lunch at the President's palace, which was where Marie Antoinette once lived.

The next annual meeting of the Governing Board of ASOSAI was held in the capital of Saudi Arabia, Riyadh. Saudi Arabia had indeed grown strong economically, investing the petro dollars it earned wisely. Conference facilities in Riyadh were excellent and the delegates were supplied with copies of the audit regulations of the country printed in English. I was curious to see one of their audit reports but was told that it was a top secret document seen only by the King! The audit report was to act as a check on the activities of the Ministers who were all members of the Saudi Royal family. When I asked him about corruption in the Government he admitted that the Ministers were officially allowed to be corrupt to the extent of twenty per cent! I wondered why India should not follow the example of getting quality work done by the contractors by officially providing in the work estimates for the bribe to be paid as in Saudi Arabia!

Back at home I visited all the States in the North East except Arunachal Pradesh. Indira accompanied me during my visits to Sikkim, Meghalaya and Assam, where we stayed at the Raj Bhawan. During our visit to Gujarat we went to the Gir Forest. Our next interesting visit was to Rajasthan where we stayed at the Raj Bhawan in Jaipur. We were invited to evening tea by Chenna Reddy, the Governor and his wife.

The Dalai Lama wished to improve the financial control over the working of the Tibetan camps by having them internally audited. The Personal Secretary to the Dalai Lama met me in Delhi to convey his request to help train Tibetans in basic audit work. Tibetan medicine dispensaries opened by the Dalai Lama also required proper financial supervision by internal audit. I agreed to train their candidates by organising a special training capsule for them. Shortly after, I received an invitation from the Dalai Lama to visit him at Dharamsala. Taking advantage of his invitation we decided to make a holiday trip to Dharamsala, Dalhousie and Yole.

The Dalai Lama was extremely gracious and spent over an hour with us; we found him to be very friendly and simple. He thanked me for the help in training his auditors and interacted with the children with his innate grace. As we took leave of him he told us that we could visit his Tibetan medicine dispensary and consult his personal physician about any ailments we may have. Before bidding us goodbye he gave me an autographed book of his biography. At the dispensary, the physician felt Indira's pulse and diagnosed that she had a back pain for which he gave her medicine. After feeling my pulse he correctly diagnosed that I had a recent heart operation. The amazing thing was that he made these diagnoses without asking us a single question!

The Auditor General of Bhutan invited me to his country. We had been training their audit officers in our institute at Shimla for some years and it was customary for Bhutan to invite every new Comptroller and Auditor General of India. Indira and I were shown around Bhutan by the Chief Justice of Bhutan who had just stepped down from the post of Auditor General. We were taken to various Buddhist monasteries and driven to the north to visit an ancient fortification against intruders entering Bhutan. The countryside was breathtakingly beautiful with trees full of orchids and wild flowers. We were then flown by helicopter to visit the Chukka hydroelectric project, a gift from India to Bhutan. The construction of the project and its initial survey was done by Indian engineers and the cost of construction, amounting to Rs 250 crore, was borne by the Indian Government. I used to supervise the release of money for this project when I was the Additional Secretary in the Ministry of Finance. On my return to Delhi I recommended to the Prime Minister that Rao, the Chief Engineer of the project, be awarded a Padma Shri for his excellent work. He was honoured the very next year. The dam had been constructed in record time and after completion had been handed over to the King of Bhutan by the President of India at a special function.

On my second day in Thimpu, I addressed the audit officers of Bhutan, most of whom had been trained in India. Later, we met King Wang Chuk in his palace and thanked him for his Government's hospitality. He, in turn, thanked me for training his auditors and the Government of India for financing the Chukka hydroelectric project. He said that the project was yielding a revenue of Rs 50 crore annually, with ninety-five per cent of the electricity being supplied to India. He added that the rate per unit of electricity being supplied to India was fixed ten years ago and was very low. He wanted me to request the Prime Minister of India to revise this. I conveyed the message and the necessary relief was, indeed, provided to Bhutan.

Russia, like China, set up an official Government organisation under an Auditor General rather late in the day and after joining INTOSAI wished to become a member of the European Organisation of Supreme Audit Institutions in the regional grouping. Their membership was refused by the European organisation and INTOSAI advised them to apply to the Asian organisation for membership. Their application for membership was received by ASOSAI when I was the Chairman of the organisation. Shortly after that I received a personal invitation to visit Russia by their Auditor General who also held the post of Deputy Prime Minister of the country. In Russia, instead of audit being independent of administration, it was part of administration. A strange combination indeed! I decided to take Indira with me on this visit at my own expense as I had done previously when I visited China. We stayed in Moscow for three days as State guests—one day being devoted for official work and the rest to sightseeing.

We visited the famous Red Square and paid our homage at Lenin's mausoleum. I am lucky to be one of the few persons in the world to have visited the mausoleums of the three iconic figures of communism—Mao Tse Tung, Lenin and Ho Chi Minh.

We also went to the Russian Orthodox churches that dotted the Red Square with their onion-shaped domes. An old Russian woman followed us, begging for alms. Taking pity on her, I gave her a big Russian currency note. She could not believe her eyes when she saw the note and raising her hands she blessed me in Russian. She followed me all over the Red Square, blessing me all the time. That memory has stayed with me.

During our visit to Moscow, Ronen Sen was the ambassador in Russia. We were invited to attend the cocktail party he was hosting on Independence Day at his residence. I was happy to meet the Deputy Prime Minister of Russia here. He took me aside and over a glass of vodka requested me to process his application quickly for admission as a member of ASOSAI. Russia became a member of ASOSAI by the time the year was over.

In Helsinki I called on the Auditor General of Finland and discussed their computerisation programme. On the basis of their own experience they told me about some of the pitfalls one should avoid when introducing computers in audit offices. I invited them to attend a training seminar on computerising that we were organising in Delhi. Helsinki was drab as compared to other European capital cities but we enjoyed a boat ride round the city. The next day Laxman Rao (from my office) and I flew to Istanbul, where we halted for a couple of nights on the way back home to Delhi.

We were auditing the office of the UNHCR in Mexico and I visited the city along with Laxman Rao to supervise the work of the audit team. Later, as Chairman of the Electronic Data Processing (EDP) Committee of INTOSAI, I was invited to Sweden to inaugurate a seminar on audit computerisation. The Auditor General of the country was a pretty Swedish lady who received me at the Stockholm airport with great charm and grace.

After the seminar was over a day was spent sightseeing in and around Stockholm. I visited the venue where the annual Nobel Prize ceremony is held and the gold room in the Museum of National Antiquities where there were more than three thousand gold items on display. Sweden has perhaps the richest collection of prehistoric gold and silver gathered by the Vikings than anywhere else in Europe.

On the way back from Mexico we visited Buenos Aires the capital of Argentina and Rio, the biggest and raunchiest town in Brazil. We went to the Eva Peron Memorial and had dinner with the UNHCR local head at a lovely restaurant located next to the Platt River. Later, we went to a nightclub where the show included the famous Spanish flamenco dance and the tango. At Rio we took a late evening walk along the famous Copacabana beach and were witness to near naked men and women in amorous embrace, oblivious to their surroundings. We also visited the famous Redeem statue of Jesus Christ perched on Sugar Loaf hill, overlooking Rio.

As Chairman of the UN Board of Audit I visited Cyprus to supervise the work of our auditors there. A distinguished Kodava had landed in the island years earlier. He was General KS Thimayya, the former Chief of the Indian Army, who headed the first UN Peace Keeping Force deputed to Cyprus.

That evening, at a reception hosted by the Prime Minister, I was asked by him where I hailed from. When I replied Karnataka, he pressed me for details. I was puzzled at his curiosity and when I answered I was from Coorg, the Prime Minister smiled and summoned his Ministers. He introduced me to them as a person from the same place as the legendary General Thimayya. I was greatly honoured by this introduction and consider this my brush with glory.

In Cyprus, with a UN passport, I had access to the part of the island held by the Turks. The Indian Ambassador, Tiwari, invited me for a dinner with some of his Greek friends. Tiwari is an exceptionally good bridge player and we had an interesting game of duplicate bridge after dinner.

My work in connection with the UN audit took me to a dozen African countries as well. These included Angola and Mozambique, two of the poorest countries which, after attaining independence, had been wracked by warfare between different tribal forces involving the deployment of UN Peace Keeping Forces.

The UN Habitat Centre, which we had the responsibility to audit, was in Nairobi. I went there along with Indira and we visited the nearby Masai Mara game sanctuary. It was an amazing experience to land on an improvised landing strip in the middle of hundreds of animals.

I visited Ghana on the invitation of its Auditor General who was also a member of the UN Board of Audit. I found it to be one of the more prosperous countries in Africa.

After the London Commonwealth Conference of Auditor Generals, the next similar conference was held in Harare, Zimbabwe, three years later. During our four-day stay there, Indira and I saw different kinds of African tribal dances. At a nearby zoo we had our first sight of the dreaded African snake, the Mamba. Tanzania was another interesting country that I visited. The famous African explorer Dr Livingstone lived in Dar es Salaam, the capital of Tanzania and I visited his house, which now houses a museum. I took a boat ride to the nearby Zanzibar Island and went round the spice garden smelling all the aromatic spices of the world just as a tourist would.

Azerbaijan, one of the Central Asian States (that broke away from the USSR), was my next stop. I was invited there as

Azerbaijan wished to become a member of ASOSAI. I had read about the famous oil wells of Baku, the capital city, in school and was taken round these wells on a sightseeing tour. I also saw a Shiva Temple erected by some Indian pilgrims in the late eighteenth century.

In between our travels abroad, Indira and I visited the IA&AS academy located at Yarrows in Shimla and spent a delightful day in the company of the young probationers undergoing training there. From Shimla we drove to the beautiful Kinnaur Valley, which is the take-off point to Lahaul and Spiti in Ladakh. On the way we visited the hydroelectric project being constructed by JP Industries, a private firm. This was the first such project in India where, under a power-sharing agreement with the State Government, the entire project was entrusted to a private firm to finance and construct.

27

Matters of Duty

All officers posted to Delhi, needing residential accommodation, are required to apply to the Estate Officer of the Ministry of Works and Housing for allotment. A waiting list is published every month indicating the position of each applicant in the list and allocation is made in serial order. In exceptional cases, the Minister in charge has overriding powers to make out-of-turn allotments. One of my officers, posted to Delhi, was approached by a tout of the Minister for getting him out-of-turn allocation of accommodation for a consideration. There were also press reports of largescale out-of-turn allocations being made by the Minister. I ordered an audit probe of the working of the Estate Office, which revealed a huge misuse of power. During this probe the Estate Officer, under instructions from the Minister, stopped access to files to Audit, saying that as no irregularity of Government finances was involved, we had no business to look into the files. When this was brought to my notice I addressed a demi-official letter to the Minister, explaining the inherent powers that I had to audit such illegal activities and asked for all the relevant papers. When I received no reply I wrote to the Prime Minister, requesting him to direct the Minister to produce the records. I got a prompt reply from the Prime Minister assuring me that it would be done.

Meanwhile, the Supreme Court was apprised of the matter through a Public Interest Litigation (PIL). On receiving a notice from the court, our preliminary audit report was produced before them. They passed severe strictures against the conduct of the Minister, including her attempt to muzzle audit and issued an interim order staying the powers of the Minister to grant out-of-turn allocation. After dilly-dallying a bit, the Minister was forced to submit her resignation. The name of the Minister was Sheila Kaul.

Seshan, two years junior to me in service, was a surprise choice to fill the post of Chief Election Commissioner, a constitutional post charged with the responsibility of the conduct of free and fair elections in the country. He distinguished himself in the post, bringing credibility in the process of elections in the country. His attempts to discipline the political parties and at times his brash behaviour brought him in conflict with politicians. The Central Government tried to rein him in by getting a controversial legislation passed to empower them to appoint two Election Commissioners of their choice with powers equal to that of the Chief Election Commissioner. It was also provided in the enactment that all major decisions of the Commission would have to be made by the majority of the three-member Commission. On the appointment of the two Election Commissioners, Seshan filed an appeal before the Supreme Court, challenging the action of the Government as being mala fide and ultra vires of the Constitution of India. During the pendency of the case in the Supreme Court, he ordered his office not to submit any files to the two newly-appointed Election Commissioners.

The Supreme Court, after an early hearing, pronounced their judgment in favour of the Government. It was a controversial decision considering the fact that the Chief Election Commissioner enjoyed protection under the Constitution against his unjust removal from office while the two Election Commissioners did not have any such protection, thereby reducing their ability to function with independence and impartiality. Seshan filed a review petition before the Supreme Court, which was thrown out after a summary hearing. The Supreme Court was not happy with some of the antics of Seshan, including his efforts with the Government to raise his status in the official warrant of precedence, to the level of a Supreme Court judge.

For nearly a month after the final judgment of the Supreme Court was delivered Seshan refused to fall in line and did not call a meeting with the Election Commissioners, let alone meet them. One fine morning there was a hint in the daily news that some lawyers of the Supreme Court were planning to file a contempt petition against Seshan for not obeying the orders of the Supreme Court. It was at this stage that I decided to intervene to prevent a constitutional authority from being punished for contempt by the Supreme Court.

Pria had become a friend of Seshan's and I told her that she and I should advise him to immediately comply with the Supreme Court order. We decided to visit him together and were received cordially by Seshan and his wife. Within two days of our meeting him, he convened his first meeting with the Election Commissioner and averted a major embarrassment to his office.

There was another case of a very high dignitary whose financial misdeeds brought to light by Audit contributed to his downfall.

Justice V Ramaswamy was the Chief Justice of the Punjab High Court before he was elevated to the position of a Supreme Court judge. During his tenure in the Punjab High Court, he had committed many financial irregularities. He had very lavishly furnished his residence using public funds. He had also sent an official car from Chandigarh all the way to Chennai at Government cost for his daughter's wedding. When this car met with an accident on the way back to Chandigarh, Justice Ramaswamy had incurred heavy expenditure on its repair from Government funds. He had also obtained Rs 72,000 from his office towards the payment of telephone charges incurred on his residential phone in Chennai, though he was posted and staying in Chandigarh and had the facility of a free residential telephone there.

The Accountant General of Punjab met me with the draft audit report and sought my instructions on whether he should issue the draft report to the Registrar of the High Court to elicit their comments before finalising it. He was aware that it was a delicate matter involving the integrity of a judge who was a member judge of the Supreme Court. He was also not sure whether he would be liable to any contempt proceedings. This is because judges had barricaded themselves against any probe into their conduct by a self-serving previous judgment that even truth about the misconduct of a judge was not a defence in contempt procedure. I convened a meeting of my senior officers and they were all of the unanimous view that it would be dangerous for Audit to take on the might of the judiciary.

I was not happy with their advice and it took me two days of deep thought to make up my mind. I was a constitutional authority who had taken an oath before the President of India that I would perform my constitutional duties without showing fear or favour. I was bound by that oath to act correctly even in adverse circumstances. I recorded a note to that effect on the file and gave written orders to the Accountant General (in order to protect him from any adverse judicial action) to issue the draft audit report to the Registrar of the Punjab High Court. Obviously Justice Ramaswamy had many enemies in the High Court he had graced earlier and within a week the allegations contained in the draft audit report (which was marked confidential) started appearing in the newspapers.

The Chief Justice of the Supreme Court, after examining the draft audit report, ordered that Justice Ramaswamy stay away from case work until the allegation against him, enquired by a collegium of three judges senior to him, gave its report. After six months the judges unanimously came to the conclusion that the charges against Justice Ramaswamy were true. Strangely enough, he never appeared before the enquiring judges though he was served notice to do so. The Chief Justice of India forwarded the judges' report to the Law Ministry, which initiated impeachment proceedings in Parliament against the errant judge for his removal from the bench of the Supreme Court.

At this stage the story took a strange twist. The large number of Members of Parliament (MPs) from the southern States wished to have a compromise solution and Seshan, the Election Commissioner, propelled himself to be a mediator. He got Justice Ramaswamy to agree to step down on condition that the impeachment proceedings in Parliament are dropped. The Speaker of the Lok Sabha did not agree to drop the proceedings. However, the proceedings failed to get the requisite majority (seventy-five per cent of the strength of the Lok Sabha and also seventy-five per cent of the number actually voting) when the southern MPs abstained from voting on the proceedings. Justice Ramaswamy continued in office without any work for a long time until he eventually retired.

When I visited Nagpur to inspect the Auditor General's office, I made a quick trip to the Gandhi Ashram located in Wardha. Most of Gandhi's life was spent in his *ashrams* (spiritual centres) at Wardha and Sabarmati. I was taken round the cottages where Gandhiji and Vinoba Bhave stayed and the whole area was well maintained and teeming with spinning activity.

During one of my official visits to Chennai, Indira and I drove up to Kanchipuram to visit the famous Kamakshi temple. Here, we ran into R Venkataraman, the former President of India. We also drove down to Puducherry and Indira and I stayed at the Raj Bhawan. We visited the Aurobindo Ashram where we meditated for some time, sitting in the newly-constructed meditation room with soothing blue light. We also visited the *samadi* (tomb) of Aurobindo and saw the room where he spent his life. Being on an official visit, the Chief Minister of Puducherry hosted a dinner where Indira and I were introduced to the Cabinet Ministers and senior officers of the Union Territory.

I had a meeting to attend in Turin. I was travelling via Rome and I had work in Geneva and Paris. Pria accompanied me on this trip. Anand's turn to go on a holiday abroad came when he accompanied Indira and me to the UK on an invitation from Sir John Bourne, the Comptroller and Auditor General of the UK. Our visit to the Lake District had a magical effect on all of us. The beauty and serenity of nature found there has no parallel anywhere in the world. On our way out of the Lake District we visited Dove Cottage in Grasmere where the famous poet Wordsworth once lived. His house had been turned into a museum. I re-read there his beautiful poem titled 'Daffodils', which was part of my English curriculum in school.

My next trip abroad was to Amsterdam where I had a day's halt on my way to the USA. Laxman Rao and I visited the windmills, took a boat ride on the canals, went to the museum of Anne Frank beside the canal and bought cheese in the local market. We visited the picture galleries of Van Gogh and Rembrandt. We hired a taxi and drove to Kokenhoff to see the tulip fields in full bloom, drove further to The Hague where we visited the building housing the World Court and then on to Rotterdam, the busiest port in Europe.

My last visit to Europe was in October 1995, when I visited Paris. It was a cold morning with bright sunshine when we walked from Arc De Triomphe to the Eiffel Tower where Laxman Rao and I climbed the nine hundred and eighty-two steps to go up to the last viewing platform.

Laxman Rao was in charge of the division handling external audit in my office. He was also a good tennis player. During our foreign visits we used to carry our racquets and played wherever it was possible to do so. In New York, the UN Plaza Hotel had a tennis court on the thirty-second floor and we played there often.

More than two hundred students of Loyola College were members of the Loyola Alumni Association, Northern Chapter, located in New Delhi. I succeeded Justice Natrajan of the Supreme Court as the Chairman of the Association for three years from 1991 to 1994. During my chairmanship, special efforts were made by all the members to collect funds to help our alma mater. We were able to raise Rs 100,000 each year, which was donated to the college. In the third year, instead of donating the money, we put it in a fixed deposit, which gave us an annual interest of Rs 15,000. With this amount we established three annual scholarships of Rs 5,000 each. The college was then authorised to select suitable candidates for these scholarships.

As Chairman of the Loyola Alumni Association, I invited L Subramaniam, the famous violinist, also a student of Loyola, to appear for a ticketed music performance in Delhi. He agreed to come all the way from the USA, at his own cost. We requested Alla Rakha, the famous *tabla* (Indian percussion instrument) player to provide the necessary accompaniment. There was full-house attendance at the function, which was presided over by Shankar Dayal Sharma, the Vice-President of India and attended by Father Inchakal and Father Sundaram from Loyola College. Never before or after my tenure as Chairman has there been such a big and sustained fund-raising activity to help the college.

28

Changing Track

My six-year tenure as Comptroller and Auditor General was coming to a close and I looked back with satisfaction at the work done by me at both the international and national levels. In India I had brought out more than five hundred audit reports relating to the annual accounts of the Centre and the States. In addition, we had brought out special audit reports on projects and programmes. These included the National AIDS Control Programme (1991), Technology Mission on Immunisation (1993), the Janata Cloth Scheme (1993), Nehru Rozgar Yojna (1994), Scheme of Creches for Children (1994), Oil Pricing Policy (1995) and the Programme for Enhancing Facility for Treatment of Cancer (1995). An excellent review report was brought out in 1993 on the Ganga Action Plan. This was a plan that was imaginatively introduced by the Planning Commission when I was functioning as its Secretary. It helped to control pollution and clean the sacred river.

A quick audit review was done in 1994 about the initiatives taken by the Government to privatise the public sector. This report helped the Government to improve the disinvestment process in subsequent years. Based on the audit of the revenues and receipts of Government audits, many suggestions to amend the laws and procedures of tax collection were readily accepted by the Government; these helped to plug the loopholes in tax administration. The first report on public debt was made in 1987 and, in 1995, a further report was brought out informing Parliament and the public of the alarming exponential increase in both the internal and the external debt of the country.

At the international level, I simultaneously held the post of Chairman, United Nations Board of Audit, Chairman of the Asian Organisation of Supreme Audit Institutions and Chairman of the EDP Committee of INTOSAI. I was a member of the governing board of INTOSAI and was elected Vice-Chairman of the INTOSAI conference held in Cairo in October 1995. As Chairman of ASOSAI, I was invited to visit Israel. I made two other visits abroad before demitting office. On the invitation of the Auditor General of Australia I attended a meeting of the Governing Board of ASOSAI, which was held in Sydney. After the conference we took a boat ride in the beautiful bay of Sydney, made memorable by the fact that it was the Sydney regatta sailing day. On the third day we flew to Canberra and called on the Governor General of Australia. I also met my friend Akbar Khaleli, our High Commissioner in Canberra, whom I had helped to trace the murderers of his wife when I was the Home Secretary. On my return journey I halted in Singapore and did extensive sightseeing.

The Comptroller and Auditor General on his return from a tour abroad is personally received in the VIP lounge by the Head of Customs. I was delighted to see that the same person who had accosted me at the custom barrier twenty years ago on my return from Oxford was now Head of the Airport Customs. He was surprised when I declared the import of a video cassette recorder and paid the requisite customs duty. He had never before seen a VIP declare anything while passing through Customs.

As the time for handing over charge as Comptroller and Auditor General came nearer, we started packing, for we had decided to shift to Bengaluru to live our retired life. We felt very sorry for our dog Ouzo who had the run of our lawns. I was not a dog lover until Ouzo arrived in our house and stole our hearts with his lovable and playful antics.

The story of my official life will not be complete without a mention of the two stalwarts of my personal staff. Khanna, my Personal Assistant, joined me in 1981 in the Ministry of Finance and migrated along with me to the various posts I held. He had developed such a wide link of contacts in the various Ministries that my friends sought his help rather than mine in attending to their problems. He served me faithfully till the end and I

With Indira and our favourite dog, Ouzo, in Delhi, 1996.

rewarded him by promoting him to the gazetted rank. I also gave him two years extension in service, using my discretionary powers as Comptroller and Auditor General. We are in touch with each other and I meet him when I visit Delhi.

Das, my official driver, joined my personal staff when I was Home Secretary. He was the envy of my colleagues who marvelled at his diligence in spotting me when getting out of crowded functions, so that I could make the quickest getaway. He followed me as my official driver when I was posted as Central Vigilance Commissioner and later as Comptroller and Auditor General. He was due to retire in the same month that I demitted office as Comptroller and Auditor General and though I offered to grant him two years extension of service, he politely declined, stating that he would not like to work for anyone else after me. He settled down in his village after retiring and I met him again in December 1997 when I invited him to attend my daughter's wedding in Delhi.

On 11 March 1996, when I turned sixty-five, I handed over charge to my successor Vijay Shungloo. He was a surprise choice as his seniors were lobbying hard for the post. I was required to vacate my residence within one month of demitting office. There have been hundreds of cases on the part of officers and Ministers overstaying in their Government houses for years but I had set myself the highest of standards and there was no question of not obeying the rule. Normally there should have been no difficulty in doing so, but Indira's birthday fell on 12 April and she expressed a desire to spend the day with her friends in Delhi before leaving for Bengaluru. We dispatched our heavy luggage by railway container service to Bengaluru on 9 April and I booked myself accommodation in the nearby Orissa Bhavan for a day, before boarding the morning train to Bengaluru on 13 April.

I had stayed continuously in Delhi from 1981 and Indira had been there ten years longer. It was a big wrench for her to leave behind all her friends and Pria, too, in Delhi. I gave Pria my Maruti 800, which I had bought in 1983. The car is still with her and she plans to use it as a vintage car. All our good friends, along with Pria, were there to see us off at the railway station. Shungloo and his wife, accompanied by some senior officers, also turned up. There were many moist eyes as our train slowly chugged out of the station on its journey to Bengaluru. After all, I was changing track, once again.

Being presented the Rajotsava Award by
SM Krishna, Chief Minister of Karnataka, Bengaluru, 2000.

Honoured at the All India Intellectual Conference of India
by the Governor of Gujarat, Ahmedabad, 2001.

Some of my favourite people—Pria and Nikhil with their son Rian, seen with Anand and Devika, Delhi, 2003; Below: With Indira, Rian and Laila, Bengaluru, 2004.

With Indira and the three gems in our life—our grandchildren Rian, Laila and Anandi, 2006.

Ode to Life

In the hush of dawn
The beauty of the rising sun
Sets ablaze the heart
With light, hope and happiness
In the quiet of the evening
The slanting rays of the setting sun
Bring in their wake
Peace, tranquility and bliss
For an enlightened soul
Both are important
For the wisdom of the message they convey

CG Somiah